Music Making and Civic Imagination

Music, Community, and Education

Series Editor: Lee Higgins

Music, Community, and Education is a focused monograph series that provides scholars and researchers with a platform for disseminating conceptually rich and empirically distinguished work that explores questions related to the impact music-making can have on those that participate and the cultural, political, and economic context through which it happens. To be accepted for publication, manuscripts must be judged as providing significant contributions to advancing cutting-edge research, promoting a wider discourse, and promoting the application of research and scholarship to policies and practices that improve our understanding of music, community and education. Monographs are intended to address their topic without being unduly narrow. They should be comprehensible to and engaging for, a general readership whilst valuable for scholars with shared research interests. Each book is expected to be written in a single voice even when it involves a collaboration between multiple scholars. Book proposals are welcome in any of the following areas that address questions relating to music-making; inclusivity, participation, social justice, democracy, power, community and pedagogy.

Building Community Choirs in the Twenty-First Century: Re-imagining Identity through Singing in Northern Ireland, by Sarah Jane Gibson (2023)

Music Making and Civic Imagination

A Holistic Philosophy

Dave Camlin

intellect

Bristol, UK / Chicago, USA

First published in the UK in 2023 by
Intellect, The Mill, Parnall Road, Fishponds, Bristol, BS16 3JG, UK

First published in the USA in 2023 by
Intellect, The University of Chicago Press, 1427 E. 60th Street,
Chicago, IL 60637, USA

A catalogue record for this book is available from
the British Library.

Copy editor: MPS Limited
Cover designer: Holly Rose
Production manager: Laura Christopher
Typesetter: MPS Limited

Hardback ISBN 978-1-78938-802-2
Paperback ISBN 978-1-83595-178-1
ePDF ISBN 978-1-78938-803-9
ePUB ISBN 978-1-78938-804-6

Series (Print) ISSN 2755-3302
Series (Online) ISSN 2755-3310

To find out about all our publications, please visit our website.
There you can subscribe to our e-newsletter, browse or download our current
catalogue and buy any titles that are in print.

www.intellectbooks.com

This is a peer-reviewed publication.

Contents

Foreword

The world needs this book right now. The messages it contains speak so poignantly to our current moment in time. As our lives become increasingly shaped by war and conflict, escalating geopolitical and economic uncertainty, widening social inequities, and accelerating climate change, many of us musicians, educators and scholars have been grappling with how to respond. In this book, Dave Camlin gives us a gift, a generous invitation to deeply consider a far more expansive view of musicing, its interconnected relationship with the world, and how it might allow us to radically reimagine and respond to these existential crises.

For years I have been yearning for a book on music like Dave has written here. The kind of book that tackles the very questions I have personally been grappling with as I explore the role of music in complex contexts of social inequity and injustice. The kind that addresses the pressing concerns of many arts organisations, music learning institutions, governments, and funders I have worked with, keen to harness the power of music in their local communities. The kind that jolts our field into new lines of questions, considerations, enquiries, and modes of being in the world. The kind that departs from the well-worn circular, and often siloed, tropes about music's capacity to 'heal the world.' The kind that not only poses the big and challenging questions, but offers multiple possible answers, and pathways for meaningfully developing our own responses in our own contexts.

At its heart, Dave's book offers a profoundly holistic view of music, conceptualising it as a complex adaptive system. Resisting old reductionist conceptualisations of musicing that explain its significance in dissected slices, he presents a fundamental departure from such narrow ways of thinking and fully embraces complexity theory. By assembling a staggering array of literature, theoretical ideas, conceptual frameworks, intellectual apparatuses, and practical musicing examples, Dave challenges us to think about music in the most holistic sense possible. To do this, he travels across many borders of intellectual and creative possibility from human evolution to quantum theory. While these fields may seem impenetrable to some musicians, Dave traverses these fields of ideas in such a grounded and relatable way that always comes back to the act of musicing. This will no doubt spark curiosity, wonder, awe and imagination in all who read it. Moreover, he weaves these ideas together in such a dynamic, interconnected and relational way, I am sure it will engender fruitful dialogue across many different cultural contexts and worldviews.

This book is a must-read for any socially-engaged, ethically-minded musician, focused on deepening, questioning, and enhancing their praxis, wherever they may be on their journey. Likewise, it is a must-read for those working in music higher education institutions, such as the one I have worked in for years, especially as we increasingly turn our attention to how we support emerging musicians to become more socially and ethically aware in their work. Indeed, every music training institution and every music research entity would do themselves a favour by setting this book on their annual reading lists. Fuelled with the ideas that this book covers, and the inspiration it provides for us to think and act more deeply as musicians, educators and researchers, I can only imagine the widespread impact that it will have on our field. Beyond professions and institutions, I can also see this book finding resonance in many community settings, and being valued and enjoyed by everyone who engages in music in any capacity. I also hope this book falls into the hands of policy makers, decision makers, local council officers, and politicians. If it does, it might well offer a powerful and potentially transformative vision for how music could be more fully integrated into the civic imagination of their communities.

What is so different about this book is the way the ideas continue to stay with you long after you have closed the cover. While the vastness of the intellectual ideas and creative examples are so striking, what is more impressive is the emotional and spiritual level on which it operates. I suspect this is due to the deeply sensitive way Dave holds space and connects with the people and surroundings where he makes music, but also how he crafts his words on a page and holds the book's overarching architecture in his hands. This realisation takes me back to the 2016 International Society for Music Education's (ISME) Community Music Activities Commission (CMA) in Edinburgh, which Dave and I co-hosted with a group of community music colleagues. We wanted to bring a strong cultural presence to the experience for delegates, so planned an ambitious daytrip to Sage Gateshead, following the songlines of the spectacular countryside that runs through Northumberland. For us, we wanted our delegates to walk away with a collective memory that was not only cerebral in nature, but deeply felt in their relationships and sense of place. To our delegates' surprise and delight, Dave arranged for his choir to greet us along the way with song and a beautiful picnic they'd personally prepared. As the warm glow of twilight descended over the surrounding hills, Dave pulled out his guitar and his choir serenaded us in one of the most moving evocations of 'communitas' I've ever experienced. It was not only the embodiment of all the ideas, dialogues, and practices we'd been sharing about community music that stood out. It was how the experience felt for all of us present on a deeply emotional, spiritual and embodied level. It is exactly that masterful 'holding space' that I can feel quietly present within this book. A gentle, considered space that invites is into a deep dialogue and reflection on the most personal and spiritual levels. One that leaves you with a feeling that you have been in the presence of great wisdom long after you have closed the cover and let the words settle on you.

This book feels like a life's work. Truth be told, I devoured it all in one go, hungry to feed a craving I have had for a deeper, more sophisticated discussion about music's possible role in addressing our current existential crises. I read it in the heat and haze of an Australian summer, recovering from the dreaded COVID virus. It was such a relief to finally read a book like this, I treated it more like a page-turning holiday novel. I suspect like-minded musicians, educators and researchers might respond in the same way. Our field has been yearning for a book like this for a long time. As I said in my opening words, it is sorely needed right now. However, my sense is that this book is best taken in slowly. The ideas and concepts are so rich and vast, it is worthy of deep pause and reflection. Through this book, Dave has created an intensely moving space for us to be in that is worth savouring and deeply listening to. I feel so grateful the world has it in its hands right now.

Brydie-Leigh Bartleet
Co-Editor of *Music as a Global Resource* (2020)
and the *Oxford Handbook of Community Music* (2018);
Professor at the Creative Arts Research Institute,
Griffith University, Meanjin (Brisbane),
Turrbal and Yuggera Country,
Australia.

Acknowledgements

I should like to acknowledge the support of some wonderful and supportive colleagues who have kindly assisted by reading early drafts of the book. Fiona Evison, Mary Stakelum, Katherine Zeserson and Tim Palmer – thank you. I'm eternally grateful. I should also like to thank the two anonymous academic peers who reviewed the book – your insightful comments and helpful suggestions have improved the book considerably. Thanks also to my colleagues Jessica Pitt and Mary Pells at Royal College of Music who have been so supportive to me during the writing process. A particular note of thanks is due to Brydie Bartleet, for kindly agreeing to write the foreword to the book.

Thanks are also extended to the many students and participants who have helped to shape the ideas in the book, whether knowingly or inadvertently. The various discussions and musicing we have undertaken together are what lies at the heart of this book. I'd also like to extend a general thanks to all of the wonderful musicians and artists I've had the good fortune to work with over the last decade or so – you know who you are. Special thanks to all of the musicians from Sage Gateshead's Learning and Participation team whose collective praxis helped to spark many of the ideas that have occupied my own reflections.

I should like to dedicate this book in loving memory of my late father Gerry Camlin, who died before I was able to finish it but was proud that I was working on it.

Above all, to Angie for everything you have done to support me in getting this book finished. Your love is what makes everything else worthwhile.

PART 1

INTRODUCTION

1

Music in an Uncertain World

FIGURE 1.1: Wild Chorus in Crow Park, Keswick 2021.

This is a book about the potential of music making as a resource to imagine possible futures. In it, I suggest that music making – or 'musicing' for short – is a way for human beings to build kinship relations by collectively 'performing' humanistic values of love, reciprocity and justice, and thereby temporarily inhabiting alternative social realities that can help us imagine the kind of world/s that we might wish to live in. When we make music with other people, we establish a space outside of everyday life where we can encounter our musical collaborators in a spirit of kinship. This feeling of kinship is a potent reminder of our common humanity and is a vital resource that we can put to service as we face the challenge of how to live in a more sustainable way as the dominant species on an increasingly fragile planet. Taking participation as the most accessible and democratic form of musicing, this book is an attempt to understand and articulate what conditions of musicing might mobilize civic imagination as a resource for global sustainable development.

Music is a discourse which permeates all levels of society: any understanding of humanity – of ourselves, our society, our history and our future – is incomplete without an understanding of music. In western societies, we have grown accustomed to the idea that music is something performed by talented (and often highly trained) musicians for others to listen/dance to, whereas a more holistic view of music recognizes that it is something that people *do* – and that *all* humans have always done – throughout our species' 230,000-year history. It is only in the last few hundred years that a separation between performers and audience has emerged, resulting in many people self-identifying as 'non-musical', a statement of identity that would not make any kind of sense to our ancient ancestors, steeped in musicing as a part of the fabric of social life (Mithen 2007; Turino 2008).

Building on traditions of community music and 'praxial' music education (Elliott 1995, 2009; Elliott and Silverman 2013; Elliott et al. 2016) which recognize that being musical is a human birth-right, the main argument of this book is that recovering musicing more generally as a human capability is a way of fostering attitudes of kinship which not only bring people together through music but which also have the potential to develop attitudes of global human kinship. Musicing fosters affiliations of biographical identity – whether to a place, a people or tribe, a sports team, a religion, a country or a nation-state. It is a logical extension to be able to invoke a more global biographical identity through musicing, imagining bonds of human solidarity which extend worldwide to everyone facing the same challenges of being human in the twenty-first century; all members of the same dominant species on the same increasingly fragile planet. As I shall discuss, it is also of critical importance to a sustainable human future that this sense of solidarity extends beyond the human species and includes *all other species* on the planet, as well as the planet itself.

In this book, I explore not just how musicing can be an important resource for the recovery of civic life following the recent pandemic crisis but also for addressing the complex nexus of existential crises facing humanity over at least the next 30 years or so, by using it to invoke civic imagination. Strengthening civil society is one way in which progress can be made towards addressing the complex challenges we face, following the maxim: 'think global, act local'. Because of its capacity for developing social cohesion, musicing is one way in which civil society can be strengthened, and long-term sustainable human development depends on the *local* choices we make, now and in the immediate future. Individuals may not be able to change the world on their own but fostering humanistic values of love, reciprocity and justice through musicing is one of the many ways to 'change the world within my reach' (Erelli 2006).

An uncertain future

The challenges currently facing our species are many and complex, with features of our immediate future that, arguably, should concern us all:

- Global population is predicted to increase by over 30 per cent – 9.6 billion up from 7.3 billion in 2015 – by 2050 (United Nations 2015: 2), with most of this population explosion occurring in sub-Saharan Africa.
- In the United Kingdom, like in many western countries, the number of people aged 60 or over is set to rise by a third by 2050 (30), while the ratio of people in employment to retired people – known as potential support ratio or PSR – is set to fall from its current ratio of 3:1 to more or less 1:1 over the same period (7).
- Because 'fertility in all European countries is now below the level required for full replacement of the population in the long run' (4), mass migration and the movement of people across the globe is almost certainly likely to be an enduring feature of our sociocultural experience, with attendant challenges of displacement and cultural integration.
- The uneven exploitation of the earth's resources over centuries means that material and economic wealth is more unevenly distributed than ever, with the world's 2153 billionaires (0.00003 per cent of the population) having more collective wealth than the poorest 60 per cent, a staggering 4.6 billion people (Oxfam International 2020), with the fortunes of the ten wealthiest billionaires doubling during the pandemic while 160 million people were 'pushed into poverty' (Oxfam International 2022).
- This rising inequality is alarming in the context of predictions that in the period to 2060, 'global growth prospects seem mediocre compared with the past,' (OECD: 6) whilst 'earning inequality in the average OECD country may have risen by more than 30%' (7) over the same period.
- Dramatic increases in earning inequality are likely to result from the prospect that, even in the United Kingdom, '35% of current jobs are at high risk of computerisation over the following 20 years' (Lee 2015), leading to higher levels of unemployment or under-employment.
- The effects of the rise of information as a technology – disruptive as well as innovative – are felt everywhere, from the work we do and the way we shop, through to the vehicles we drive, and how we socialize, relax or find a partner.

Perhaps now more than ever in our history, we are less able to predict how the rapid pace of technological and environmental change will continue to impact on our experience of the future. As a globally connected species driven by technological innovation, living longer but working less (due to computerization and automation of labour), dealing with global population explosion coupled with ageing populations and low fertility rates, climate change, mass migration and displacement, increasing inequality, facing the possible onset of a 'pandemic age' (UN Environment 2020) and reliant on systems of education and governance designed for a previous era, it is little wonder that we can find the world a bewildering place to be human. The twenty-first century is a complex, uncertain and challenging time to be alive. As a result of so many challenges, and so much uncertainty, significant numbers of the world's population are becoming more unhappy, and our younger, most digitally connected generations appear to be becoming more unhappy more quickly (Twenge 2017). An expanding, ageing, depressed and more culturally diverse population with more time on its hands and less money might sound like disastrous conditions for existence. The future sounds like a deeply uncertain destination that it is easy to get despondent about, so where is the hope in all of the gloom?

The value of musicing

Musicing may sound like an improbable solution to all of the above, and I'm certainly not advocating learning the ukulele or joining a choir as an alternative to concerted global political efforts to address the complex existential challenges we face. That sounds like a strategy for avoiding the issues altogether, or worse, developing ways to help people 'cope' with these challenges rather than doing something about them, an uncritical approach which disrespects both the value of music *and* the human agency, and which I hope to avoid as my argument unfolds. The particular ways in which musicing might be a valuable resource in *how* we address some of these challenges is because – to do it well – it requires us to 'perform' the best of our ethical human selves, to 'reveal' ourselves to the 'other' and be vulnerable with them and to find in that exchange a mutual care and compassion which can foster ethical attitudes of kinship which extend beyond the musical encounter. This book is a hopeful book, not least because it assumes that the humanistic values invoked during musicing are indeed universal human qualities which transcend more partisan, biological or cultural identities, because of the opportunities they afford for interpersonal neurobiological attunement. Connecting with or amplifying those qualities is an important way of being able to put aside one's differences – e.g., religious, ideological, cultural, national – and focus our attention more on our common concerns as a species.

If we are to understand – and perhaps even mobilize – musicing as a resource to support our transition to a global species, such an understanding needs to start with a holistic understanding of music itself. I suspect that it is only possible to think about music differently in the present moment because music's value is changing – and has been for twenty years or so. In this period of transition, my hope is that there may be insights to be gleaned which can point towards a more sustainable future. Thinking differently about music means re-assessing a number of assumptions we have about it, the biggest of which is its economic value. Over the same period of the last few hundred years of industrial revolution and global population expansion, music has become a valuable commodity that has made a significant contribution to the wealth of nations. Its value is often measured by its contribution to GDP and export value, as well as the number of people employed in the industry. In the United Kingdom in 2019 (pre-pandemic), the contribution of the music industry to GDP stood at £5.8 billion (*c.*0.18 per cent of UK GDP) and £2.9 billion worth of exports, with the full-time equivalent of 197,168 people (*c.*0.6 per cent of the UK workforce) employed in the sector.

Hysteresis

This relative strength in music's economic value represents a significant resilience in the face of a considerable disruption to the economic value of music – 'cutting the costs of consumption by democratizing distribution' (Anderson 2009: 55) – with the advent of digital distribution of recorded music at the end of the last millennium. The transformation of the market for recorded music from a 'hit' economy to a 'niche' one (177–91) – and the general expectation that music ought to be 'free' – has had profound effects across the whole of the field of music, following Kevin Kelly's broad predictions that as things become plentiful in a 'network' economy, 'they become devalued' (Kelly 1997).

The impact of these radical changes to the way music functions as a 'field' is still playing out and is by no means complete. New technologies e.g., 'live' video streaming, advances in gaming technology – especially 'immersive' environments like virtual reality (VR), online musical tuition services and platforms for musical collaboration – continue to evolve faster than many of us can adapt to them. The speed of change, and the disruption they cause to established practice, would suggest that we are currently in a period of 'hysteresis', where the field of music has changed substantially, but where musicians (more specifically their 'habituses') are still adjusting and adapting to – or lagging behind – those changes. Bourdieu describes hysteresis as,

> the structural lag between opportunities and the dispositions to grasp them which is the cause of missed opportunities and, in particular, of the frequently observed incapacity to think historical crises in categories of perception and thought other than those of the past.
>
> (Bourdieu 1977: 83)

While it is clear that the familiar field of music may be in the process of a radical transition – with increasing blurring of boundaries between producers and consumers of music; performers, audiences and participants; 'professionals' and 'amateurs'; presentational and participatory forms – in terms of cultural production, it is not yet clear what we are in transition *to*. Such is the nature of hysteresis.

This hysteresis – brought about by the disruptive effects of information technology – is not confined to the field of music; other art forms like film and photography are being directly affected too, as the development of markets for 'non-fungible tokens' (NFTs) illustrates. Recorded music may have been one of the first casualties of infotech and its drive towards 'zero marginal cost' (Rifkin 2015: n.pag) but is certainly not the only casualty, or the last. However, building a critical understanding of what happens to the field of music as it undergoes these radical transformations will potentially give us useful insights into our future cultural lives. The massive social, political, economic, environmental, cultural and technological transformations currently disrupting human experience across the globe will almost certainly increase in complexity over time, and what music means to citizens 30 years hence is likely to be radically different to what it meant to citizens 30 years ago. In the course of a single generation, what it means to be a musician in western civilization has changed dramatically and irrevocably. The last wave of technological innovation in music i.e., digital distribution – has disrupted the economic model of music so much that now, people generally expect recorded music to be free. This obviously has serious implications for how musicians might hope or expect to make a living.

Changing value of music

However, within this disruption, there is also opportunity, as music's value goes far beyond its economic value. The 'value' of the abundance of, and free access to, recorded music is not something that can be 'captured' simply in terms of its economic capital, but instead in terms of the opportunities for choice, it provides for consumers, as well as in terms of increased opportunities to produce as well as consume music (Matarasso 2010; Comunian and Gilmore 2016: 46). A consequence of the changing economic value of music has therefore been a resurgence in its symbolic value – its social and cultural value. As well as its ongoing contribution to both entertainment and leisure, we have therefore seen the academic rise of Community Music (CM) (Higgins 2012; Bartleet and Higgins 2018; Willingham 2021), health musicking (Stige 2013) and (community) music therapy (Pavlicevic and Ansdell 2004; Stige et al. 2013), alongside a renaissance in Socially Engaged Art (Bishop 2006; Helguera 2011; Jackson 2011), Everyday Creativity (Hunter et al. 2016) and Cultural Democracy (Gross et al. 2017) movements. Music is beginning to be re-evaluated as much for its impact on people as for its impact on GDP, if not more so. Music is, after all, 'not a single, uniform entity but a far-flung, evershifting constellation of human practices' (Bowman and Frega 2012: 21).

The cultural value of music also might be seen to reside in its utility in relation to national political aims, in terms of its potential for social impact and/or associated positive health and well-being outcomes, which we might think of as having 'proxy' economic value, saving government funds through 'social prescription' of the Arts (Hancock 2018). In the 25 years, since it was suggested that 'participation in arts activities brings social benefits integral to the act of participation' (Matarasso 1997: 10), considerable knowledge has been developed about the positive 'paramusical' effects of musicing such as its positive impact on health and well-being (Clift et al. 2010; DeNora 2013; MacDonald et al. 2013; Creech 2014; Perkins and Williamon 2014), including recent reports by government bodies (Public Health England et al. 2016; All-Party Parliamentary Group on Arts, Health and Wellbeing 2017) which highlight its potential in this regard.

However, this too represents only a partial understanding of music's potential for broader human development. Much of the knowledge outlined above builds an understanding of how music can help people 'cope' with the various existential challenges and everyday hardships they face, rather than focusing on what the structural reasons for increasing ill-health and dissatisfaction might be in the first place. At least, a part of the problem is that information technology – and capitalist systems generally – calls us into global relationships which transcend national boundaries, while our political systems reinforce those same boundaries, resulting in a dissonance of how to *be* in the world. Humanity is struggling to bridge the conceptual gaps between the localized nature of individual circumstances, the global world of information and the *inter*-national world of politics. A key part of my argument is that musicing helps us to bridge these gaps, making connections between multiple human social and biographical identities, from the *actual* social cohesion which is established in the musical moment through to the more *imagined* bonds which unite people in cultural, religious, political, regional, national, inter-national and global identities. Musicing creates opportunities for people to experience others in uniquely human ways, and which transcend their biographical identities, in turn helping us to think differently about how to be in the world, as evidenced very clearly in the most recent compendium of music projects contributing to the United Nation's Sustainable Development Goals (SDGs) (Bartleet and Hesser 2020). The 'worlds' we create when we make music together may only be temporary, lasting only so long as the resulting sounds vibrate in the air, but the sense of communitas which underpins such acts of 'worlding of the world' (Barad 2007: 177) lingers long in our collective memory.

Key themes

In advancing an over-archingly holistic perspective on musicing as a praxis, the book ranges across a number of key themes, and the style of the book is broadly recursive, in that I return to many of these themes as a way of making connections between what may at first appear to be quite separate ideas. In approaching the writing of the book in this way, what I hope to illustrate is how these different conceptual lenses combine and re-combine in different ways to illuminate different perspectives and provide a richer understanding of the subject at hand. While I address these themes in more detail in different chapters, it is worth summarizing some of them beforehand, so that a reader may have a sense of the sorts of conceptual lenses I am going to use to focus my argument. In particular, I want to be clear about what I mean when I talk about (i) musicing, (ii) the human and the posthuman, (iii) diffraction and (iv) Terrapolitanism.

Musicing, musicking, 'musicians' and musician–researchers

You may have already noticed that I use David Elliott's contraction of 'music making' into the term 'musicing' to mean 'all five forms of music making: performing, improvising, composing, arranging, and conducting' (Elliott 1995: 40). I could perhaps instead have chosen to use Christopher Small's term of 'musicking' as a verb meaning 'to take part, in any capacity, in a musical performance, whether by performing, by listening, by rehearsing or practicing, by providing material for performance (what is called composing), or by dancing' (Small 1998: 9). Small's inclusion of listening and dancing as 'musicking' encompasses more experiences which involve musical entrainment and emphasizes the interpersonal relationships which are performed during the act of 'musicking', whereas Elliott's concept – while restricted to those activities which are directly contributing to the resulting sounds – emphasizes the ethical dimensions of praxis. Both definitions are valuable refinements to the term, and both are central to the arguments developed in this book. I toyed with the idea of using the hybrid term 'music'ing' to imply both definitions of music as a verb, but thought a reader may find its repetition rather awkward, so instead settled on Elliott's more ethically inclined term (musicing) as a reminder of (a) the centrality of an *ethical* sensibility underpinning musical action (Bowman 2009b: 162; Regelski 2011: 81) and (b) its contraction of 'music making' in the more restrictive sense of activities which directly contribute to the resulting sounds.

It is therefore also worth highlighting from the outset that the focus of this book is on *the 'live' act of making music together with other people* as distinct from a more passive engagement with music as purely a listener, say. My argument will suggest that there are particular benefits from the mutual musical 'entrainment' associated with active participation in musicing which are pertinent to the formation of identity in quite specific ways but I am also aware that in restricting my focus to active music making, I potentially miss some of the complexity associated with more 'responsive' musical activities e.g., listening to pre-recorded or 'live' music, and dancing. There is of course much to be said about these activities but each represents an entire field of scholarship in itself, and their inclusion would therefore dilute the focus of my argument too much. This working definition of musicing as a 'live' experience also excludes both online and virtual musical experiences, and while these are both of considerable interest to me (Daffern et al. 2018; Camlin and Lisboa 2021) – especially in the context of posthumanism which I discuss in Chapter 6 and musicing during the pandemic crisis which I discuss in Chapter 7 – the main focus of the book is in developing a deeper understanding of face-to-face group musical experiences in order to understand the potential of such experiences as a resource for the collective civic imagination.

I also use the term 'musician' throughout the book to describe any person actively engaged in the act of musicing – to mean both professional, student and/or amateur performers and/or composers; leaders, conductors or facilitators of musicing; other participants and also to some extent listeners. In initial drafts of this book, I kept the quotation marks around the term 'musician' as a reminder that I mean this more inclusive use of the term, especially with regard to both amateur and professional musicians. For the sake of readability – even I found it annoying encountering the term 'musician' (with quotation marks) every few pages – I have removed the quotation marks but I encourage the reader to see the term 'musician' as this broad and inclusive category of biographical identity.

Musician-as-researcher

A further recurring theme throughout the book is the situated nature of the perspective presented here, as the ideas have arisen from within my own musical practice, in dialogue with academic literature. I do not attempt to hide this or gloss over it. In keeping with a diffractive understanding of music, I acknowledge that I am a part of the situation I am trying to understand, just as every musician is. The book was not conceived and written somewhere *outside* of my practice as a musician, but very much entangled within it. I highlight this truth because I want to suggest that if we are to develop a critical understanding of musical practices in such a rapidly changing cultural landscape, the role of the musician-as-researcher is one to be encouraged. To that end, I have included a couple of biographical chapters which 'book-end' the main section of the book, which illustrate how the ideas in the book have emerged in and through my practice as a musician, highlighting the situated nature of the knowledge presented.

Being human

Throughout the book, I draw heavily on the notion that musicing is something that only humans do, pointing to it as a uniquely human characteristic. Active involvement in music making – the act of musicing – is a practice believed to be present in all human cultures throughout our long history, and it therefore represents a fundamentally human capability. As Bowman (2002) suggests, 'when we talk about music we stand on fundamentally human ground, because music is fundamentally human' (57). As a result, much of my argument is grounded in concepts of humanism and humanity, both of which are terms which come with some intellectual baggage, and worth unpacking. Critics of philosophical conceptions of the Humanities often base their criticism on what they see as a culturally specific view of 'what is "human" about humanity' (Braidotti 2013: 13). Anti-humanist traditions centre around the idea that 'man is an invention of recent date [...] and one perhaps nearing its end' (Foucault 1966: 422). Braidotti suggests that da Vinci's Vitruvian Man epitomises the humanist ideal of a white, able-bodied male, which is both alienating and limiting in terms of human aspiration, and instead uses the term 'posthuman' to indicate the need to think beyond the 'historically specific construction called the human' (Hayles 1999) in order to 'think critically and creatively about who and what we are actually in the process of becoming' (Braidotti 2013: 12). Much of Braidotti's line of thinking forms a substantial part of my own argument, especially in Chapter

6, and a consideration of the 'posthuman' thinking found in New Materialist approaches to philosophy and the need to extend concepts of flourishing beyond the human species to include all life on the planet, and indeed the planet itself. In this sense, it is important to recognize that even concepts of musicing might be anthropocentric, privileging particular human musical behaviours over the kinds of communication enjoyed by other species as a 'higher' order of musical communication. Musical entrainment – in and of itself – is not an indication of a more evolved biology but simply an adaptation which has allowed humans to do some things that other animals do not.

Nevertheless, I also maintain that there is much to be gained from a broader consideration of the notion of humanity than an anti-humanist stance allows. The modern humanist movement might be seen to arise in response to the horrors of the global conflicts of the early twentieth century (Camlin 2021c), especially in the resulting 'search for meaning' (Frankl 1946) which followed the Holocaust, and in particular the work of Hannah Arendt around the 'human condition' (Arendt 1958), which considers humanity from a more universal perspective than the Vitruvian ideal. Furthermore, much of my argument develops around the role of music in the 230,000 year history of human evolution (Aiello and Dunbar 1993; Cross and Morley 2010; Dunbar 2012), as well as its enduring function in human ontogeny (Tomasello 2019) or how humans develop over the lifespan. My argument also rests in part on a consideration of human interpersonal neurobiology, and it simply doesn't make sense to me to talk of *post*human neurobiology – neurobiologically we are still more or less the same human organism we were 230,000 years ago, even though there is of course much about modern humans that would no doubt be unrecognizable to even our more recent ancestors, and vice versa.

As a result, a reader may notice what appear to be inconsistencies in my use of the terms 'human' and 'posthuman'. I like both terms, for different reasons, and am therefore reluctant to abandon either term altogether. A notion of humanity which is predicated on neurobiological similarities – rather than on biological, physical, cultural, racial or religious differences – seems to be one worth defending, and both terms speak to such a definition, although it does not make them interchangeable. Therefore, to clarify, when I refer to the 'human', it is specifically with the long history of the human species in mind, and when I refer to the 'posthuman', it is with the sense of transcending the Vitruvian ideal which grounded study in the Humanities for much of the nineteenth and twentieth centuries. Between these two – often fiercely contested – distinctions, there is much common ground about what it means to be human. Certainly, the values in Chapter 6 which I argue are materialized through musicing – love, reciprocity and justice – might be viewed as both human *and* posthuman.

Diffraction/waveform interference

At the heart of musical experience is the experience of the ways in which different sounds combine to produce particular effects. If we take as a foundation the classic definition of music as 'organised sound' (Varèse 1966: 18) and that what we mean by 'sound' is simply vibrations in the air which fall within the range of human hearing, then this book is a logical extension of the consequences of that basic premise, as it applies in the way that humans organize sound (and other waveforms, as I shall discuss) through their disparate activities and traditions of musicing.

Throughout the book, I refer to the concept of diffraction/waveform interference which I have borrowed from the work of quantum physicist Karen Barad – in turn developing the work of atomic physicist Niels Bohr – to discuss the organization of sound. In lay terms, waveform interference is to do with how waveforms behave when they encounter other waveforms, either becoming amplified or attenuated through such encounters. In music, we talk of such encounters in terms of the consonance and dissonance of soundwaves, and the resulting patterns created when sounds mingle is really at the heart of what makes a musical experience satisfying or not.

Diffraction, by contrast, is perhaps a more slippery concept. In more literal terms, it describes what happens to a waveform when it passes through an aperture which is shorter than the wave's length, causing the waveform to bend and spread on the other side of the aperture, for example flood water pouring through a narrow gap in a wall. Barad also suggests that we can think of diffraction in more metaphorical terms, not just about what happens to a waveform when it encounters an obstacle but about the 'patterns of difference' (Barad 2007: 84) which emerge from such an encounter, and in a more general sense, about 'patterns of difference that *make* a difference' (85, emphasis added). In conceiving of diffraction in this more figurative way, Barad opens up the concept to be useful to consider other kinds of experience. I draw on both a literal *and* a metaphorical understanding of diffraction, first to develop an argument about the intra-active way in which a number of waveforms (principally sonic and neurobiological mechanisms) might become entangled during the act of musicing, and second to highlight the importance of pedagogical approaches which respond to the uniquely situated nature of all music education situations (the 'diffractive pedagogy' I introduce in Chapter 8).

Music is not just a sonic experience, and my argument also rests on an assumption that diffraction/waveform interference is experienced in other ways too through musicing. While we can hear (and feel) the sounds music produces as vibrations in the air and in our bodies, musicing also entangles other aspects of our physiology – our interpersonal neurobiology in particular – such that the sounds we hear can also be understood as the physical manifestation of the experience of human vitality, of other kinds of diffractive experience deep inside us which connect us to others. I discuss these issues in more detail in Chapter 3, as a hypothetical explanation for some of the commonly reported experiences of 'magic moments' (Gabrielsson 2011: 746; Pavlicevic 2013b: 102) in musicing. While there are obvious limits to this kind of hypothetical thinking about musicing when compared with empirical observation, they can also help to illuminate these transcendental experiences in different ways, largely because such moments tend to evade a more scientific understanding. As well as being physically present in the form of organized sounds that we can hear, music also therefore stands as a temporary resonance signifying the interpersonal connections which underpin it. To build on Varèse' perspective, we might say that music is *sound organised through attuned bodies*.

For quantum physicists like Barad and Bohr, paying close attention to the whole of the apparatus wherein patterns of diffraction can be observed means above all recognizing that the observer is inescapably 'a part of that nature that we seek to understand' (Barad 2007: 35). In other words, the observer can never be somehow 'outside' the system they are observing. This is important to my argument in a number of ways. First, it introduces the notion of 'entanglement' which is important throughout the book, especially in Chapter 3 where I discuss the well-being effects of musicing as arising from a complex 'entangled state' of multiple mechanisms. Second, it justifies my inclusion of two biographical chapters – Chapters 2 and 7 – as a means of accounting for the situated and practical nature of my perspective – my own entanglement within the subject as a practitioner of music – and how it inevitably influences the things I write about, and the thoughts I think with. Third, it helps to focus my discussion in Chapter 4 about the different musical traditions of performance and participation, drawing on the universal experience of diffraction/interference to highlight the similarities of what might often be considered quite separate traditions. Finally, it underpins the development in Chapter 8 of the notion of a 'diffractive' pedagogy, as a reminder to music educators to account for their own presence and influence in the particular material circumstances of their practice.

Terrapolis

In relation to some of the above discussion, I draw on Donna Haraway's conception of Terrapolis (Haraway 2016) as a way of understanding how we might make the transition from a human world in conflict with itself, to one that exists more harmoniously and sustainably with the planet and its other cohabitants. Many geologists concur in demarcating the current period of the earth's history as the dawn of a new epoch – the Anthropocene – in which 'conditions and processes on

Earth are profoundly altered by human impact' (Anthropocene Working Group 2019). Haraway, like some geologists (Bauer et al. 2021), prefers to view this period of human impact on the earth as a 'boundary event' – a period of disruption *between* epochs rather than a new epoch altogether. What matters to Haraway is what comes *after* the Anthropocene, and what kind of journey we take to get there.

Rather than Cosmopolitanism – and all of the complex and chequered history of that term (Goldberg-Vååg 2018) – Haraway invokes the notion of Terrapolis as a fictional political system beyond the Anthropocene, an '*n*-dimensional niche space for multi-species becoming-with' (Haraway 2016: 11) where humans co-exist with other species and natural systems without bringing them – or us – to the point of destruction. Because Terrapolis is a fictional place in the future, it calls on us to prepare for the journey by carefully selecting those resources that will be of most use when we arrive. Of course, the journey to Terrapolis is itself the destination, so the selection of resources for the journey becomes about how we *imagine* that future world into existence. I discuss these ideas in more detail in Chapter 6 but what is of pertinence to this introduction is that whatever journey we take beyond this period of the earth's history, it requires both imagination and a leap of faith: imagination in the sense of having to think of different ways of 'becoming-with' the planet and faith in the sense of knowing where to turn to find appropriate resources for the journey.

This is precisely where musicing may have a role to play. In Chapter 5, I discuss at some length the different ways we have put our human musicality to service in our evolution from small social groups of hunter-gatherers to the current orthodoxy of nation-states consisting of millions of individuals. In this book, I suggest that it is this uniquely human capacity of musicing – of 'tuning in' to the internal states of others through musical entrainment – which might be a practical collaborative resource which helps to stabilize the vicissitudes of more complex social realities, reminding participants of our common humanity as a foundation wherein more complex affiliations can be grounded. It is into such liminal spaces – a step outside of everyday realities – where civic imagination can be brought vividly to life, through the 'performance' of positive interpersonal relationships leading to strong bonds of human connectivity which reach out to possible futures – a resource of kinship to help us face the existential challenges which threaten all life on the planet. As Donna Haraway suggests,

> The task is to make kin in lines of inventive connection as a practice of learning to live and die well with each other in a thick present. Our task is to make trouble, to stir up potent response to devastating events, as well as to settle troubled waters and rebuild quiet places.
>
> (Haraway 2016: 1)

Bumps in the road

As well as these various over-arching themes, there are also a number of underlying complexities and challenges which underpin much of the discussion in the book. I cannot claim that my argument is able to resolve these (although I do hope it may help to question some of them more critically) but it is important to highlight them from the outset, so that they are present for a reader in what follows. I'm very aware that presenting musicing as a possible complementary solution to global challenges might seem naïve and even frivolous, given the scale of threat represented by the particular combination of existential challenges currently facing humanity. Therefore, throughout the book, I have attempted to prevent my argument from falling into the various traps and pitfalls associated with an 'advocacy' agenda (Belfiore and Bennett 2008: 7), and a blind belief that music can 'save the world', by approaching it with as much critically as I am able.

Inequalities of cultural access

Music is clearly *not* a panacea for all social ills and is by no means a universal social 'good'. Whether any given instance of musicing is in fact capable of producing any kind of social 'good' depends entirely on whether 'the need for ethical foresight and prudence' (Regelski 2011: 81) is materially present:

> Since performing is not good in and of itself, whether it helps or harms depends upon how we engage in it and upon what we perform. But that is not a sign of deficiency: it is, rather, a natural consequence of its power and import. The outcomes of musical performance are not "just musical"; they are personal, social, and political, involving important moral and ethical considerations – and not tangentially, but centrally. We need to be critically vigilant not only about the musical quality of what we perform, but of everything we are performing musically.
>
> (Bowman 2009b: 162)

Paradoxically, as well as being liberating and empowering for many, music making can also be seen to be 'at once inclusionary and exclusionary' (Bowman 2016: 59–80), instrumental in mobilizing partisan national, religious or cultural identities which might be seen to *impede* matters such as global sustainable development. When it comes to matters of social justice, it might also be seen to be part of the problem, a kind of 'symbolic violence' (Bourdieu and Passeron 1977: 6–68) against those excluded from cultural participation, perpetuating and reinforcing structural inequalities. Indeed, there is a growing recognition that despite the best efforts of a series of political initiatives over many years, widening access to publicly funded cultural experiences has not advanced in the way many may have imagined it would. It is alarming that, following twenty years of heavy investment in the Arts in the United Kingdom, we are still reporting that,

> The wealthiest, better educated and least ethnically diverse 8% of the population forms the most culturally active segment of all: between 2012 and 2015 they accounted (in the most conservative estimate possible) for 44% of attendances to live music, benefitting from £94 per head of Arts Council music funding.
>
> (Neelands et al. 2015: 33)

We can see the apparent proliferation of more culturally democratic initiatives as being part of the solution, but if we want to see a world where 'everyday creativity' (Hunter et al. 2016) is part of society's fabric and 'making art is a daily experience' (Fox 2009) for everyone, then clearly there is much distance yet to travel. Much of the research around the social impact of the arts has tended to start from a deficit position, assuming that arts activities are primarily interventions in ill health or disenfranchisement, rather than exploring the potential of the arts for addressing the root causes of structural inequalities, which are more ideological. Rather than skirting over these uncomfortable issues, I address them directly by suggesting that musicing can only be considered as a *potential* resource of civic imagination – a disavowal of political solutions to complex problems, and a means of making democracy happen by doing something about one's immediate situation. The extent to which it is *able* to achieve such ambitions is entirely dependent upon its ethical character and delivery.

My argument rests to no small degree on the assumption that musicing can foster the 'performance' of 'ideal relationships as the participants in the performance imagine them to be' (Small 1998: 314), and one of the challenges of writing about music from this kind of idealistic perspective is that it is easy for the intended goals of musicing (e.g. social connection) to become part of its pre-requisites, resulting in a circular and self-defeating argument. In other words, that people who are more capable of or motivated to develop interpersonal relationships because of their position in society can use musicing as a means of reinforcing that privilege which they already enjoy as socially connected individuals.

In Chapter 5, I suggest that it is precisely this kind of 'dead end' of cultural thinking which has prevented more democratic access to cultural resources. As a practitioner, it is something which continually disturbs my reflections on what I do and why I do it, attempting to ensure that I am not inadvertently becoming part of the problem of cultural injustice I am hoping to address through my practice (Camlin 2017a, 2018b) by reproducing cultural norms which mitigate against participation. Through the book, I hope my argument illuminates at least some of these ethical concerns facing musicians who want to use their musical capabilities to make a difference in the world. While critically examining the ethical considerations which motivate such practice – and which help transform it into *praxis* – might not provide a guarantee of producing social 'goods', the absence of such critical examination is much more likely to result in practice which is only superficially 'good', or worse, actively harmful.

Hesmondhalgh's (2013) critique of the idealist perspectives of theorists on which my argument is built – Christopher Small, Charles Keil and Thomas Turino – which he characterizes as 'primitive sociality [being] made the basis of a quest for an ideal future' (88) might also be levelled at the idea of music making and civic imagination in that it might be seen to advocate 'a notion of collective flourishing which is only likely to lead to misunderstanding and disappointment' and which may 'miss the more ordinary ways in which good sociality continues to be a feature even of the damaged worlds of capitalist modernity' (88). My defence of musicing as a way of encountering more idealized social relations is to suggest that such encounters foster agency – not necessarily to change the world in its entirety but at least to 'change the world within my reach' (Erelli 2006). As Tia DeNora suggests, music is as 'a resource in and through which agency and identity are produced' (DeNora 2000: 5):

> Music may contribute to the sense that actors make of themselves and their social circumstances. Music is active within social life, it has 'effects' then, because it offers specific materials to which actors may turn when they engage in the work of organizing social life. Music is a resource – it provides affordances – for world building.
>
> (DeNora 2000: 44)

Devaluation of music

Whilst suggesting that the changes in the economic value of music have given rise to a relative revaluation of its symbolic – cultural and social – value, it is also worth noting that in other ways music's more precarious relationship to economic capital makes it a target for disinvestment by neoliberal administrations. In the United Kingdom, despite the music industry's significant ongoing contribution to GDP, we have seen ongoing disinvestment in music through government policy. In the United Kingdom during the recent COVID-19 pandemic, significant numbers of musicians received no government support to sustain their incomes and businesses, and a third of the workforce was lost (UK Music 2021). One of the first policy decisions post-pandemic in the UK was a 50 per cent cut in government support for music courses in higher education (Office for Students 2021), a move that is believed will lead to many such courses ceasing to be viable, thereby choking the supply of education for aspiring professional musicians. A recent report by the Incorporated Society of Musicians (ISM) suggests that music education is a 'subject in peril' because of educational policy failures over many years (Underhill and ISM 2022). Increasingly, music appears to be falling through the cracks, and it is a cause of much frustration and concern for many in the industry and those involved in the education of musicians.

However, we might take some comfort from the fact that it is often in such cracks that the seeds of new ideas germinate and take root. I hope that music making as an act of civic imagination is one such idea. We are so used to our thinking being conditioned by the economic value of things that we can struggle to make sense of a rapidly changing world. As Slavoj Žižek (2018) notes, 'change is already happening in broad daylight: capitalism is openly disintegrating and changing into something else. We do not perceive this ongoing transformation because of our deep immersion in ideology' (226). If civic imagination ultimately leads us towards Terrapolis, where new relationships between humans and the world take shape, it is to be expected that there will be bumps in the road.

Perhaps the biggest barrier on our journey to Terrapolis is that it is not really a journey that the current political and economic order wishes us to make. The orthodoxy of political discourse is centred around what Bruno Latour (2017) terms the 'sovereignty of the states', and thus all discourse around how to live with our fellows is constrained by the assumption of the nation-state as 'the only viable basis for political community' (Hesmondhalgh 2013: 151). It is an invisible discourse, so taken for granted that it is barely possible to think outside of its constraints. And yet the 'sovereignty of the states' must be no less a discursive practice than any other, consisting of 'a body of anonymous, historical rules, always determined in the time and space that have defined a given period, and for a given social, economic, geographical, or linguistic area' (Foucault 2002: 126). It is an issue which I address directly in Chapter 5 of the book but the implications of this discourse permeate all threads of my argument.

Musicing provides one such means of thinking outside of the political box. When we are musicing, we cease to be citizens of a particular state (although we can of course imagine ourselves as such) and instead become citizens of the temporary republics of harmony that we build together in the air through the diffraction of the waveforms our musicing creates. Therefore, in musicing, we inhabit the possibility of existing within an alternative discourse of political affiliation, a discourse that is centred around the temporal relationships which are formed and dissolve as we build patterns of diffraction together, through our collective communicative musicality. While critics of the idea of musicing as a resource for the political imagination suggest that, 'the whole point of liminality is that it cannot last, and so cannot sustain societies or communities' (Hesmondhalgh 2013: 72), this is only partially true. Musicing presents us with a way of relating to one another that is emergent, dynamic and interpersonally sensitive, and the experience of these kinds of (albeit temporary) relationships can be an ongoing source of inspiration and aspiration which endures long after the sounds themselves have dissipated. However, these are not neutral spaces – there are no guarantees that they can be used to further the public 'good', and history has taught us that often – and especially without ethical underpinning – they can be spaces where prejudices and assumptions can be reinforced, rather than challenged. However, because the liminal space which musicing facilitates is conditioned by our collective intentions, when infused with an ethic of love, kinship and mutuality it can also be somewhere where we begin to imagine alternative ways of being, with and for each other, and with and for the planet.

Summary

Making music together is one possible way of enacting our fundamental ethical obligations to each other as fellow human beings, as a part of a general commitment to what bell hooks terms ethical living: 'living ethically ensures that relationships in our lives, including encounters with strangers, nurture our spiritual growth' (hooks 2000: 120). In turn, encountering each other in a way which represents our collective responsibilities to one another also reminds us of our collective ethical responsibilities as the dominant species on a fragile planet. The earth calls us to find more ethical, just and equitable ways of living in harmony – with each other and with the fragile resources of the planet. Making kin through making music is one way of answering that call.

A commitment to living ethically will be a vital attitude as we navigate towards an uncertain future. In a world facing enormous challenges, there is a clear need for activities like musicing which form part of the social 'glue' that will be required to prevent our species from falling into terminal conflict with itself. Kwame Anthony Appiah notes that, 'conflicts between people of different identity, usually have at their base something other than the identity itself,' namely 'competition for resources' which creates the conditions for those more divisive and conflicting identities to be 'mobilised' (Appiah 2016: n.pag.). We might see the recent resurgence of nationalism across the globe as evidence of these more partisan identities – along racial, religious, class and territorial lines – becoming mobilised in order to compete for what appears to be increasingly scarce resources. We might also therefore reasonably expect that the challenging conditions outlined at the start of this chapter will increase the likelihood of further conflict not just across individual societies, but across the world.

In such a divided world, it is worth remembering that while music in general may play a significant role in reinforcing *differences* in cultural identity because of the ways in which it represents 'public presentations of the deepest feelings and qualities that make a group unique' (Turino 2008: 2), it is also the case that it can also be instrumental in *transcending* those same differences. Making music together – when underpinned by an ethical sensibility – can help us express our common (post)humanity, providing us with a common language of empathy, emotion, enjoyment and understanding where other forms of communication fall short. Musicing might therefore be seen as a valuable way of mediating some of the divisions which threaten to disrupt the fabric of our society in an increasingly uncertain future.

Perhaps *because* the field of music has been among the first to feel the impact of the radical economic changes which are already transforming our world, the experience of musicians is perhaps of some value in navigating a course through the troubled times ahead. Perhaps *because* musicing has been an essential part of our capacity to transcend our individual differences and connect with our fellow humans since the origin of our species (Dunbar 2012; Mithen 2007), we can turn to it now as a uniquely human resource to help build trust and empathy within our communities and across the globe. For these reasons, perhaps we need music now more than ever. Not only as a way of maintaining positive health and well-being in an ever more complex and challenging world but also as a way of forming bonds with our fellow humans which transcend our cultural, ethnic, geographic, political and religious backgrounds and differences – a way of expressing and celebrating what makes us uniquely and collectively human.

Faced with an uncertain future, we shall clearly need our wits about us. Understanding the value of music and musicing in ever more critical terms is essential if we are to meet the challenges the future holds. Hence, the need to build up a more critical understanding of the situated and pluralistic nature of ethically guided musicing practices. We do not need to reach a 'consensus' about what these should look and sound like; the rich diversity of our practices calls on us to articulate our various perspectives in 'dissensual' ways (Camlin 2017b, 2016c, 2015a), in order to allow our combined voices to become a clamorous and polyphonic truth, helping to raise the level of discussion about the value of music in an increasingly uncertain world. In doing so, we play our part in building a body of knowledge that will, in turn, contribute to a more hopeful vision of Terrapolis – a future society where being musical is a part of everyone's daily experience, and an essential human activity which helps unite us as a species and as a planet.

Who is this book for?

I hope this book will be of interest to anyone with a practical and/or scholarly interest in music, CM in particular, and music making. Above all, the people who I most imagine reading it are fellow musicians – from diverse backgrounds and all levels of experience – who are looking for insights into how to connect their musicality to a bigger purpose. In particular, I hope that if you're a musician who also thinks of yourself as an educator, that you will find something in here to help you develop insights into your own practice, and perhaps be inspired to pursue your own line of critical inquiry. Perhaps most of all, this book is for you if you are just finding yourself as a musician and would like some reassurance that your way of being musical is absolutely fine. This is the book I wished I'd had to hand for many of the young musicians I've worked with over the last 30 years or so. I hope it is the kind of book I'd come across when I was just starting out as a musician myself, which may have helped me to think about music differently, and sooner.

I hope it is also a helpful reference for other professionals – e.g., health workers, youth workers, social workers, occupational therapists – who use music as part of their work with people, or who want to find a reason to. Music can play an important role in health recovery (both physical and mental) and in identity development, and I hope that the arguments I make will convince or confirm for you that music is more than 'auditory cheesecake' (Pinker 2003: 534) or a bit of fun. Music is (or should be) fun, but it also speaks very deeply and directly to the heart of what it means to be human. With that in mind, I hope that the content of the book will speak to cultural policy makers, cultural managers and cultural institutions as well as other arts professionals, in helping to develop a more nuanced discourse about the value of music to people and society, and the need to be 'vigilant' about how we deploy it so that we avoid reinforcing some of the structural inequalities of access to culture which have beset our sector over its recent history.

Structure and contents

I have structured this book in three parts, which I hope will help to accompany the reader on a journey through the ideas raised and developed. In this current Part 1: Introduction, I outline the book's structure and the development of my own perspective on the issues under discussion. This current Chapter 1: 'Music in an Uncertain World', provides a summary of the rest of the book and the various themes discussed throughout its pages, where I introduce the potential of musicing in the context of some of the existential challenges currently facing the human species, and the implications of this, particularly for those just emerging into professional practice as musicians. In the following Chapter 2: 'Libraries Gave Us Power', I use some of my personal biography as a music practitioner – performer, composer, teacher and researcher – to illuminate the origins of the ideas which have led to this book. I also advocate the importance of this kind of practice-based enquiry as a way of expanding our knowledge of the field of music generally, and practitioner experience as a valuable source of knowledge in a changing world. This might be of particular interest to other musicians embarking on a more critical inquiry into their practice but I hope also provides some useful context for how this book came to be.

Part 2: Thinking About Music is the greater part of the book, where I present an array of conceptual lenses and thinking tools which focus on the central issues of music making as a holistic practice which engages and inspires civic imagination. Chapter 3: 'Music as a Complex Adaptive System' opens the lid on the complex ways in which musicing comes to 'mean' something, both in the hundreds of intra-active mechanisms which might be at play, and the way in which we generally experience this complexity as a totality rather than in its isolated parts. Drawing on an evolutionary history of music, I highlight the importance of music as a uniquely human form of communication, founded on the kind of 'communicative musicality' (Malloch and Trevarthen 2010) which survives in all relationships between infants and their care-givers, and grounded in notions of musical 'entrainment' (Clayton 2012) underpinned with an ethic of love. I elaborate on why the idea of love is central to a holistic philosophy of music, underpinning such vital concerns as human attachment and social bonding, which in turn underpin the act of musicing itself. I then refer to contemporary accounts of 'agential realism' (Barad 2007) and 'vitality dynamics' (Stern 2010), to suggest that we might consider the perceived benefits of musicing as an 'entangled state' between the music, on the one hand, and its effects on those participating, on the other.

In Chapter 4: 'Performing Works, Performing Relationships', I consider some of the complexities which arise from this holistic perspective on music in relation, recognizing a creative tension between three complementary dimensions of musical experience: the presentational or aesthetic – the performance of musical works, or music for *listening to*; the participatory – music as the 'performance' of relationships, or music for *doing*; and the paramusical – the significant benefits which 'go along with' musical experience. I consider how over time, these different dimensions have become separated into different musical traditions, a move which has tended to limit our understanding of music's value as a totality. Re-uniting these traditions into a holistic philosophy of music where all three dimensions are active provides valuable insights into the complexities surrounding the issue of music as a social 'good', including its potential as a resource for 'healthy publics' (Hinchliffe et al. 2018; Camlin et al. 2020) and health and well-being more generally.

An important implication of the reunification of music's complementary dimensions is that traditional notions of musical 'quality' are insufficient in terms of understanding music in its complex totality. I highlight a number of important notions which help to make sense of some of these complexities: the notion of dialogue as a way of discovering perspectives different to our own, in music as in life; the notion of diffraction as a way of considering the complex ways in which music's different dimensions *intra-act*; the notion of dissensus as a reminder of the pluralistic and contested nature of musical experience; the notion of praxis – 'theory imbricated within practice' (Nelson 2013: 33) – as a way of exploring the particular and situated ways in which divergent musical practices evolve and are sustained.

In order to make an argument about how musicing might provide imaginative possibilities for future ways of co-existing more harmoniously on the planet, in Chapter 5: 'Music, Politics and Society', I examine some of the current political contexts of music and its value to people and society. I consider how music can be seen to be instrumental in the forming of both social and biographical/political identities, by reviewing the role of music in the evolution of human political affiliations up to the present day, and the conceptual barriers that the present 'sovereignty of the states' (Latour 2017) – the orthodox view of the nation-state as the highest possible political affiliation imaginable – presents for imagining more global identities. I also consider some of the ways in which national cultural agendas have reinforced this orthodoxy, even at the expense of the well-being of a nation's citizens due to rising inequality and historical injustices, and some of the ways in which more culturally democratic initiatives can address these complex issues.

Chapter 6: 'Music Making and Civic Imagination' draws the preceding chapters together into an argument for music as a means of imagining – and beginning to inhabit – the kinds of future world we might wish to inhabit as *citizens of the planet*, or Terrapolitans. Following a discussion of the different 'dialects' of civic imagination, and its general disavowal of politics as a more promising solution for addressing complex global issues, I consider how musicing might be considered a form of civic imagination, a 'performance' of the humanistic values – love, reciprocity, justice – that might be mobilized as a part of an ethical underpinning to our relationships with all human and non-human life on the planet, and the planet's ecological systems.

In the final part of the book – Part 3: Practical Applications – I consider some of the practical implications of the book's main themes. In Chapter 7: 'This Musician', I outline how the ideas developed in the book and the development of my own practices as a musician have fed into each other, including the development of approaches to research – e.g., Sensemaker® as a 'distributed ethnography', which I have pioneered to understand those practices. In particular, I focus on socially engaged undergraduate music projects at Sage Gateshead and Royal College of Music which have directly informed my thinking, as well as how ideas about musicing and civic imagination have emerged from a number of recent artistic projects I have been involved with.

Chapter 8: 'Musician Education' makes some suggestions as to how these holistic principles can be applied in supporting emerging musicians to prepare for a professional portfolio career in music during a time of global transition. Our uncertain future lies not just in the hands of our politicians but also in the creative imaginations of our artists and musicians, and it is for this reason that the education of musicians needs to evolve too. Both the current hysteresis in the music industry and an increasing awareness of the need for globally sustainable musical practices means that the focus of musician education is already different to what it was twenty years ago and is steadily evolving.

Historically, the education of musicians has focused on training them to take up roles within the existing economic model. Now that this model is changing, musicians find themselves trying to make sense of the complex ways to get by against a background of diminishing returns. Most musicians who sustain a career in music now do so with some form of music education – e.g., 1:1 studio teaching, classroom teaching, community music or music therapy/health musicking – as part of a broader portfolio of skills and practices. As educators, musicians therefore need to develop a sophisticated set of capabilities to help them move across a range of different teaching-learning situations, by sensitively 'tuning in' and responding – musically and pedagogically – to observable behaviours in their students/participants/clients. However, the process of developing these capabilities also means re-thinking what it means to be a musician; not just changing musicians' practices and habits but the whole way we think about music itself, what it is for, and what we do with it. Instead of *training* musicians to take up a place in society where their contribution is primarily understood as economic through the taxes raised on their recordings and public performances, we need to re-focus our efforts instead on *educating* musicians to be a source of inspiration for civic imagination, to be at the centre of creative new ways of 'becoming-with' all life on the planet.

I hope you enjoy reading this book as much as I have enjoyed writing it, and I also hope it raises questions and insights which help you to reflect on the role that music has in your own life and the musical lives of the individuals and communities which intra-act with your own. Above all, I hope it may inspire you to view musicing as a resource that you can put to service in your particular situation, and to feel that, collectively, music is something we can *do* to address some of the existential challenges we face.

2

Libraries Gave Us Power

FIGURE 2.1: Tryckster and Choirs at Sage Gateshead 2017.

In this brief chapter, I provide some biographical background to the development of the ideas in this book. I do so to make it clear that this is not an attempt at an objective account but rather very much a personal and therefore subjective perspective. My interest in research has been driven by questions that have arisen from my practice as a musician, in particular the significant part of my career which has been dedicated to leading or facilitating musical activities and being involved in the education of other musicians and artists. My intention, therefore, is to lay bare my lack of objectivity; it is not possible for me to pretend that my perspective on the things I write about is impartial.

One of the assertions I repeat in this book is that all musicing is uniquely situated, by which I mean not only that all musicians operate in unique situations but that we are intimately a part of those situations and often influence them considerably. Therefore, to be a musician is always to be *this* musician, making music in *this* situation with *these* people and *these* materials, within *these* cultures and traditions. This is an important point as it raises a number of questions to do with how possible it is to infer any general insights into musical situations and also to do with the transferability of any insights, practices and approaches between those different situations. The ideas in this book feel useful to me because I think I can *do* something with them in my practice. If you can do something with them too, that will make it worth me having written them down, but more than that, I hope that my approach inspires you to want to tell your own story.

This is my truth ...

My own development as a musician originates from being a self-taught singer/song-writer, very loosely from within informal traditions of folk, rock and popular music. I have written songs since my adolescence when I learned that being able to write songs and sing them was a way of building some small degree of cultural capital within my immediate peer group. My first band was formed in school and called Sky Blue Formica, named after the brand of table covering in use throughout the school. We reasoned that as it was already written on the underside of every table in the school, it would look like a viral graffiti campaign to help promote our band. Needless to say, the fact that you haven't heard of Sky Blue Formica (until now) rather betrays our hopeless naïveté.

I continue writing songs and singing as a key part of how I identify in the world and, apart from a couple of albums with different bands on a small folk label in the early 2000s, have been largely untroubled by commercial success. As a younger musician, I found this rather dispiriting but over time I have come to appreciate the space it has given me to develop my musical identity in ways that are motivated much more by my own creative ideas and urges, collaborations with other musicians and a commitment to the place where I live and the community of people who live here.

Some days I think my career has been based around saying 'yes' to every opportunity I possibly can. A lot of the time, following the advice of Eleanor Roosevelt – 'you must do the thing you think you cannot do' – borrowing the confidence of friends, family and peers when my own confidence wasn't quite enough. As a result, I've enjoyed a varied career as a musician. I've performed all over the world in different musical guises, from Glastonbury and Scafell Pike to RSC Stratford and the Royal Opera House; I've supported hundreds of young musicians to develop their skills and knowledge; was part of the organizing committee for the Solfest music festival for ten years; and founded SoundWave, a charitable community music (CM) organization which is still going strong more than a decade after I stepped down as its founding Creative Director. Most of that I did with little idea of the road ahead, doing what I imagine most musicians do; seizing every opportunity as it presented itself and giving it my best shot.

Becoming a researcher was not part of any great career plan. The idea of academic study couldn't have been further from my mind while I was busy in bands in my twenties and thirties. Having trained as a teacher, I spent eight years with multiple identities – a secondary school teacher by day; a gigging folk musician at the weekends; and a community musician in the spaces in between. When the music side of things took off a bit more, I gave up the school teaching and just concentrated on the music. Gradually, I integrated my music and teaching/facilitation skills into a 'portfolio' career with CM as a key ingredient. Historically, community musicians have been resistant to conceptualizing their practice (McKay and Higham 2012: 5; Brown et al. 2014: 2), and I completely understand why. CM is a practical activity, and, as practitioners, our practices have evolved in response to the particular situations we find ourselves in, often in contrast to more orthodox approaches to music education. To attempt to create a 'general theory' of CM practice is therefore often to miss the situated and emergent nature of such practice. Although I attended the occasional conference, research was definitely 'not for the likes of me'. I saw academics as people in lofty towers with equally lofty ideas, one step (or many) removed from the 'real world' of professional practice. So, what changed?

While never really thinking of myself as 'academic', studying philosophy at university had introduced me to the notion of dialogue as a form of knowledge development, very much in the Socratic tradition. I hope that I have always, therefore, taught from the perspective of facilitating students' autonomy and agency through critical reflection and dialogue, asking questions and promoting peer dialogue. I didn't realize that the way I taught was in the tradition of Freirean dialogics (Freire 1970) and Critical Pedagogy (Giroux 2011; Abrahams), because I didn't know what those things were.

Sage Gateshead and beyond

My research journey started properly in 2010 when I was appointed as Head of Higher Education & Research (HE&R) at Sage Gateshead, NE England's flagship music venue on the south bank of the River Tyne. I'm aware of making myself sound supremely unqualified for such a role, whereas actually since 2001, I had developed a role as a senior manager within the organization's Learning & Participation programme before founding SoundWave, so what I lacked in academic knowledge I made up for in the confidence that comes from having practical skills and experience. During this period, I had developed a more critical understanding of reflective practice through my leadership roles in a number of national and regional initiatives involving artists in reflecting on their practice through peer–mentor relationships (Renshaw 2008; Camlin 2012; Cooper 2013).

My new responsibilities included the organization's innovative BA (Hons) Community Music degree, and finding myself responsible for undergraduate learning and knowledge development was a daunting prospect, especially in such a new academic field as CM. Although CM scholarship has flourished in recent years, at the time, knowledge of CM certainly wasn't 'book' knowledge. The practices of CM have tended to evolve in very practical ways, amongst communities of practitioners and their communities of participants (Camlin 2015a: 236). Authentic CM knowledge is therefore both situated and situational, i.e. it emerges from within the particular situations where it evolves, and it changes as those situations change. In that sense, it is always emergent and unique (248). Because of this, developing a 'theory' of CM practice through research has been complex and contested, and the endeavour of doing so is viewed with suspicion by some of its practitioners, including myself.

However, it became clear to me very early on in my new role that relying on how I'd grown accustomed to reflecting on my work as a teaching musician – personal experience, opinion, intuition and gut instinct – was clearly insufficient when it came to backing up approaches with evidence, and especially when sign-posting undergraduate students to the academic knowledge they would need to underpin their own ideas more critically. So, I read. A lot. And the more I read, the more I realized that the knowledge I was acquiring through study gave me more robust critical frameworks to articulate my own practice as an educator and as a musician more generally.

In 2011, I signed up for a self-funded Professional Doctorate (DProf) with the University of Sunderland. This was a route that worked for me because it required me to build up a critical understanding of my own professional situation. Very quickly, I was able to see that what I was involved with at Sage Gateshead was a kind of Action Research (McNiff 2013), using the opportunity of undergraduate programmes situated inside a cultural organization to build up a stronger critical understanding not just of the undergraduate experience of CM but also of Sage Gateshead's wider artistic practices, and of the situation itself – a cultural organization in a collaborative partnership with a HE institution. This particular arrangement was a unique opportunity for research, and I threw myself into the task, quickly forgetting my former reticence and suspicion of academia.

Therefore, my doctoral research dealt directly with my own situation as a musician and senior manager within Sage Gateshead – an organization which at the time expressed its artistic programme as consisting equally of performance and participation. As part of its early history, the organization had to evolve ways of conceiving of and delivering a diverse artistic programme which did not unduly privilege either the aesthetic dimension (e.g. the resident Royal Northern Sinfonia orchestra), the participatory dimension (e.g. adult music classes) or the more 'socially engaged' (Helguera 2011; Roche 2006) dimension (e.g. work with NEET groups, music therapy). Under the leadership of its founding directors, Sage Gateshead's artistic programme from 2000 to *c.*2015 became a vibrant professional situation where undergraduate students and professional musicians alike developed their own praxis, not as *either* performers *or* teachers *or* community musicians, but often as all three. The vision of music espoused by the organization during this period as pluralistic, multi-dimensional, socially engaged, transformational and above all dialogic – by turns contested, joyous, messy, contradictory and willing to adapt – was instrumental in seeding the ideas which I have developed since into academic research, the results of which you are now reading.

I finished my doctorate in 2016, submitting a 30,000-word report alongside a 170,000-word portfolio of supporting evidence (Camlin 2016a). As anyone who has completed a doctorate will tell you, the whole process certainly wasn't a 'walk in the park', but neither was it impossibly difficult. Studying one's own practice is a deeply rewarding and stimulating pursuit and comes with its own rewards. The contribution to knowledge made by my doctorate is in the articulation of a model of music which I refer to as 'music in three dimensions', emphasizing the 'creative tension' (Wegerif 2012: 4) and interdependence between the aesthetic, participatory and paramusical dimensions of music's power (Camlin 2016a, 2016b), an updated version of which I outline in Chapter 4.

The ideas developed through my doctoral studies have become the foundation of my particular contribution to academic knowledge and a passport to my current professorial roles in HE institutions. Since 2014, I have been part of the lecturing team on Trinity-Laban's postgraduate course The Teaching Musician, which supports other music educators to develop a critical understanding of their own practice, and in 2018, I left Sage Gateshead and took up a part-time lecturing role at the Royal College of Music, where I am privileged to be part of the institution's Music Education team, supporting students at undergraduate and postgraduate levels to find their own journey into being critically reflective music educators.

Praxis

I share this brief biography partly as a way of helping to explain my own research journey – which I suspect may be less conventional than most – but mainly to emphasize the importance of a concept that is integral to research in Arts and culture, the idea of praxis. For those unfamiliar with the term, it has multiple meanings to different writers (Camlin and Zeserson 2018) which I discuss throughout the book, but here I'm really invoking Robin Nelson's definition of praxis as an 'imbrication' of theory and practice, where 'theory is not prior to practice, functioning to inform it, but theory and practice are rather 'imbricated within each other' in praxis' (Nelson 2013: 62). I'm also invoking Wayne Bowman's idea of praxis as 'mindful doing', i.e. 'action guided by attention to variable procedures, traditions, and standards' (Bowman 2005: 53).

Within music education, praxialism has become a central concept since it was introduced by David Elliott in his seminal work Music Matters (Elliott 1995b), a 'post-aesthetic paradigm' (Regelski 2011: 82) representing a pedagogical turn from technical to ethical concerns (Bowman 2009a: 117, 2018: 172) and which 'connects musics with their social worlds, instead of reducing music to works and elements alone' (Elliott and Silverman 2015: 86): 'The praxial concept of education [...] situates *socially* each person's efforts to construct his or her knowledge [...] in and through *ecological relationships* with his or her environmental circumstances' (Elliott and Silverman 2015: 146, original emphasis).

As such, 'focusing on praxis emphasizes all forms of [musicing], not just performances dominated by technical standards' (Regelski 2011: 80). Central to such a conception is the sense that 'musics can only be understood and experienced in relation to contexts of socio-musical contexts' (Elliott and Silverman 2015: 103) and is a theme I elaborate further on in Chapter 7 in relation to the socio-musical context of my own practice. Crucially, this conception of praxis and praxialism is bound up in an ethical sensitivity towards education: 'conceived as praxis, there's an ethical dimension to almost every decision we make and act on as [music educators] because these cannot exist without ethical guidance' (Elliott and Silverman 2015: 20). The ethical and political dimension of praxis is also central to my argument about musicing as a resource of civic imagination, given its capacity for imagining alternative ways of being (musically) in the world, where a neo-Marxian concept of praxis represents:

> action undertaken in and on one's lifeworld to improve it for one's self and, by extension, for others [...] Thus conceived, music is a source of personal and social agency [with an] important role in performing sociality and for creating socio-musical worlds.
>
> (Regelski 2011: 80)

Praxis in the broader sense also preserves the centrality of practice, whilst emphasizing the importance of critical reflection. As Freire notes, without practice, critical reflection can become 'armchair revolution' (Freire 1970: 48), where more abstracted theories of practice appear remote from the everyday experience of practitioners. However, without critical reflection, or a theoretical grounding, the practice itself can become 'mere activism' (48). Praxis is therefore a call to every musician working in every situation within music's diverse territories to develop and articulate their practice in ever more critical ways. If we allow that every situation of musicing is materially different and uniquely situated, it follows that every such situation has its own unique contribution to make to the ever-expanding body of knowledge about the value of music to individuals and society. New knowledge drives debate, reveals new perspectives and is the foundation of discourse which in turn leads to more new ideas. And now, more than ever, we need new ideas to help us understand the potential value of music as a resource to address the complex challenges we face as the dominant species on an increasingly fragile planet. Making practice the focus of research ensures that the tacit knowledge that is generated through innovative and creative practices is not lost. Moreover, as Ben Goldacre points out, 'understanding how research is done also enables [practitioners] to generate new research questions. This, in turn, ensures that the research which gets done addresses the needs of everyday [practitioners]' (Goldacre 2014: 215).

There may also be a parallel to be found between the task of articulating our own professional truths as musicians in academic terms and the challenge of inspiring and facilitating active participation in publicly funded music for those who do not currently do so. In both instances, individuals are expected to cross a threshold that may feel unsettling, unsafe or even disruptive to their sense of personal identity, inhabiting situations and experiences where they may initially feel uncomfortable, or which they may feel are 'not for the likes of me'. The challenges musicians may face, in coming to a more critical understanding of ourselves, may well help to generate the kind of insights we need, to facilitate a broader cross-section of society to make similar journeys of self-discovery of a musical identity. It starts with each one of us finding the words to articulate our own truth, even if – or especially if – we feel that such an endeavour is 'not for the likes of me'. In doing so, we put ourselves in the position of those on the threshold of participation in the activities we facilitate, but who waver at the door. If we 'do the thing we think we cannot do', we learn from that experience more about how to help others do the same.

As such, this book is certainly not intended to be the final word on any of the subject matter it addresses. Rather, it is one musician's perspective on the world as I find it, a single voice borne out of practice in a complex and constantly unfolding dialogue about music and its value to people and society. I hope it encourages others – other musicians especially – to want to articulate their own truths about their own practical experiences in more critical terms. In Chapter 7, I continue this biographical account to show in more detail how the ideas in the next part of the book have emerged through the particular circumstances of my practice, but first I must share those ideas with you.

Thinking about music

My studio at home is packed full of musical instruments – various tuned and untuned hand percussion and a myriad of other acoustic and electronic instruments for specific purposes, from a hammered dulcimer and a pair of amboxes to a Cajun accordion, a box of harmonicas and a p-trumpet, as well as microphones and boxes full of leads, connectors, adaptors, amplifiers and speakers. And lots of (probably too many) guitars. For any particular musical job outside of my studio, I will assemble a selection of instruments that I think will be most useful to make music with, bearing in mind who I'll be playing with (and who might be listening).

When it comes to thinking about music, I take a similar approach. In my metaphorical battered leather briefcase (really a kindle and a computer with extensive notes on it), I have a multitude of other people's ideas which I think of as conceptual 'lenses' – each of which might provide a unique insight into the issue under investigation. Much like an itinerant optician or astronomer, opening the briefcase and arranging the lenses is how I hope to develop a clearer understanding of the subject at hand, and in this instance, focus the idea of music making and civic imagination. As Donna Haraway (2016) reminds us, 'it matters what thoughts think thoughts' (12), so this section is my way of laying out my intellectual apparatus. My approach to this is somewhat recursive, in that re-arranging these conceptual lenses in different ways helps to reveal different perspectives, and so the book's narrative is spiral in nature, building up a rich picture of praxis by examining it through different combinations of these conceptual lenses.

In the chapters that follow, I use this briefcase of lenses to explore four main areas of enquiry which, when taken together, form an array of concepts that I hope will make it easier to understand what I mean by music making and civic imagination. In Chapter 3, I explore the notion of music as a 'complex adaptive system' (CAS), a vitality of different aspects of music's power which are intra-active. Chapter 4 explores three complementary traditions of musicing in more detail to understand how aesthetic, participatory and paramusical dimensions of musical experience intra-act. Chapter 5 examines some of the ways in which this adaptive complex of musical potency has been put to service historically in the service of political ends, while Chapter 6 considers how music's potential might be re-purposed as acts of civic imagination in the service of global sustainability.

My overall argument runs something like this: Music is a CAS, which means that it achieves its effects in many different ways and through a range of complementary traditions – aesthetic, participatory and paramusical. Uniting these traditions enables us to recognize the role that music has played in human evolution and political affiliation, as well as some of the limits of such development. Despite our conditioning to accept the nation as the highest level of political identity available to us, an examination of the way that musicing has been instrumental in the formation of biographical (e.g. national) identities also points to the ways in which it might also be instrumental in the formation of a higher level of political identity as a citizen of the planet, what I will refer to as a terrapolitanism.

PART 2

THINKING ABOUT MUSIC

3

Music as a Complex Adaptive System

FIGURE 3.1: Girt Dog Building at the Universe Next Door 2019.

This chapter discusses the idea of music as a complex adaptive system (CAS), in other words, the idea that music in its totality has multiple meanings which it arrives at through a series of complementary mechanisms which are broadly psychological, biological, social, behavioural and, of course, musical. This is a central foundation to my argument, as it highlights the complex ways in which music comes to 'mean' and what we might therefore consider as musical knowledge. The chapter uses this perspective of complexity to reflect on music's enduring intrinsic value over the history of the human species, and how we might therefore view it as a potential resource in our transition to a more sustainable future.

An enduring characteristic of this web of musical meaning over human history is the capacity for humans to entrain – or 'tune in' – to one another through musical activity, highlighting music's communicative potential as an ambiguous medium for communicating internal emotional states and social intentions. I also draw in some reflections on the apparently similar neurobiological underpinnings of music and love, before turning to a consideration of how this complex intra-action of music's many dimensions is experienced in practice. First, using the theoretical frame of 'agential realism' (Barad 2007), I consider some insights from the world of quantum theory about how to consider musicing as an 'entangled state', by applying 'diffractive' thinking. Second, through Daniel Stern's account of the time-based arts as 'forms of vitality' (Stern 2010), I consider how music is experienced in more holistic terms as a totality, or gestalt.

600+ Mechanisms

In 2021, a team of researchers at University College London (UCL) led by Dr Daisy Fancourt produced a ground-breaking report which suggested that there are more than 600 'mechanisms' which may underscore the health and well-being benefits of leisure activities (Fancourt et al. 2021). If we take the term 'mechanism' to mean 'entities and activities organized in such a way that they are responsible for the phenomenon' (Illari and Williamson 2012: 1), Fancourt et al.'s report points to a very complex network of possible explanations for why leisure activities (including the time-based performing arts, and therefore music) can play a positive role in people's health and well-being. As they elaborate, 'these mechanisms can be categorised as psychological, biological, social, and behavioural processes that operate at individual (micro), group (meso), and societal (macro) levels' (Fancourt et al. 2021: 329). The comprehensive nature of the report is staggering and covers in considerable detail the many ways already known through scientific investigation of how leisure activities including music can support positive mental and physical health in individuals (331–32).

Despite the comprehensive detail and scope of the 600+ mechanisms identified, the researchers highlight that the framework is by no means exhaustive:

> although this framework brings together a large number of potential mechanisms of action, it is not, and could never be, complete. There might be mechanisms of action that have not yet been identified, or that might not yet exist but could still emerge as patterns of leisure activities and behaviours evolve. Further, many of the

> mechanisms activated by leisure engagement will not be unique to leisure, but will also be activated by non-leisure activities in everyday life.
>
> (Fancourt et al. 2021: 334)

Complex adaptive systems (CAS)

It is worth remembering that these mechanisms are purely those which characterize the relationship between leisure activities and health and do not include the many musical mechanisms which are also at play e.g. synchronization or dissonances of pitch, rhythm, tone, timbre and articulation – complexities which Charles Keil refers to as the 'participatory discrepancies' (Keil 1987) between those aspects which give music its vitality. Even without these musical considerations, the sheer scale of complexity when it comes to thinking about music can be overwhelming, as the UCL researchers highlight. As well as each mechanism having a *direct* impact on physical and mental health outcomes, they also 'interact with one another both across levels and between domains' (Fancourt et al. 2021: 332). In other words, the different mechanisms act with and upon each other to produce ever more complex ways in which affordances for health and well-being are realized. Moreover, 'the mechanisms involved in complex interventions are non-linear and can involve positive and negative feedback loops, recursive causality, self-reinforcement, disproportionate relationships, and emergent outcomes' (332).

This is what we might understand as an 'adaptive complex', where 'the functional significance of each characteristic is amplified by the others' (Whiten 2007: 155) or a CAS. CASs have a number of characteristics. They are 'open, irreducible, non-linear, sensitive to initial conditions, carry their history with them, are constantly changing, display path dependency, and are fundamentally unpredictable' (Koch 2020: 249). Additionally, 'complex systems do not exist in equilibrium and are not static. Rather, they constantly adapt to feedback from interactions between elements within the system, and between elements and their environment' (Fancourt et al. 2021: 334). Viewed in this way, it requires no great leap of understanding to locate music as a complex phenomenon.

So why start our discussion here, in the thick of complexity? My main purpose here is to be clear from the outset that I intend to avoid more dichotomous ways of thinking about music's value to people and society. The pressure to evidence causal relationships between musical 'interventions' and the social 'goods' they are intended to produce has driven much cultural policy in the early part of this century, leading simultaneously to a perceived cheapening of the intrinsic value of the arts (art for art's sake), *and* an instrumentalization of those same art forms in serving social agendas e.g. social impact, health and well-being (Arts & Humanities

Research Council 2014). Rather than being drawn into the dichotomous debate about 'instrumental' vs. 'intrinsic' value of music (or any other dichotomous view of music, for that matter), recognising music as a CAS from the outset steps over that discourse, at least to some extent, by recognizing that the fullest understanding of music's value accounts for both what it is, but moreover what it *does*.

Music as a polyvalent system

Merely scratching the surface of music as a social phenomenon as we have done here reveals a rather prosaic truth that music sustains 'polyvalent significance' (Cross and Woodruff 2009: 2) – it 'means' different things to different people, in very different ways and in very different situations. As Bowman (2002) asserts, 'the unique phenomenal nature of music fosters experience with a richness and complexity found almost nowhere else in the world' (59), and the sheer number of ways in which music might come to 'mean' something – either intrinsic to it or as an affordance of it – further confounds the issue of its effect on us. As MacDonald, Kreutz and Mitchell (2013b) highlight in their summary of the role music has on human health and well-being, music is 'ubiquitous'; it is everywhere, an inescapable feature of our everyday lives. As a medium, it permeates our day-to-day existence in a multitude of very direct and very indirect ways, from the music we choose to listen to or play, to the music that is imposed on us through media platforms and retail sites.

As a resource, 'music is appropriated by individuals [...] for the ongoing constitution of themselves and their social psychological, physiological and emotional states' (DeNora 2000: 47). Not fully appreciating the complexity of how music impacts on people and society therefore risks missing music's full potential as a resource for human flourishing. Attempts to quantify music's value ultimately fail when they reduce the complexity of its power to just some – or as is more often the case, just one – of its many elements. As the UCL researchers acknowledge, 'attempting to break down a complex system such as leisure engagement into individual elements (e.g. research attempting to test specific mechanisms artificially isolated from other mechanisms) risks altering the processes that we seek to understand' (Fancourt et al. 2021: 333).

The advocacy trap

Viewing music as a CAS therefore limits – at least to some extent – the evangelical claims which are often made for it by its staunchest advocates, myself included. As well as being selective and reductionist about what evidence will support particular claims, an evangelical belief in the power of music to bring about every kind of social impact possible in every circumstance is both naïve and simplistic, and means we are likely to pay less attention to situations where music is not the answer, or worse, where it might in fact be part of the problem. When it comes to social impact, if music is good for *everything*, then we can start to lose sight of what it is that *only* music can do, which in turn weakens more specific claims about music's potential to bring about particular 'goods' in particular circumstances. The honest answer to the question 'what is music good for?' is 'it depends'. For instance, if actively making music is good for everyone, why does it remain a minority interest? We can make arguments about people being disenfranchised from their birth-right to be musical which sound plausible and convincing – and the thrust of this book is very much along those lines – but the reality is not so simple as dragging everyone in the world kicking and screaming into a community music workshop.

In my role as Creative Director of the SoundWave music organization, I once met the manager of a charitable trust to discuss a possible partnership, who very quickly lost patience with my insistence that whatever thorny social problem he wanted to address through the work of the trust that music would be able to form at least part of a valuable solution. What he really wanted to know was what was it that *only* music could do, and for *who*, so that he could understand where best to deploy it as a method for addressing social inequalities. The meeting ended quickly, and the partnership never really blossomed.

As Francois Matarasso reminds us, 'nothing worth having about artistic experiences can be delivered; it can only be enabled' (Matarasso 2014: 5). Any transformation which occurs through music happens at a local level – that of the individual and/or the group – and it cannot be forced to happen. No-one can *make* me or anyone have a transformational musical experience: 'Music, and its benefits, can only be allowed to happen. It cannot be forced' (6).

All roads lead to complexity

As well as limiting evangelical claims about music, a critical examination of music as a social phenomenon is perhaps inevitably going to lead us – whichever route we pursue – to reflect that 'I think you'll find it's a bit more complicated than that' (Goldacre 2014: n.pag.). When it comes to thinking about music, all roads lead to complexity. My own thinking as a musician has led me towards a similar picture of complexity as the one presented by the UCL researchers, albeit starting from questions I asked of my practice as a musician and then working steadily towards a growing awareness of complexity over twenty years or so. Rather than every musician following a similar winding path to understanding, it is surely better to be mindful of the complex system of intra-active mechanisms which underscore musical experience as a foundation of musical knowledge. I know that if I had developed more of an understanding of these complex intra-actions earlier in my own career as a musician, it would have enabled me to have refined my practice and approach sooner. Thinking about music in the most holistic sense possible – as a CAS – will help us work with it in more sophisticated ways, especially if we think that music might have a role to play in addressing global existential threats to human flourishing.

Music as gestalt

Of course, this leaves us with an epistemological challenge, namely if music is a CAS, how do we come to 'know' the full value of music? By understanding it through its various elements, or in its totality? Or both? Daniel Stern highlights the challenges associated with developing a scientific understanding of cultural phenomena:

> The sciences are in a difficult situation. On the one hand, they are led by their nature to understand events at smaller and smaller levels of greater reduction, and in greater isolation one from the other, to understand better how they work. This results in a fragmentation of the world as we normally know it.
>
> (Stern 2010: 5)

In the same way that taking a motorbike to pieces to understand its essence is going to tell us little about what it feels like to ride one: 'at times the reductive sciences can take apart a wrist watch to better understand its workings, but then cannot put it back together again so that it works' (Stern 2010: 29). He suggests that instead of this fragmented understanding of musical experience, we should instead invoke something more holistic – that music in its essence is a form of what he terms a gestalt of 'vitality' – a holistic experience of multiple inter-related phenomena simultaneously – and that the many mechanisms which give it its vitality are not experienced in isolation, but rather as an inseparable whole:

> Starting with movement, we get five dynamic events linked together. Movement, time, force, space and intention/directionality – taken together give rise to the experience of vitality. This natural Gestalt gives rise to the experience of vitality in one's own movements and in those of others.
>
> (Stern 2010: 4)

This is a more phenomenological way of knowing, where our understanding starts from 'the standpoint of everyday life, from the world as it confronts us' (Husserl 1931: 3). Scientific enquiry can give us explanations about why we might experience something in a particular way – the interconnection of hundreds of individual mechanisms being a case in point – whereas a more phenomenological understanding can help us understand what that experience *feels* like. Crucially, both perspectives are necessary for a comprehensive understanding of music's power and potential to 'mean' in so many complex ways.

Music in human evolution

To explore this complex relationship between music as a CAS and our experience of it as such, it is worth considering music's enduring presence throughout the history of the human species. It is generally accepted that musicing is a feature of all human cultures (Cross and Morley 2010: 67) and that such practices pre-date a contemporary western understanding of music – as a performance given by performers for listeners – by tens of thousands of years (Elliott et al. 2016: 3):

> It is only in the last five hundred years that music has become a spectator activity – the thought of a musical concert in which a class of 'experts' performed for an appreciative audience was virtually unknown throughout our history as a species.
> (Levitin 2008: 257)

Understanding music as a means of human communication – that serves a different communicative purpose to spoken language – may help us appreciate its evolutionary value and enduring ubiquity across human pre-history right up to the present age of recorded music. Such an understanding has grown in recent years in critical response to the suggestion made by cognitive psychologist Steven Pinker that 'music is useless' (Pinker 1995: 528) in evolutionary terms; that it is in fact mere 'auditory cheesecake' (534) in terms of human evolution, 'a pure pleasure technology, a cocktail of recreational drugs that we ingest through the ear to stimulate a mass of pleasure circuits' (528). In direct contrast to this notion, a range of theorists argue quite the opposite – that music has an important evolutionary function in promoting collaboration and cooperation across large groups (Mithen 2007; Levitin 2008; Cross and Morley 2010; Dunbar 2012, 2014) and may be one of the contributing factors to our evolution as cooperative social animals. Recent scientific discoveries suggest that 'the human brain contains a neural population specific to the analysis of song' (Norman-Haignere et al. 2022: 3) further highlighting the long-standing independent presence of singing and music within our biological make-up, rather than as an affordance of our linguistic capabilities.

Music as communicative medium

While the principal means through which human alliances and allegiances are achieved and sustained might be considered to be through linguistic means, 'allowing hominids to exchange information about individuals not immediately present' (Aiello and Dunbar 1993: 185), the evolution of human language is presumed to have involved a musical phase of development as well:

> At the earliest stage, tone and emotion would be the essential components of vocalization; information content would not necessarily be important. The function of this type of enhanced vocalization would be vocal grooming, an expression of mutual interest and commitment that could be simultaneously shared with more than one individual.
> (Aiello and Dunbar 1993: 187)

Contrasting with language, music might be considered 'a communication system specialising in the expression of emotion' (Mithen 2007: 286). It serves a different basic purpose as a communication system to that of language: 'As a tool for activation of specific thoughts, music is not as good as language. As a tool for arousing feelings and emotions, music is better than language' (Levitin 2008: 268). A potent truth about music is therefore that language cannot be a substitute for it; music expresses and communicates things that words cannot, by which we might mean the profundity and range of emotional communication through music and the vitality which carries such expression. This value of emotional communication 'appears incompatible with Pinker's view that music is no more than a spin-off from language and has no biological value' (Mithen 2007: 50).

Furthermore, music also has a powerful role to play in the evolution of group communication. The ambiguous nature of musical communication means that it is 'a communicative medium with features that are optimised for the management of situations of social uncertainty' (Cross and Woodruff 2009: 1). Similarly, 'music can transmit emotional information to many people at once, equalising the emotional state of the group, which results in a bonding effect between the group members' (Cross and Morley 2010: 62). If we view language as a development of music – i.e. a pre-linguistic medium of emotional communication – it becomes easy to see how 'music may be the activity that prepared our pre-human ancestors for speech communication and for the very cognitive, representational flexibility necessary to become humans' (Levitin 2008: 260).

Taken together, these perspectives suggest a very different view of music's evolutionary purpose to that of Pinker: 'It would be impossible to do away with music without removing many of the abilities of social cognition that are fundamental to being human' (Cross and Morley 2010: 77). What is communicated along with any musical content is important; not just the sounds that are made but the way in which they are made and communicated which give clues as to the sounder's social intentions. From a broader perspective of human ontogeny, 'human cultural learning is not just about acquiring important skills and knowledge, it is also about establishing important social relationships [...] displaying, and hopefully reinforcing, one's social solidarity with others and the group' (Tomasello 2019: 123). Musical communication is thus a performance of relationship, in the sense in which 'vitality forms of interpersonal happenings are part of implicit relational knowing' (Stern 2010: 111) and a theme which I develop in more detail in Chapter 4.

Entrainment

At the heart of this musical communication is the notion of entrainment, or the capacity to synchronise one's musical expression to that of another, or to a group. Broadly defined, entrainment is 'a phenomenon in which two or more independent rhythmic processes synchronize with each other' (Clayton et al. 2004: 1) and involves 'the interaction and consequent synchronization of two or more rhythmic processes or oscillators' (2). In the case of music, we might think of an 'oscillator' as anything which vibrates at a frequency that is perceivable by human hearing, including the human voice as well any instrument which is struck, bowed, rung or otherwise manipulated to make a sound. Entraining to a rhythmic pulse is a fundamental musical skill as is being able to manipulate an instrument or one's voice to vibrate at a particular frequency that attunes sympathetically with sounds being produced by others. Entraining to one another in a musical exchange leads to a sense of 'coupling' – 'when people synchronize the sounds and movements they make, [they] enter similar emotional states, and hence attune their nervous states to one another' (Mithen 2007: 216) – and is a uniquely human capacity:

> Apart from some insects or frogs (which produce synchronous courtship sounds), humans are unique in the animal world in their ability to synchronise or entrain their behaviour to an extrinsic common or isometric pulse. This capacity for entrainment is prefigured in the 'coordinated interpersonal timing' of vocal interactions between mothers and infants as young as two months of age.
>
> (Dissanayake 2010: 539)

The fact that entrainment is something we are hard-wired to from before we are born is significant – it is a fundamental part of the process of 'attachment' which ensures that a dependent infant's needs are met by a primary care-giver, usually a mother. Some theorists suggest that infant–carer relationships which lacked 'the drive to vocalize musical sounds, conceivably would have had an important disadvantage for survival' (Roederer 1984: 353). The most fundamental form of entrainment is what survives in the proto-musical exchanges between an infant and a primary care-giver variously referred to as 'motherese', 'baby-talk' or Infant-Directed Speech (IDS) where 'the usual melodic and rhythmic features of spoken language – prosody – are highly exaggerated so that our utterances adopt an explicitly musical character' (Mithen 2007: 74). The function of this kind of communication may in itself be complex, a direct means of communicating emotional experience and social intentions, as well as a preparation for linguistic development:

> Prosodic characteristics [of speech] such as intonation, rhythm and stress help partition the discourse into meaningful articulatory units. These units serve not only to reinforce syntactic and semantic structures but also to signal the communicative intentions of the speaker.
>
> (Cross and Woodruff 2009: 8)

Communicative musicality

This foundational musical experience has become the focus of a significant amount of research drawn together by Stephen Malloch and Colwyn Trevarthen into a comprehensive field of research known as 'communicative musicality', which they summarize as follows: 'to capture the essence of movement and its values we use the metaphor of "musicality". To recognise that our experience in movement is shared by a compelling sympathy we call this activity "communicative"' (Malloch and Trevarthen 2010: 9).

As Daniel Stern clarifies:

> 'Musicality' does not refer to music as usually thought about, but rather to the duet of movements and sounds between two people expressing motives and intentional states – a synchronising of two people's behaviours. This coupling occurs on a scale of milliseconds and seconds.
>
> (Stern 2010: 51)

Stern also suggests that this kind of musical exchange might also be considered a sharing of 'vitality forms' and 'probably the earliest, easiest, and most direct path into another's subjective experience' (Stern 2010: 43). He elaborates:

> Communicative musicality is largely based on the coupling of vitality dynamics between people. 'Musicality' is composed of pulses that are formed by timing, in the rhythmic sense, and its temporal contouring, and the deployment of force in time. This is the backbone of vitality dynamics where 'being with another' is accomplished by sharing the vitality dynamic flow.
>
> (Stern 2010: 52–53)

We might view this relationship made between infant and primary care-giver as lying at the heart of musical experience. We first come to know that we exist through the way that our communicative musicality binds us in this primary dyad. We might therefore consider communicative musicality to be the foundational underpinning of all musical communication. That music exists at all as a human behaviour – whether as a technology or an adaptation – is dependent on this foundational experience of the sharing of emotional states and vitality dynamics through patterns of soundings between an infant and an adult care-giver through musical exchange. Whatever we might want to 'do' with music, the fact that we can 'do' anything at all with it is inescapably bound up in its evolutionary purpose to build human attachment.

Recognizing that the musical exchanges of communicative musicality are largely pre-linguistic is also significant, as in a wider sense, it may be music's ambiguous and polyvalent nature which makes it more potent as a communication system, especially in situations of social uncertainty (Cross and Woodruff 2009: 2). As well as the communication of any musical, emotional or intellectual content, musical communication is always about communicating social intent, establishing mutuality and 'a common cognitive context for the act of communication' (8).

What's love got to do with it?

To conclude this discussion of music in human evolution, it is worth turning briefly to a rather neglected concept in music research but one which helps to deepen our understanding of why music forges interpersonal bonds of connection so well. As we can see, communicative musicality and the relational quality of the infant-carer dyad is very much about interpersonal connection; it is also therefore very much about love. It is a subject I have written about in more detail elsewhere (Camlin 2021c), but here I outline some of the main points of discussion.

Love might seem a rather nebulous concept to think about music with but love and human connection are intimately related, as are music and human connection, so there is a clear correspondence between the two (Camlin 2021c). And yet love is not something we really talk about outside of our intimate kinship relationships.

In music education circles, it is almost taboo. Child protection and safeguarding procedures – for the safety of both students and staff – mean that the boundaries between professional and personal teacher – student relationships are carefully monitored. So, it came as a shock when one of my undergraduate students at Sage Gateshead asked me, during a workshop, 'do you love us?'

At this point, I should provide a little context. As a part of their studies, small groups of students had been exploring a selection of texts they'd chosen to review. Two of them, getting their academic teeth into Paulo Freire, had come across a passage in *Pedagogy of the Oppressed* which had particularly caught their attention: 'The naming of the world, which is an act of creation and re-creation, is not possible if it is not infused with love. Love is at the same time the foundation of dialogue and dialogue itself' (Freire 1970: 70).

It was only in the act of giving their presentation that the penny dropped for them. Education, in its broadest sense, is only partially fulfilling its purpose if the only thing students learn from it is how to be better skilled at something, in their case, music. Education is only really living up to its potential when it leads to learners' holistic development and actualization as human beings, and love – for Freire – is a pre-requisite for such development. Hence, to teach, in any capacity, is to carry the responsibility of providing a 'secure base' (Ainsworth 1963) for learners' future development, which as Freire observes, is not possible unless such a responsibility is 'infused with love' (70). As the realization dawned that this situation must also apply to their own learning, and their relationships with their own teachers, one of the students turned to me and asked directly, 'do you love us?' I'm pleased to be able to say that I barely hesitated before affirming that yes, of course, I loved them all. However, it made me think about it. What is love and what has it got to do with music? It is a question worth asking, not least because so much of music's power lies in its capacity to bring people together, often to share intense, intimate, emotional experiences.

What is love anyway?

Of course, it is worth making some clear distinctions about what kind of love we might be referring to. Love is variously represented as an emotion or a poetic metaphor or a feeling (more of which later) but here what I'm referring to is an inter-personal (neuro-) biological phenomenon. While all of 'our adult romantic and other intimate relationships develop out of, or are scaffolded by, our early experience of mother–infant relationships' (Dunbar 2013: 16), Dunbar also highlights that 'neuroimaging suggests that maternal love and romantic love are actually two different things' (17). It is the close attachment of maternal/platonic love which is invoked here, rather than any romantic/sexual connotation. For bell hooks, 'the essence of true love is mutual recognition – two individuals seeing each other as they really are' (hooks 2000: 215).

Silverman (2012) invokes hooks' notion of 'love-as-action' as an underpinning ethic of musicing – especially in relation to themes of social justice – as love calls us to act: 'with love we exist for others and with ourselves' (158). In specific relation to intercultural musical practices, Bartleet (2016) also invokes hooks in suggesting that love is 'a verb, a participatory emotion, and a social practice' (91). In other words, love is an ethical attitude towards engaging with other people which entails 'a specific focus on the good of the other' (95). Such attitudes of mutual care which constitute ethical musicing foster empathy and its social equivalent 'copathy' which refers to the 'social function of empathy, including that interindividual empathic states become more homogeneous, thus decreasing conflicts and promoting cohesion of a group' (Koelsch 2013: 206).

Of course, love as an ethical attitude can condition and mediate all social encounters, not just musical ones: 'Commitment to a love ethic transforms our lives by offering us a different set of values to live by' (hooks 2000: 120). However, a stronger claim to musicing's capacity for fostering close and intimate attachment might be seen to arise from the various entanglements between musical entrainment, interpersonal neurobiological attunement and neurohormonal activation/s. The same theories of attachment developed by Bowlby and Ainsworth (Bowlby 1969, 1988) which help to explain communicative musicality similarly underpin the concept of maternal love. Because our earliest experiences of feeling loved arise in the prosodic exchanges of communicative musicality, the experience of love is bound up in a musical process and similar feelings of intimate connection, of 'unconditional positive regard' (Rogers 1961: 62), can also be experienced during musicing throughout the lifespan. To understand these various complexities, it is worth a brief overview (in lay terms) of human interpersonal neurobiology.

The limbic system

A group of researchers led by Thomas Lewis developed 'a general theory' of love (Lewis et al. 2001) building on Paul MacLean's model of the 'triune brain' (MacLean 1990), which suggests that one of the functions of a key part of mammalian neurobiology is to promote attachment between parent mammals and their infants. This same neurobiological hardware is what predisposes us as humans to continue to seek out and develop bonds of trust and attachment as adults. Social bonding is not something that is restricted to humans – all mammals have evolved similar ways of strengthening the bond between mother and infant, which extends to developing cooperative 'communities' (Lewis et al. 2001: 25). The means through which these strong attachment bonds are formed and sustained are complex but include the part of the brain which all mammals possess but which other animals – reptiles, for example – do not: the limbic system.

The limbic area 'evolved when small mammals first appeared around two hundred million years ago,' [and] 'works closely with the brainstem and the body proper to create not only our basic drives but also our emotions' (Siegel 2011: 16). As Siegel explains:

> The limbic regions help create the 'e-motions' that 'evoke motion', that motivate us to act in response to the meaning we assign to whatever is happening to us in that moment. The limbic area is also crucial for how we form relationships and become emotionally attached to one another.
>
> (Siegel 2011: 16)

Crucially, the limbic system is considered to be an 'open-loop arrangement' for regulating a range of physiological parameters including, for example, hormone levels, cardiovascular function, sleep rhythms, immune function but which cannot be undertaken in isolation from others. Such regulation requires the limbic system of at least one other mammal, usually (but not exclusively) of the same species and usually a significant attachment figure, to 'tune in' to, where 'the first person regulates the physiology of the second, even as [they themselves are] regulated' (Lewis et al. 2001: 84).

This kind of interpersonal 'limbic regulation' is an important factor in maintaining homeostasis. When it is disrupted, the results can be catastrophic, especially for dependent animals (Lewis et al. 2001: 78). Limbic regulation is therefore significant for our general health and well-being (Siegel 2011: 27). Siegel refers to this as a core part of our 'resonance circuitry' (61) which explains 'how we can come to resonate physiologically with others – how even our respiration, blood pressure, and heart rate can rise and fall in sync with another's internal state. This is the pathway that connects us to one another' (71). In other words, neurobiology is interpersonal: 'the internal states of others – from joy and play to sadness and fear – directly affect our own state of mind' (71). Siegel explicitly connects this to the idea of love: 'When we see the mind of another person, we bring the qualities of being present – curiosity, openness, and acceptance – into our relationships. These qualities seem to me to be the essence of that overused, often misunderstood word: love' (Siegel 2011: 188).

Interpersonal neurobiology

When it comes to the arts, there is little attention given in the scientific literature to interpersonal neurobiological effects and limbic attunement and synchronization.

Of the 108 biological mechanisms outlined in the UCL report, all relate to individual biology. Perhaps the reason why one of the most significant studies in this area (Vickhoff et al. 2013) is not referenced in the report is because the kind of knowledge it represents does not fit easily into the model. In other words, the 'unit of analysis' when it comes to a scientific understanding of biological mechanisms underpinning well-being effects of the Arts is generally taken to be the individual, which is perfectly understandable:

> It is true that neuropsychologists and physicists feel more 'comfortable' with the more quantifiable, experimentally more accessible and more structured cortical functions of cognition than with the diffuse, qualitative, electrophysiologically much less accessible limbic functions – but the two must be studied together.
>
> (Roederer 1984: 352)

However some cultural theorists believe that 'by focusing on the individual we have been working with the wrong unit of analysis' (Crossick and Kaszynska 2016: 39). Apart from anything else, the notion of the 'individual' is 'ontologically and semantically indeterminate' (Barad 2007: 348) outside of a social context. If the experience of human connection is an interpersonal one, we need ways of understanding those experiences which account for the complex ways in which meaning is negotiated and experienced *between* individuals, which is to say neither at the level of the individual nor at the level of group *per se*, but rather in the spaces in between. Recent developments in the field of interpersonal neurobiology (Siegel 2012) provide us with new ways of understanding this most fundamental of human emotional experiences, in particular a deeper understanding of the neural correlates of the experience of love and attachment (Siegel 2011), and the 'resonance' that exists between individuals as a function of shared neurobiological networks.

I first came across the field of interpersonal neurobiology in my role at Sage Gateshead, when we hosted a seminar in partnership with University of Northumbria featuring the eminent psychotherapist–researcher Professor Dan Siegel. As a part of his presentation, he convened what he terms a 'complexity choir' (Siegel 2011: 64–66) from delegates to illustrate the point that neural integration is about navigating the territory between rigidity and chaos and also that 'tuning in' to each other is something that comes quite easily to us, and that fundamentally changes our experience of a situation. First, the assembled 'scratch choir' of volunteers are called on to sing a single note in unison, which quickly becomes – literally – monotonous. Then, they are required to sing aloud individually and at the same time as each other but whilst covering their ears and without paying any attention to the sounds the other singers are making. The result is a cacophony of competing musical ideas which is satisfying for neither the listening audience nor the singers themselves. Then the exercise is repeated a third time, but this time by singing a well-known song together, and 'tuning in' to the sounds that the other singers are making and adjusting their own expressions accordingly. The resulting sound, while perhaps unlikely to become a chart-topping hit, was clearly recognizable as a musical improvisation, with the singers converging both rhythmically and harmonically into a collective expression.

Feeling felt

Siegel uses the example of the complexity choir to highlight the power of interpersonal attunement and also gives us the expression of 'feeling felt' to highlight the reciprocal nature of attachment, expanding on Carl Rogers' (1961) more directional sense of 'unconditional positive regard':

> When we attune to others we allow our own internal state to shift, to come to resonate with the inner world of another. This resonance is at the heart of the important sense of 'feeling felt' that emerges in close relationships. Children need attunement to feel secure and to develop well, and throughout our lives we need attunement to feel close and connected.
>
> (Siegel 2011: 27)

While our resilience to isolation may be stronger as adults, the impact of regular limbic regulation is still significant for our general health and well-being: 'this stance of curiosity, openness, acceptance, and love is at the heart of secure attachments' (Siegel 2011: 188).

What's music got to do with it?

What I hope is clear from this discussion is that in talking about love and attachment, a musical perspective might have a good deal to contribute. Musical communication – building on the foundations of communicative musicality – may be an active manifestation of the 'open-loop' nature of interpersonal attunement, leading to the activation and synchronization of human neurobiological 'resonance circuitry'. Not just metaphorically, but literally. Music is a simultaneous dialogue between voices – 'each one expressing itself to the fullest while at the same time listening to the other' (Barenboim 2009: 20) and as such provides not just a metaphor for human cooperative communication, but a medium as well. Music is the audible evidence of our otherwise invisible neurobiological attunement to other people.

However, while one of the great unspoken truths about musicing may be the opportunities it affords for limbic regulation in this way, it isn't something that has been widely studied. Even though participant narratives suggest that we seem to know it when we experience it (Camlin et al. 2020), a more communicable understanding of the interpersonal 'resonance' and attunement, or this sense of 'feeling felt' during musicing, evades a more scientific explanation. Siegel suggests that such interpersonal 'resonance' is something which *can* be measured in more scientific terms, because of the fact that different neural circuits of the brain are not only activated but become synchronized with others when in attunement: 'internal and interpersonal forms of attunement each lead to the growth of the regulatory circuits of the brain' (Siegel 2011: 86). Even more significantly, it may also be the case that through musicing, we can help to strengthen these 'resonance circuits' and build our attunement to others – something that is critical to our own well-being. If we set out – as we do when we make music together – to breathe together, or to synchronise our movements around a mutually agreed musical pulse, to match others' pitch, harmonies, onsets and so on – we activate the same parts of our neural architecture that are naturally synchronized when they are in a state of attuned resonance with others.

Because musicing works on the basis of attuning one's breathing and movement to that of others – often in a non-auditioned and hence 'unconditional' setting – it means that these positive relationships can be even stronger and have more positive impact on the health and well-being of all involved. Far from being a 'second-hand emotion' as Tina Turner would have us believe, love is a basic human need. My suggestion is simply that musicing can address that need, capable of making a space where people can begin to form, or reinforce, healthy bonds of trust and attachment through 'tuning in' to one another, not just metaphorically, but literally. Such acts of attunement not only contribute positively to participants' individual and collective well-being but actively engage our collective neurobiological functioning in a sympathetically virtuous tangle of music and vitality.

At an individual (intra-personal) level, a scientific approach to understanding these kinds of exchanges might draw our attention to certain biological or 'motivational–structural' (Cross and Woodruff 2009) mechanisms which might be at play, including the way that 'synchronized exertive movements' might lead to the release of endorphins (Tarr et al. 2014: 1) and the consequent sense of 'self-other merging' (5–6) whereby 'musicians' become a 'we' rather than separate 'I's. We might also look to the way that the mirror neuron system (MNS) might become activated:

> When an observer watches someone execute a goal-directed action, the mirror neurons in the observer will fire in the same pattern as if the observer himself had

> performed the same action. In other words, the observer has a virtual experience of the actual experience.
>
> (Stern 2010: 47)

At a group (inter-personal) level, we might also look to the way that interpersonal 'resonance circuitry' (Siegel 2011: 61) including heartrate variability (HRV) may become synchronized during the musical moment (Vickhoff et al. 2013), further enhancing the effect of the entrainment. We might also want to examine the specifically musical qualities of any entrainment, how synchronization comes in and out of phase and what effect this has on any of the above. And of course, we might identify any number of the 600+ other mechanisms which might be implicated in such an exchange.

However, the way in which we experience attunement is not through any of these phenomena in isolation, but rather through them as a totality, in the way that they adapt and change in relation to each other. Furthermore, each of the various mechanisms that underpin a powerful music experience might be present to a greater or lesser degree in different people's experiences. How do we therefore develop accounts of the experience of musical attunement which allow for such complexity? In the final section of this chapter, I turn to two different schools of thought which shed some light on these issues – an agential realist account (Barad 2007) which recognizes the complex intra-action between human and nonhuman 'materials', and the idea of music as a 'vitality', as expressed in the ideas of Daniel Stern (2010).

Agential realism

Agential realism is Karen Barad's (2007) theory of matter and meaning which has emerged from within quantum theory discourse and is a foundation of the 'performative' school of the 'new materialist' approaches to material existence (Gamble et al. 2019). It is 'agential' in the sense that it describes how different entities (both human and nonhuman) act upon each other (intra-act) in the production of phenomena, and 'realist' in the sense that these intra-actions produce real effects. Whilst a diversion into quantum theory might seem unwarranted in a discussion of musicing, Barad's ideas provide a number of helpful insights, concepts and terms to help us make sense of music as a CAS. Appreciating some of the subtleties of Barad's argument has been important in the development of my own thinking, as it points towards a different way of 'knowing' about musical experience which I will draw on in what follows in the next section, when I discuss music as a 'vitality'. I summarize these contributions in the following section as: first, the notion of 'intra-action' and 'entangled states' as they relate to our discussion about mechanisms; second, the concept of 'diffraction' of waveforms as it relates to musical experience in general; third, the concept of investigative 'apparatus' and the kind of 'agential cut' that needs to be made upon experience in order to observe it. Each of these conceptual lenses provides us with interesting new ways to think about musicing.

Entanglement and intra-action

Central to Barad's perspective is the notion of 'intra-action' as a subtle replacement for the term 'inter-action', to recognize the difference between a more 'unidirectional' relationship between one phenomenon and another (inter-active) and one which is 'iterative and mutually constitutive' i.e. 'intra-active' (Barad 2007: 4). From a quantum perspective, 'reality is not a fixed essence. Reality is an ongoing dynamic of intra-activity' (Barad 2007: 224). This entangled nature of musical experience is especially pertinent to our discussions, as it has implications for how we can understand the complexity of music as a polyvalent system. The notion of 'entanglement' calls into question the apparent separateness between phenomena. An 'entangled state', Barad explains, is different to a 'mixture':

> The entangled state of systems A and B cannot properly be understood as a composite system, for example, a mixture, composed of two independent components, that is, separately determinate systems A and B. Rather, the entangled state of A and B, must be understood as a single entity.
>
> (Barad 2007: 297)

When it comes to exploring the complexity of musical experience, it therefore matters whether we think we are looking at a mixture, where the individual constituent parts of the phenomenon are separate systems which can be understood independently, or whether we are looking at an 'entangled state' which is not reducible to its constituents. When considering the 600+ mechanisms which may be implicated in a musical experience, this has profound implications. Common sense might seem to suggest that if we could develop ever more sophisticated ways of measurement, we might ultimately be able to quantify the precise ways in which these mechanisms *inter*-act to produce particular effects. However, this is to assume that it is the complex *inter*-actions of a mixture of different mechanisms that we're trying to understand, rather than an *intra*-active 'entangled state'.

Conversely, if musical experience is about the experience of an 'entangled state', isolating just one (or a few) of the underlying mechanisms as a way of understanding the phenomenon is to miss the essentially entangled nature of the experience. Similarly, choosing which mechanisms to study in combination as a set of variables is fraught with problems, not the least of which is that to look at a set of particular variables is not to look at others (Barad 2007: 163), as well as the fact that 'entanglements are highly specific configurations and it is very hard work building apparatuses to study them, in part because they change with each intra-action' (87).

More significantly, from a quantum perspective, choosing to set up the 'apparatus' in a particular way to look at a particular phenomenon is to make a 'cut' in the experience in order to be able to observe it (127), and this act of 'cutting' – in and of itself – changes the phenomenon under observation (163). Measurements themselves do not occur in some way external to the phenomenon being measured but are rather 'causal intra-actions' (375) that change the phenomena being observed. In that sense, 'measurements extend rather than resolve entanglements' (349) as they introduce yet more variables into the entanglement. In quantum experiments, such challenges are mediated by limiting 'the simultaneous measurement of complementary variables [to] only those variables that are mutually compatible (i.e., are simultaneously determinable)' (322).

In laboratory conditions, I imagine this is painstaking work of calibrating scientific apparatus in precise ways to measure infinitesimally small changes in atomic phenomena. In a real-world musicing situation, the variables to be controlled for would be simply too great to countenance, and the different situations simply do not compare. Moreover, the perspective of quantum theory reminds us that such measurement may not in fact be possible, as the act of measurement itself changes the phenomena under observation. Therefore, the combined effects of different mechanisms need to be understood not as a complex 'mixture' of different (but ultimately separable) causal *inter*-actions, but as *intra*-active 'entangled states' – entirely new phenomena in themselves.

Diffraction

I'm aware that talk of quantum theory in relation to musicing is likely to raise a few eyebrows, especially as 'Physics can't be bootstrapped into giving a full account of the social world' (Barad 2007: 32). Barad herself is also rightly critical of approaches which appear to claim validity by somehow appearing analogous to quantum theory – suggesting that musicing might be considered some kind of quantum experiment is beyond the bounds of reasonable argument and is certainly not my intention. However, it is important to remember that quantum theory is not just a theory of how atoms behave but how the universe behaves: 'Quantum physics supersedes Newtonian physics; it does not merely supplement it' (305).

Furthermore, there is an important and specific way in which musical experience may relate more directly to quantum concerns – not as an analogy, but in a more literal sense – in the experience of diffraction.

Waveform interference is to do with the way that waveforms are amplified or attenuated by each other when they meet – through the effects of consonance and dissonance – while diffraction has perhaps a more ambiguous meaning. As a physical phenomenon, Barad (2007) suggests that diffraction is about 'the way waves combine when they overlap'[1] and also 'the apparent bending and spreading of waves that occurs when waves encounter an obstruction' (87). Despite waveform interference and diffraction being somewhat discreet concepts in Physics, Barad often uses these terms interchangeably, suggesting that when waves 'interfere with each other, [...] the pattern created is called an interference *or* diffraction pattern' (89, emphasis added).

As an example, if you imagine throwing a pebble into a large, still pond, ripples of water move concentrically outward from the point where the pebble penetrates the surface of the water and continue until they either dissipate, or they encounter something else – a shore, an object or another wave. Now imagine throwing two pebbles into the same still pond – each produces its own waves, and when these waves encounter the waves produced by the other pebble, they interfere with each other. That is, they create new wave patterns which are based on the relative strength of each wave (their amplitude) and the way that the waves intra-act. Waves travel in peaks and troughs – when peaks meet peaks or troughs meet troughs, the resulting amplitude increases (the waves get bigger), and when peaks and troughs meet, they tend to cancel each other out, reducing amplitude.

Light also travels in waves, and much of quantum theory stems from experiments designed to understand how light behaves, especially when it diffracts – for example when moving through an aperture that is slightly narrower than the waveform. Hence, the importance of an understanding of diffraction to quantum scientists: 'there is a deep sense in which we can understand diffraction patterns – as patterns of difference that make a difference – to be the fundamental constituents that make up the world' (85).

Sound also travels in waves. Although invisible, we perceive sound based on the frequency with which objects (e.g., musical instruments, vocal folds) vibrate and which vibrations travel as soundwaves through the air between the sound source and our brains, via our ears. Every sound source (e.g., every musician or musical instrument) in a musicing situation produces sound in the form of soundwaves, and when these soundwaves combine in the air, they create patterns of diffraction and interference which become a materialization of the combined intentions and actions (the performativity) of the musicians. To take the metaphor of the still pond, if you now imagine the pond encircled by musicians (it is a large pond) who each throw a stone into the pond (or perhaps a note) at the same time, the resulting complex disturbance in the centre of the pond where all of the waveforms meet is the pattern of diffraction and interference. Now imagine that as sound in the air.

Diffraction/waveform interference is a unifying concept for a holistic understanding of music because it applies to all musical situations, in both a metaphorical and, more importantly, a literal sense. In the aesthetic traditions of the concert hall, great emphasis is placed on being able to precisely reproduce musical scores – which we might think of as maps for the production of particular 'diffraction patterns' of sound – in order to make manifest a composer's sonic intentions. Conversely, in participatory traditions, there may be more emphasis on the interpersonal relationships which underscore such patterns of diffraction/interference, and the particular patterns of sound participants are able to make together. In 'health musicking' (Stige 2013: n.pag.) meanwhile, there may be an emphasis on both, understanding what kinds of diffraction/interference patterns will support healing and also how the relationship between the musician and the clients/participants amplifies any such benefits.

My general contention is that musicing represents a *literal* experience of diffraction and waveform interference, not just a metaphorical one. From this perspective, musicing is not an analogue or metaphor for quanta but rather a direct experience of it, because it is fundamentally an intra-active experience of the diffraction of sound waves which are integral to the act. Moreover, because musicing is a fundamentally embodied experience, we can directly influence the resulting pattern of diffraction by the degree to which we control or manipulate our own sound source to produce particular effects. We can also hear the results of these manipulations immediately in the resulting pattern of diffraction, and we can even modify our own means of production to change the resulting diffraction pattern, in real time. In Mouthful – the vocal quartet I sing with – a performance is a careful negotiation between the four of us to adjust our own vocal production to work sympathetically with that of the other three, listening carefully to the soundwaves we co-produce and making adjustments as necessary to produce particular effects, responding to changes in the others' expressive qualities.

Even when human bodies are literally removed from music – through recording or generative composition, for example – the presence of those bodies are still inferred in the sounds we hear. A recording of a musical group *may* capture a particular pattern of diffraction as expressed in the intra-action of sound waves in performance, and this in itself can be a potent reminder of a group's identity at a particular point in time. However, the recording of a musical pattern of diffraction is not the same as the 'live' experience of the diffraction itself principally because – like the printed word – once recorded, the diffraction patterns can no longer be subject to change or revision by its co-creators, or influenced by its audience. Its vitality is captured or frozen, preserved in the medium of its recording like an insect in amber.

In addition, if the argument I make earlier in this chapter is valid – that our neurobiology becomes entangled with that of others through the act of musical entrainment and the consequent activation of pleasure-giving hormones like endorphins – then it may also be that the experience of diffraction during musicing involves other waveforms as well. HRV is understood as a frequency, as are the emission of (alpha and beta) brain waves (Clayton et al. 2004: 9) during the experience of interpersonal 'attunement' (Siegel 2015). The powerful effects of musicing might therefore be seen to be about how the various mechanisms involved combine in particular ways to produce complex 'entangled states' which are materialized as (literal) patterns of diffraction and waveform interference. A diffractive understanding of musicing is therefore helpful when it comes to thinking about 'which differences matter' (Barad 2007: 418).

The concept of diffraction also extends beyond its literal meaning of the confluence of waveforms. Clearly, we can think of musicing in *metaphorical* terms as a means of experiencing diffraction – 'tuning in' to one another, 'blending' voices, harmonizing and so on. However, for Barad, because diffraction 'attends to patterns of difference' (Barad 2007: 38), it is also a reminder of the entangled and 'intra-active' nature of phenomena more generally:

> diffraction does not fix what is the object and what is the subject in advance, [and] involves reading insights through one another in ways that help illuminate differences as they emerge: how different differences get made, what gets excluded, and how those exclusions matter.
>
> (38)

As a concept, diffraction has therefore also been 'taken up and developed by feminist scholars who have transformed it from a scientific model into an analytic tool and then, further, a methodology for dismantling patriarchal structures' (Hickey-Moody et al. 2016: 217). Donna Haraway in particular has championed the concept of diffraction as an 'optical metaphor for the effort to make a difference in the world' (Haraway and Goodeve 2018: 15) and a 'narrative, graphic, psychological, spiritual, and political technology for making consequential meanings' (275). I refer to both literal and metaphorical understandings of diffraction throughout the book.

Apparatus

A further concept illuminated by Barad's quantum perspective and pertinent to our discussions is that which she refers to as issues to do with the 'apparatus' of scientific enquiry, and how the gap between phenomena themselves (ontology) and how we come to 'know' such phenomena (epistemology) is perhaps narrower than we may think. From a quantum perspective, 'apparatuses are to be understood not as mere laboratory instruments, static instrumental embodiments of human concepts, but as open-ended and dynamic material-discursive practices, through which specific "concepts" and "things" are articulated' (Barad 2007: 368). We might see this idea as building on and extending poststructural concepts, where practices 'systematically form the objects of which they speak' (Foucault 2002: 51). However, Barad's critique of this position is that it appears to 'take for granted the materiality of nonhuman beings/bodies and do[es] not consider the productive workings of natural forces' (Barad 2007: 253). She therefore extends the idea of the 'apparatus' to include all of the human and non-human entities which constitute a phenomenon, and the way in which they intra-act in the materialization of that phenomenon: 'I take the primary ontological unit to be phenomena, rather than independent objects with inherent boundaries and properties' (Barad 2007: 367).

This ontological shift is central to an understanding not just of Barad's agential realism but has significant implications for what we consider to be 'reality' in more general terms. Rather than a world where every object exists independently with its own set of separable and discoverable attributes, what constitutes 'reality' is rather the intra-action of different entities as entangled phenomena. The 'realism' of agential realism is the fact that phenomena themselves are the basic unit of meaning rather than their separable components: 'Crucially, the objective referent of measured values is phenomena, not objects. Objectivity, then, is about being accountable and responsible to what is real' (375). For the purposes of our discussion, this is another important distinction, as it points to the value of a more holistic understanding of musical phenomena over a more reductionist approach.

A further invaluable insight into the nature of experience and how we can understand it come from what she describes as the 'agential cut' (Barad 2007: 164) that must be made somehow between subject (observer) and object (thing observed) in order to make an observation of it. In a quantum experiment, the apparatus 'enacts a cut delineating the object from the agencies of observation' (127) in order to observe a specific variable in the phenomenon under observation. Theorists like Schrödinger (he of the cat fame) suggest that the entanglement between the object and the measuring system is only fully resolved once observed by a 'cognizing agent' i.e., the researcher (311) – Schrödinger's cat's mortality is literally indeterminate until Schrödinger opens the box. The manner in which such a cut is made ultimately changes the phenomena because it 'makes a distinction between object and instrument [and furthermore] it is the materiality of the experimental arrangement that constitutes this distinction' (Barad 2016: 362). In other words, the act of measurement – by making a 'cut' in the nature of experience, and the particular nature of that 'cut' – changes the phenomenon being observed.

Again, without suggesting that we can think of musicing as some kind of quantum experiment, we can recognize that musical experience suffers in a similar way from trying to understand it by reducing it to a measurement of only some of its variables rather than as a holistic and inseparable phenomenon of entangled mechanisms. Part of the reason why music cannot be thought of as a quantum experiment is that each instance of musicing is fundamentally irreplicable, its 'apparatus' re-configured for each 'performance'. The fact that human bodies are part of the musical apparatus changes the experience in complex ways which ultimately make them unique events. Furthermore, we can see that in any given musicing situation, the musician is simultaneously:

- the 'object of observation' – the source of the sound (and other?) wave forms and therefore constituent in the resulting patterns of diffraction;
- the 'measuring instrument' – the 'body' on which the patterns of diffraction are inscribed;
- the 'cognising agent' – the means of observation of the patterns of diffraction.

Viewed as an integral part of the 'apparatus', 'musicians' are both cause and effect: they (or rather their bodies) are the objects which initiate phenomena – the very means of producing soundwaves and diffraction / interference patterns. They are also the 'agencies of observation' in that those same bodies are where the patterns of diffraction/interference and their attunement effects are felt and the 'cognizing agent' which interprets the phenomena. However, the experience of an *individual* musician is not the total experience of diffraction/interference; this is held at a group level within the whole apparatus – the bodies of all of the musicians, and also of any audience present. Choosing where, or how, to 'cut' into such complex experience – even at an individual level – in order to observe its workings is clearly no simple task, and one that risks denaturing the whole experience being observed.

Another reason why musicing cannot be thought of as a quantum experiment is because the 'apparatus' – including but not limited to the participants – differs in each instance, meaning not only that the complexity of the intra-action of mechanisms is too great to accommodate any meaningful measurement, but more importantly that any variables are not isolable. Paradoxically, for forms of musicing to *be* replicable would necessitate changing the experience so that it was no longer unique in its entangled temporality, which is an integral part of the experience. Making any kind of agential 'cut' to delineate object and measuring instrument in order to achieve replicability is almost bound to interrupt the activity, in turn denaturing it, and rendering any measurement unreliable. In other words, interrupting the musical experience to 'measure' it changes the experience, potentially negating any effects sought to be measured.

We learned this the hard way in a research experiment to understand the potential value of group singing in virtual reality, which required amateur singers in two separate choirs to be recorded using immersive audio and video technology so that they could sing 'virtually' with the other choir whilst physically isolated from them (Daffern et al. 2018). To understand any potential changes to their physiological state, we asked them to wear 'shimmer' devices to collect readings of HRV, as well as interrupting their usual weekly singing rehearsal every twenty minutes or so to undertake a short well-being questionnaire. At the end of the first session, individuals in both choirs expressed their profound dislike of the interruptions to their experience of the activity, such that for ethical reasons, we were forced to abandon the measurement processes. In this instance, even a mild re-configuration of the phenomenon under observation was sufficient to change it to something no longer recognisable as the thing we were trying to observe.

The aesthetic 'cut'

However, in another sense, the notion of an 'agential cut' is useful in understanding how particular musical traditions relate to the patterns of diffraction/interference which seem central to music's affect. Within aesthetic traditions, such a 'cut' is made explicitly between performers (the 'object' which produces the soundwaves) and audience (as both the 'agencies of observation' and the 'cognizing agent'). The purpose of such a cut is presumably to establish replicable patterns of diffraction/interference that are manifest in musical works, deploying skilled musicians to follow precise notated instructions (a musical score) to produce particular patterns of diffraction and interference which are discernible to the audience as a faithful constitution of the musical work in question. Similarly, in recorded fields of music – hi-fidelity recordings which are intended to 'index' a live performance, or 'studio audio art' involving the 'creation and manipulation of sounds [...] to create a recorded art object' (Turino 2008: 26–27) – sonic engineering and production decisions are about where and how to make a 'cut' between what is performed by the musical agents, and how that performance is perceived by a listener, using microphones and various hardware and software processors and effects to shape the final recording.

This aesthetic 'cut' which separates performers and listeners is therefore founded on an assumption that it is principally the diffraction and interference of audio waveforms that gives rise to music's affective qualities. The field of acoustic design is (literally) about how to shape diffraction/interference patterns to produce particular effects, where anticipated convergences in audio waveforms produced by performing musicians can be enhanced to give their affect more presence, thereby enhancing an audience's experience. The canonization of bodies of musical works also helps to reinforce the idea that there are particular patterns of diffraction and interference which are more potent than others in terms of their affect. Most thinking about music is predicated on this assumed aesthetic 'cut' between performers and audience, which further assumes that the audience are clearly separated from the sounds they hear, in order to appreciate those sounds as objective witness to them.

However, interpersonal neurobiological attunement implies that other waveforms are entangled in the production of musical meaning, through the process of 'feeling felt'. The presence of an audience – or rather the introduction of an audience as part of the 'apparatus' of musical production – changes the experience of the music, not just because there is a witness to the act of musical entrainment but because the audience become an intrinsic part of the interpersonal attunement which is a key constituent of music's affective qualities.

There is no such 'cut' between performers and audience in participatory musical traditions, where the musicing is a fully immersive materialist-discursive practice which (ideally) involves everyone present. This leads to quite a different experience of music as a phenomenon, where the patterns of diffraction become more emblematic of the relationships which underpin the phenomena, rather than the musical 'work' as the sole bearer of meaning – a material representation of kinship and social bonding.

To summarize, an Agential Realist perspective offers some useful conceptual lenses through which to view musical phenomena. The recognition of musicing as the experience of an 'entangled state' – the 'intra-action' of multiple mechanisms – helps us to appreciate the complex ways in which it achieves its paramusical effects, while the notion of diffraction and waveform interference helps us to appreciate the subtleties of musical and interpersonal attunement. Similarly, building an understanding of the many contributory factors underpinning musical situations as constituting the 'apparatus' whereby transformational effects are achieved further highlights their interconnectedness, while an appreciation of the way that musical experience must be 'cut' into in order to prepare it for a listening audience emphasizes some of the inherent tensions between aesthetic and participatory musical traditions, as well as raising some thorny epistemological questions about how can we can 'know' anything about musical experience in a purely objective way.

In the following chapter, I consider what happens when we view musical experience without this aesthetic 'cut', a move which I assert helps to emphasize a more holistic understanding of musical experience as a phenomenon. Before I do, however, I wish first to introduce an alternative way of thinking about music's potency, which speaks to music's complex and entangled nature in quite a different but sympathetic way to Barad, by turning to Daniel Stern's framing of time-based artistic experience in a more holistic sense as a 'vitality'.

Music as a vitality

While it may be *theoretically* possible if highly impractical – given the right instruments for measuring all of the mechanisms in the UCL report simultaneously without affecting the musical exchange itself – to build a comprehensive picture of the complex intra-activity between different mechanisms, this is not the way we actually experience music, or any other time-based art form. We experience it in its totality rather than its fragments. This is especially relevant when some of what is being communicated in a musical exchange is certainly not merely information, or even emotion, but forms of vitality which carry both:

> Vitality is a whole. It is a gestalt that emerges from the theoretically separate experiences of movement, force, time, space and intention. It is not analysed in any conscious way piece by piece, anymore than a familiar face is, even though each separate element could be taken aside and studied in isolation.
>
> (Stern 2010: 5)

The experience of vitality as a gestalt, while perhaps hard to pin down, is not unfamiliar to us: 'wholes, gestalts, and emergent properties are what we have to work with and are, largely, what the familiar world seems to be made of' (Stern 2010: 5). They are just hard to describe, partly because they are largely non-verbal, as well as pre-verbal experiences. Time and again in music research, we encounter the narratives of participation where words are simply unable to articulate a transformational experience. For want of a scientific explanation, we call them 'magic moments' (Gabrielsson 2011: 746; Pavlicevic 2013a: 197) where the music is 'known within and between all minds and bodies as one, complex, phenomenon' (Pavlicevic 2013b: 102). In my own research, one of the singers in a focus group following a mountain-top singing project expressed it as 'the stronger the feeling and the sensation was about that [sense of] connection, the less able I was to articulate it' (Camlin et al. 2020: 9). We characterized it as a form of 'communitas', or 'collective joy' (Turner 2012: n.pag.) 'driven by the power of social 'appearance' i.e. 'showing up' for each other (Camlin et al. 2020: 10).

While we can hypothesize that this experience of 'communitas' may be bound up in the experience of diffraction/interference patterns intrinsic to the musicing, as Stern highlights, the experience of 'vitality dynamics [is] about the "feel" of being alive and full of vitality' (Stern 2010: 46). A powerful musical experience may activate multiple mechanisms and neural networks but rather than experiencing this complexity as isolated elements that we can name, we experience it in its totality, as an inexpressible form of vitality: 'without vitality forms there could not be the exquisite fine-tuning of interpersonal interactions, nor creative artistic interpretations. We would also lose part of what makes us feel alive and vital' (Stern 2010: 51).

Stern argues that vitality forms 'are hard to grasp because we experience them in almost all waking activities' (Stern 2010: 10). They are never experienced in isolation but always in relation to something they contain, or carry with them: for example, 'an emotion or shifts in emotion, a train of thoughts, physical or mental movements, a memory, fantasy, a means-end action, a sequence of dance steps, or a shot in a film' (23). The experience of vitality is always as an accompaniment to other emotional or cognitive content, and as such becomes elusive:

> [Vitality forms] are obscured by the felt quality of emotions as it accompanies them. They are absorbed into the explicit meaning as the vitality form accompanies a train of thought, so we do not pay attention to the feel of the emergence of the thought, but only to its contents. It slips through our fingers.
>
> (Stern 2010: 10)

Viewed in this way, music might be said to 'mean' in a number of different ways, simultaneously: first, through the explicit content of the musical themes, through lyrics or subject matter; second, through the emotional content which underpins the explicit content e.g., joy sadness; third, information about the carrier of that emotional content, what Stern describes as the vitality content. While these might appear to be separate mediums of communication they are not experienced as such, but rather as a 'whole', a gestalt.

'Affect' attunement

Attuning to the subtle ways in which forms of vitality carry emotional and/or cognitive meaning is about tuning in to the *medium* of human communication as much as any intended *message*, 'matching and sharing dynamic forms of vitality' (Stern 2010: 42), especially when undertaken across different modalities, leading to a deeper sense of the underlying vitality dynamics. Turning to vitality dynamics in this way – as a means of understanding music as a CAS or even as an experience of music as patterns of diffraction of various kinds – is not in any way to reject a scientific understanding of the phenomenon; rather, it is a way of supplementing such understanding.

It seems unlikely that the experience of transcendence in musicing is the same experience for everyone, each time it occurs. If it were, there would be some kind of common description of the experience. Instead, we are left grappling with the language of 'magic moments' to describe unique experiences of transcendence which are profoundly personal. However, resorting to the language of 'magic' to explain the most powerful and transformational musical experiences is to do them a dis-service, because it suggests they are inexplicable; that they are not understandable by science. The opposite is also true – powerful musical experiences elude full scientific understanding *because of* their complexity, and the nature of their diffraction and intra-action. Vitality dynamics at least give us a framework for understanding that complexity, and why it is elusive:

> The final emotional experience [what we say that we feel] is the result of multiple processes acting together and in sequence, namely physiological arousal, neurological activation, attention processes, hedonic evaluation, the social context, cultural biases, 'basic' response tendencies, past history, and so on.
>
> (Stern 2010: 67)

If it is meaningful to assert that the participants in a musical encounter *are* the apparatus for understanding music as a phenomenon, then an important implication of this is the need to develop methodologies which make the fullest use of that whole apparatus – what is inscribed on participants' bodies as a result of participation and the sense they make of such inscriptions, and not just individual bodies but rather recognizing the *inter*-personal and *intra*-active nature of group musical experience. Can the experience of forms of vitality present itself therefore as an alternative – or at the very least, a powerful adjunct – to measurement? Vitality is a more ontological frame through which to view the experience of phenomena i.e., 'not knowledge of the world from above or outside, but *knowing as part of being*' (Barad 2015: 7526, original emphasis).

Conclusion

In this chapter, I have attempted to make sense of the transcendental experiences that are frequently reported as part of collaborative music making through a consideration of the complex ways in which music – as a CAS, has perpetuated throughout human evolution. Building on the foundations of communicative musicality, musicing invokes a deep and profound sense of connectedness-through-music that we might view as 'communitas', or 'moments of collective joy' (Turner 2012: n.pag.) which foster kinship. Attending to vitality dynamics and the entanglement of phenomena alongside a more scientific understanding of music requires us to look at musical experience in a different way. Understanding the full range of mechanisms and their diffractive intra-action during a musical experience is obviously important, whereas attending to vitality dynamics in people's actual experiences of the musical moment can help us to develop a better idea of the experiential significance of the intra-action of those mechanisms in practice. It will increasingly become more of an issue as we try to understand the inter-personal mechanisms which give music its vitality, even while those mechanisms – as a vitality – resist full scientific understanding because of their adaptive, intra-active, diffractive and polyvalent nature.

In the rest of this book, I will draw on this relationship – vitality dynamics as a way of experiencing music as a CAS – as a foundation for what follows. The argument I develop is that this complex system of intra-active dimensions that we call 'musicing' – when undertaken with *ethical* intent – is a potential resource for humans in our ongoing evolution as the dominant species on a fragile planet, because of its capacity for making kinship relations. At the heart of music's power as a form of vitality is a universal experience of communicative musicality, a capacity for creating deep bonds of intimate connection that we can recognize as a form of 'love'. Music making therefore verifies (literally makes true) the notion that we *can* develop kinship relationships with strangers. How we turn this experience of intimate connection – of 'feeling felt' – into a resource for sustainable human development is very much part of our developmental task as a species to 'make kin in lines of inventive connection as a practice of learning to live and die well with each other in a thick present' (Haraway 2016: 1). Music has been a feature of all known human cultures throughout history, and in this time of multiple threats to existence as we know it, musicing can continue to serve as a potent reminder of our collective humanity, as well as a form of nourishment and solidarity as we journey into an uncertain future.

NOTE

1. which may be more strictly akin to waveform interference.

4

Performing Works, Performing Relationships

FIGURE 4.1: The Gathering, Ennerdale 2019. Photographer: Dave Camlin.

In this chapter, I build on the complexity of musical experience described in the previous chapter to outline a holistic philosophy of music which unites two particular traditions of musicing which have more often been considered to be separate: the performance of musical 'works' (aesthetic traditions), on the one hand, and the 'performance' of human relationships through music (participatory traditions), on the other. Resolving the apparent contradictions between aesthetic and participatory musical traditions is an important step in the development of a holistic understanding of music's potential, because such a resolution illuminates how the complex ways in which music comes to 'mean' something play out across a broad sphere of musical practices.

Rather than thinking of performance and participatory traditions as separate fields entirely as Turino (2008) suggests, I suggest that they represent complementary dimensions of musicing held in a creative tension with each other, and united through their mutual interest in a third dimension of musicing, namely the 'paramusical' – the associated benefits which 'go along' with musical experience. This stance emphasizes the importance of both 'dialogic' and 'diffractive' thinking – the dialogic assumption that 'meaning is never singular but always emerges in the play of different voices in dialogue together' (Wegerif 2012: 3) – as a way of reflecting on these complex interdependencies, as well as a 'diffractive' understanding of *which differences matter*. I also suggest that 'dissensus' – agreeing to be uniquely different – is an essential characteristic of the ways that different musical traditions, practices and practitioners take up positions within this network of meaning. This is an important next step in my argument because it highlights some of the many different ways that people may come to think about music – what it is and what it does. Only by developing ways of thinking about music which allow us to reference its many dimensions – without falling into dichotomous views on which has greater value – can we begin to view it as a holistic concept.

Background

This model of 'music in three dimensions' emerged from my doctoral studies undertaken as Head of Higher Education & Research at the Sage Gateshead music organization in NE England between 2010 and 2016. As a dialogic construction, it has undergone a few transformations since its initial conception, from the original thesis (Camlin 2016a) and an earlier journal article which developed some of the ideas (Camlin 2014) as well as a conference paper which explored how the model might be applied in practice, as a way of understanding the complexity of issues of 'quality' in socially engaged music practice (Camlin 2018a). In this chapter, I set out a more evolved version of the model, which suggests that music is at its most potent when these three 'dimensions' of music – the aesthetic (performance of 'works'), the participatory ('performance' of relationships) and the paramusical (what 'goes along with' the music) – are actively engaged, not to the exclusion of the other two, but held in a creative tension with them.

As described in Chapter 2, this perspective emerged from the process of situating undergraduate music education within the artistic programme of UK music organization Sage Gateshead over a ten-year period 2009–18. The model was initially developed as an articulation of the complexity of the organization's public-facing practices, to support undergraduate music students to make critical sense of such complexity, and it has since become a key reference point for much of my work. What I hope is gleaned from the model is an understanding of the kind of creative tension which exists when these three dimensions of music's power are engaged in practice, and how they intra-act, leading to a very wide range of musical possibilities.

Sage Gateshead

For those unfamiliar with it, Sage Gateshead is a music organization (since 2000) and cultural venue (since 2005) whose mission is 'enriching lives through music' (Sage Gateshead). It operates from an iconic Norman Foster designed glass building on the Gateshead bank of the River Tyne in the Newcastle-Gateshead conurbation in the north of England, which is home to the Royal Northern Sinfonia.

During the earlier parts of the organization's history, the artistic programme of Sage Gateshead was conceived as consisting equally of music performance, on the one hand, and music learning and participation (L&P), on the other. Under the leadership of its founding directors, it pioneered a comprehensive programme of L&P during the 'boom' in arts funding for social impact from the end of the 1990s (Zeserson 2021). In 2013–14, the annual expenditure on the L&P programme was roughly the same as that spent on its performance programme – *c.*£6.5 million each in 2013–14 (Sage Gateshead 2014) – emphasizing the equal artistic weighting between these two elements of the organization's work. At its peak, the L&P programme employed a workforce of over 140 musicians to deliver a wide range of musical activities with a wide range of participant groups, from pregnant mothers and Early Years groups, a weekend music school for children and young people, turntablism and rock/pop workshops for teenagers, an extensive music participation programme for adults – including a 'Silver' programme for the over-50s with over 1000 weekly participants – through to 'health musicking' (Ruud 2013: 151; Stige 2013: n.pag.) in care homes, music therapy and much more in between.

This artistic vision was reflected not just in the equal weighting in its artistic programme but also in the fabric of the building itself. The Sage Gateshead building contains three concert venues of different sizes, with a suite of 26 music education rooms of varying sizes contained on the ground floor. Music education was, quite literally, the foundation around which the rest of the organization's practices were constructed. Perhaps the simple fact of this physical co-existence between the worlds of music performance and music education is responsible for some of the development of the dialogic model described in this chapter, as it meant that an intellectual separation between these 'dimensions' of music was simply not possible.

From 2009 to 2018, Sage Gateshead delivered undergraduate music education in a joint collaboration franchise model with University of Sunderland. The BA (Hons) Community Music (CM) course was established in 2009, and a pre-existing BMus (Hons) Jazz Popular and Commercial Music transferred from Newcastle College to Sage Gateshead in 2011. The central idea of establishing these programmes within Sage Gateshead was to provide an alternative route for Higher Education (HE) Music study for the region which was grounded in the practices of the music and music education sectors, giving students the opportunity to learn 'inside' industry practices, rather than just learn 'about' them.

Praxis

The knowledge that emerged as result of this situation might be said to have done so iteratively as a form of *praxis* (Bowman 2009a: 53; Freire 1970: 33; Nelson 2013: 4), with the more productive knowledge of the organization's practices – e.g. CM workshops in many diverse contexts – informing the undergraduate curriculum, and the more theoretical knowledge used to critically underpin that curriculum articulating the complexities of the organization's situation; a virtuous circle of knowledge development, so to speak. Delivering undergraduate music programmes within a music organization in this way might be seen as a form of 'action research' (McNiff 2013; Reason and Bradbury 2013), with new knowledge about the organization emerging in a 'dialogic' way (Bakhtin 1981; Wegerif 2012) through the development of the academic perspective required to underpin undergraduate learning. Students developed insights into 'real world' (Bennett 2012) music industry practices, while the organization learned how to articulate those practices in more critical terms, through the undergraduate curriculum.

Music in three dimensions

Situating undergraduate musician education within this extensive and complex offer of 'presentational performance' on the organization's three stages and the 'participatory music' (Turino 2008: 28–49) of its L&P programme required the development of a philosophy of practice to enable students to make sense of the diverse range of situations they found themselves developing skills and knowledge within. Much of this discourse centred around notions of 'quality'. Discussions of issues of quality surrounding the performance of musical 'works' have a long tradition e.g. (Godlovitch 1998; O'Dea 2000; Rink 2002; Chaffin and Lemieux 2004; Williamon 2004; Klickstein 2009) and are often to do with the development of technical skills required to undertake the execution of challenging musical materials and which are enshrined in the quality standards of the various music examination boards. By contrast, the quality standards of participatory music are perhaps more elusive (Renshaw 2010; Matarasso 2013; Camlin 2014). Turino argues that:

> The quality of [participatory] performance is ultimately judged on the level of participation achieved. Quality is also gauged by how participants feel during the activity,

> with little thought to how the music and dance might sound or look apart from the act of doing and those involved.
>
> (Turino 2008: 28)

These fundamental differences in character make comparisons between these two kinds of musicing problematic, especially as many instances of musicing do not fall neatly into either category (Camlin 2014: 106). The development of the model of 'music in three dimensions' was therefore to provide a framework for aspiring musicians to understand the complex networks of practice they would find themselves engaging with over the course of a 'portfolio' career, where they might be expected to move between performance, education, community and healthcare settings on a regular basis.

Dimensions

The 'music in three dimensions' model expresses a dialogic and intra-active relationship between three musical dimensions, namely the aesthetic, the participatory and the paramusical, as illustrated in Figure 4.2.

The model addressed the conceptual problems facing undergraduate music students by re-framing the performance (aesthetic) and L&P (participatory) elements of Sage Gateshead's artistic programme as complementary musical dimensions, held in a 'creative tension' (Adorno 1973: 153; Wegerif 2012: 158) with each other. In turn, these musical dimensions are brought further into more complex relationships with each other through the influence of the third dimension, the 'paramusical'.

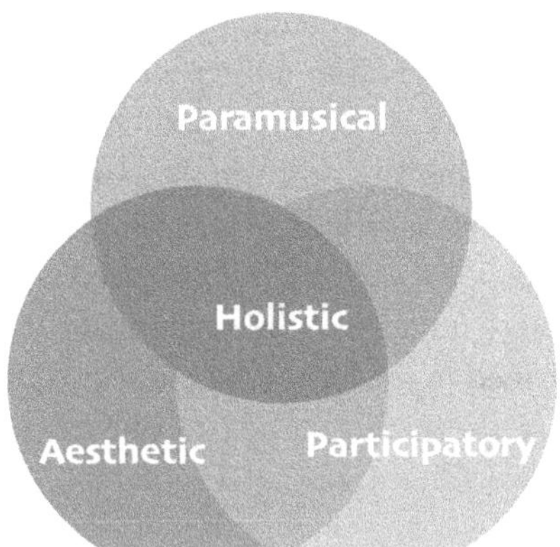

FIGURE 4.2: Music in three dimensions.

Rather than being seen as completely discreet fields of practice, this 'dialogic' philosophy of practice emphasizes the correspondences and tensions of different kinds of musical practice being pulled simultaneously towards different dimensions of musicing, the overlapping circles in the diagram representing the ways in which the different dimensions intra-act in a fluid yet stable relationship with one another.

While conceiving of the dimensions independently may appear to begin to reinforce the notion that they are somehow separate fields and can be understood as such, that is not really my intention here. The identification of complementary dimensions in the model is simply to bring them into a reader's awareness as corresponding forces acting on all musical instances to a greater or lesser degree. The extent of such influence is, of course, highly situated and responsive to the socio-cultural particularities of a given situation, and therefore emergent, fluid and susceptible to continuous change. Making a 'cut' into musical experience in this way – to view each dimension discreetly – is potentially to miss the ways in which these dimensions are truly complementary and intra-active. While some musical practices may *feel* like they belong more clearly within one dimension or another, the reality is that all musical praxes, when underpinned with an ethical intention towards actualization of the full potential of musical experience, will resonate with *each* dimension to a greater or lesser degree.

Nevertheless, in the sections that follow, I provide a brief outline of each of these various dimensions, including a short summary of the kinds of assumptions which might underpin practice oriented towards a particular dimension. Again, this is not to suggest that musicians actually undertake such conceptual leaps between different perspectives on musicing while they are being musical, but rather to highlight the different kinds of thinking and doing which occur as the different dimensions become more or less active within any given musical situation. The model is conceived as a territory that musicians move around all the time rather than one where people take up fixed positions. The contexts of music are constantly shifting, and as one moves around between and across its different dimensions, the kinds of questions a musician might be asking of themselves shift and change too. I also therefore provide some examples of reflective questions which a musician might be asking themselves in response to their orientation towards a particular dimension. These questions are intended to be examples of how a musician might put the ideas in the model to practical service.

Musical dimensions

In the model, the aesthetic and participatory dimensions along the horizontal *x*-axis are *intrinsically* musical ones, in that they are both inseparable from the acts of musicing which constitute them. By contrast, the paramusical dimension along the vertical y-axis is not specifically musical but rather represents effects which 'go along with' the musical activities, as outlined in Chapter 3.

Aesthetic – The performance of musical 'Works'

Put simply, the 'aesthetic' dimension of music (Adams et al. 2010: 20–23; Elliott and Silverman 2013; Turino 2008: 51–58) represents a concern with 'the beauty or 'meaning' of [music's] sonorous forms' (Elliott and Silverman 2013). It is therefore generally about the performance and appreciation of musical 'works', especially those which have been canonized through the act of distinction i.e. particular pieces of music which have come to represent the highest standards of musical achievement in both their composition and their execution, as agreed through the consensus of a 'rational community' (Lingis 1994: 9) of arbiters of that particular kind of musical taste. While we might associate the 'aesthetic' dimension of music with Western Art Music (WAM) in particular, the same judgements of quality of 'sonorous forms' could equally be applied to any other culturally specific musical performance practice where 'listening' is emphasized.

The use of the term 'aesthetic' is not without some ambiguity. An aesthetic experience in its fullest sense is fundamentally to do with the stimulation of the senses, and not dissimilar to Stern's account of vitality dynamics. Educational theorist Ken Robinson suggests that an aesthetic experience is the opposite of an anaesthetic one, where 'your senses are operating at their peak, when you're present in the current moment, when you're resonating with the excitement of [whatever] you're experiencing; when you are fully alive' (Robinson 2010). While different acts of musicing might achieve different aesthetic effects – compare the auditory pleasures of a seated orchestral concert with the more embodied frenzy of a Heavy Metal mosh-pit, for example, or the collective joy expressed in a 'loved-up' festival dance tent. Despite these clear differences in terms of aesthetic experience, the term has generally come to mean the former i.e. a construct of 'the specific historical, social, cultural, economic, and political circumstances of the age of enlightenment (approximately 1685 to 1800] and in a specific location: Western Europe, especially Germany and England' (Elliott and Silverman 2015: 68).

Assumptions

If music's power lies in the quality of its 'sonorous forms', then a basic assumption underpinning the 'aesthetic' dimension of music is that music is for listening to: it requires 'listeners'. Turino refers to music from the aesthetic dimension as

Presentational Music: 'a field involving one group of people (the artists) providing music for another (the audience) in which there is pronounced artist-audience separation within face-to-face situations' (Turino 2008: 51). Central to this practice is an inherent separation between listeners and performers: 'presentational music is prepared by musicians for others to listen to, and this simple distinction has many ramifications' (Turino 2008: 52).

If the purpose of musical activity is for a (group of) performer/s to realize a particular aesthetic effect for the benefit of attentive 'listeners', then a number of further assumptions follow. First, that musicians need to be skilled at manipulating and organizing sound, which implies that technical skills are therefore the foundation of good musicing. A logical conclusion of this line of thought is that virtuosity is the quality standard of musical excellence.

Reflective questions

Examples of the kinds of reflective questions that a musician might therefore ask themselves, if oriented towards the aesthetic dimension, could include:

- How do I (we) shape/control the musical sounds to achieve something emotionally 'affective'? What aesthetic effect are we aiming for?
- What techniques/skills do I (we) need to deploy/develop to achieve this?
- How do I refine my awareness to express myself clearly and effectively, whilst listening to all the other voices?
- How can I support others to express themselves?
- How do we work together for maximum aesthetic impact?
- How do we interpret the work, within generic/stylistic constraints (e.g., composer intention, previous recording, performances, religious/spiritual/social traditions)?

Participatory – The 'Performance' of relationships

Because the 'aesthetic' dimension of music is so prevalent within everyday life in most parts of the world – pitch-perfect recordings and performances honed to often impossibly high standards by the use of algorithms in post-production audio manipulation, for example – it is very easy to think of the 'aesthetic' dimension as lying at the centre of all musical experience rather than at one end of a continuum. Comparing classical music with pop music, sociologist Simon Frith characterizes this problem as one of an assumption of value: 'serious music matters because it transcends social forces; popular music is aesthetically worthless because it is determined by them (because it is "useful" or "utilitarian")' (Frith 2007: 257). CM and practices such as 'health musicking' (Stige 2002) – which might be seen to be more closely connected to participatory and paramusical dimensions of musicing respectively – might be further yet from the centre of a world with aesthetic traditions at its heart.

Even Daniel Stern tends to conceive of vitality dynamics in music in relation to the aesthetic dimension and notions of performer-audience "transmission" rather than anything more participatory: 'the difference between a technically adequate performance and a transporting interpretation lies in the unique vitality dynamics that a great artist can bring to the work and transmit to an audience' (Stern 2010: 20). It may be that a particular casualty of the rise of recorded music was musical participation itself. Perhaps the higher presentational standards of recorded music mitigated against participation, where 'changes in the ways in which music is manifested [have resulted in] the discouragement of alternative and often older ways of engaging with music, particularly as an active element in everyday life' (Cross and Morley 2010: 66).

However, participatory musical traditions have their own vitality. They are 'not just informal or amateur, that is, lesser versions of the "real music" made by the pros but, in fact, they are something else' (Turino 2008: 25). Whereas in the 'aesthetic' model of 'presentational' music our attention is directed to the performance of musical 'works', in the participatory dimension of music – which holds that music is, 'a human practice that is procedural in essence' (Elliott 1995: 247–49) – our attention is directed more to the 'performance' of relationships. As one of the contemporary architects of this idea, Christopher Small perhaps sums this up most clearly:

> The act of musicking establishes in the place where it is happening a set of relationships, and it is in those relationships that the meaning of the act lies. They are to be found not only between those organized sounds which are conventionally thought of as being the stuff of musical meaning but also between the people who are taking part, in whatever capacity, in the performance; and they model, or stand as metaphor for, ideal relationships as the participants in the performance imagine them to be: relationships between person and person, between individual and society, between humanity and the natural world and even perhaps the supernatural world.
>
> (Small 1998: 314)

Or, as Turino puts it, 'participating in music and dance is more about the social relations being realised through the performance than about producing art that can somehow be abstracted from those social relations' (Turino 2008: 36). We might say that within participatory traditions music is an integral part of social life, a means of expressing and performing particular 'intimate relations with others' (Hesmondhalgh 2013: 2) and enhancing 'feelings of shared experience, attachment, and solidarity towards other human beings' (87). Therefore, 'in participatory music making one's primary attention is on the activity, on the doing, and on the other participants, rather than on an end product that results from the activity' (Turino 2008: 28). It is important to emphasize that this attention to the 'other' in participatory traditions does not make them any less musical than their aesthetic counterparts. As I discuss in Chapter 5, the purpose of music for most of human history has been about its affordances for social bonding as an *intrinsic* part of the musicing, not separate from it; participatory musical traditions are *inherently and inseparably musical* traditions.

However, because of this emphasis on the 'performance' of human relationships, the characteristics of participatory music are therefore different to that of its more presentational counterpart, with an emphasis on 'open' musical forms i.e. music that can be looped and repeated 'for as long as the participants and situation requires' (Turino 2008: 37), so that 'newcomers and people who have not carefully prepared or rehearsed the music won't be caught off guard and be made to feel awkward' (38). Participatory performance (musicing) also has a range of both 'core' roles for the less experienced that are easy to join in with, and 'elaboration' roles for those with more musical confidence and experience (31). Wide intonation systems, fewer musical dynamic changes and 'buzzy' instrumental timbres help to further 'cloak' individual contributions so as to 'inspire musical participation' (46).

Assumptions

These musical characteristics lead to a very different set of assumptions about what music is and what it is for. Principally, music is for *doing* – it is the *act* of musicing that gives it value, and this is an ancient and universal human activity: 'long before there were musical compositions there was in the sense of singing and playing remembered renditions and improvisations; many cultures still view music as something people do' (Elliott 1995: 49). Because of this ancient and historic social function of music, musicing remains a fun social activity that brings people together and unites them in a common purpose. With that purpose in mind, accessibility is paramount, so that 'everyone present can, and in fact should, participate in the sound and motion of the performance' (Turino 2008: 29).

In turn, this suggests a further assumption that everyone is – or can be – a musician and is able to participate at a level appropriate to them, especially when participation doesn't require an audition of someone's skill level prior to participation: 'participants in a non-auditioned group are welcomed for who they are and what they can bring to the group' (Camlin 2021c: 299). In other words, participatory musicing is about 'encouraging people to join in regardless of the quality of their contributions' (Turino 2008: 36), and where the primary measure of quality is about how many of those present *do* join in (28).

In this context, music therefore consists of a series of 'acts of hospitality' (Higgins 2007, 2009, 2012: 133–43; Bartleet and Higgins 2018: 10–11), and the role of the musician in society is to welcome people into practical musical opportunities and ensure as many people as want to are involved. This entails structuring musical opportunities so that there are multiple ways of participating, for those with both greater and lesser experience: 'participatory traditions usually include a variety of roles demanding different degrees of specialisation, so that people can join in at a level that offers the right balance of challenge and acquired skills' (Turino 2008: 31). As noted above, 'the inclusion of people with a wide range of abilities within the same performance is important for inspiring participation' (31).

Reflective questions

Examples of the kinds of reflective questions that a musician might therefore ask themselves, if oriented towards the participatory dimension, could include:

- Who's in the room? What do they (we) want (today)? What are they (we) capable of? How can I (we) build on previous experience?
- What do the others need/expect from me? How can/do I inspire them? What's my unique contribution?
- Who isn't in the room? Why not? Where are they? Why?
- How can I (we) make this easier/more accessible for those with less experience?
- How can I (we) make this more challenging for those with more experience?
- When do I – or someone else – need to direct proceedings? When to facilitate? When to delegate? When to just 'get out of the way'?
- How do I (we) create a 'safe space' where everyone feels welcome, and not judged?
- How do I (we) make space for each other's creativity?
- What are the expectations of others in terms of content, outcomes?

Musical continuum

Recognizing the functional differences between the aesthetic and participatory dimensions of music goes a long way to understanding the complex social contexts of musical performance, but can ultimately result in a polarized perspective on musicing which is not necessarily reflective of the complexity of 'real life' situations

(Camlin 2014). Turino goes so far as to see the aesthetic/presentational and praxial/participatory dimensions as 'different form[s] of art and activity entirely – and that they should be conceptualised and valued as such' (Turino 2008: 25). While the motivation for thinking along these lines of separation might be to highlight the unique nature of participatory music as distinct from its more presentational counterpart, it could also contribute to a more dichotomous view of music, where different musical traditions become embroiled in the familiar but stale discourse of competing interests – process vs. product, access vs. excellence and so on – rather than being viewed as complementary influences on musical quality. While arguments about 'aesthetic' vs. 'praxial' models of music education may have been a consistent feature of academic debate around music education for some time (Bowman 2005; Elliott 1995, 2009; Elliott and Silverman 2013), critics argue that such distinctions 'don't do anyone any service, they don't really have any meaning' (Mullen 2015).

In practice, there is perhaps more commonly an integrative tension between these dimensions: musical participation often leads to public performance (Camlin 2015b), and even highly presentational forms need to widen participation, increase access and broaden inclusion, in order to resist becoming what Daniel Barenboim describes as an, 'ivory-tower community [which has] lost a great part of the connection between music and everything else' (Rusbridger 2013: 210). Hence the idea of aesthetic and participatory dimensions of music existing in a creative tension with each other recognizes the complexity of real-life situations of musicing where the boundaries between these apparently discreet fields of music are often blurred or transgressed (Camlin 2014). A dialogic perspective highlights the fact that these musical dimensions (aesthetic and participatory) call on us as musicians to attend to them *both*, which in turn helps us not to stay in a fixed and static relationship with either one.

Musicality is something which has been present in all human cultures for the entire 230,000 year history of our species (Dunbar 2012; Mithen 2007) and only relatively recently separated in western cultures with the evolution of 'aesthetic' forms (Elliott and Silverman 2013; Ranciere 2003: 115–33). Or, as David Byrne puts it, 'before recorded music became ubiquitous, music was, for most people, something we did.' (Byrne 2012: 70). Because of the ubiquity of presentational forms of music, there is a tendency – perhaps not surprisingly – to judge the quality of participatory forms of music by the standards of its presentational counterpart, without recognizing that the intentions and concerns of participatory music might be different, and require different quality measures. However, recognizing these differences also highlights the fact that the quality standards of presentational music – e.g. 'organised beginnings and endings, individual virtuosity, contrasts, transparent textures' (Turino 2008: 45) – often *do* apply to participatory settings as well, leading to a complex web of inter-related meaning. To illustrate the blurring of these boundaries, it is worth remembering that some forms of music actively reach across this conceptual divide. Without wishing to create further divisions along a continuum between the aesthetic and the participatory, it is also the case that some forms of musicing at different points along this continuum share similar characteristics. I highlight some of these firstly to make the point that apparently separate traditions of musicing have more in common than may first appear, and also because a consideration of these create tensions help to illuminate an important concept in my argument, namely the power of public 'appearance'.

Performance-as-participation

Performance events which are conceived as 'presentational' events but which inspire or facilitate participation might be loosely considered to be 'performance-as-participation' (Camlin 2014: 110), where the presentational elements invite those present to move between being listeners and active participants in the performance. Stadium rock immediately comes to mind, or musical theatre, where highly virtuosic musical displays by professional musicians are structured so as to inspire participation. At different times in the performance, those present might be expected to listen attentively to a particular solo performer, sing along with a familiar song, or get up and dance. Doing so provides no particular conceptual obstacle for those present; they fulfil the different roles expected of them without really having to think about it.

Participation-as-performance

Similarly, towards the other end of the continuum, we find performance events designed more specifically around a celebration of participants' public and social identities as performers. In these instances, which we might term 'participation-as-performance' (Camlin 2014: 109), the audience are applauding the participants' participation as much as (or maybe more than) they are the quality of the works performed. At the heart of the audience's involvement is their role as 'witness', recognizing and validating the participants' public 'appearance' in the form of musical performer, essentially celebrating the realization of individual identity and social relations through performance.

Although the idea of social 'appearance' through music may seem at first glance to be a minor affordance of public performance, there is much to be said about it. The Humanist philosopher Hannah Arendt suggests that to 'appear' in public is really an important part of the process of self-actualization – that one's identity can only ever be partially actualized until such time as it 'appears' in public:

> Everything that appears in public can be seen and heard by everybody and has the widest possible publicity. For us, appearance – something that is being seen and heard by others as well as by ourselves – constitutes reality. Compared with the reality which comes from being seen and heard, even the greatest forces of intimate life – the passions of the heart, the thoughts of the mind, the delights of the senses – lead an uncertain, shadowy kind of existence unless and until they are transformed, deprivatized and deindividualized, as it were, into a shape to fit them for public appearance.
>
> (Arendt 1958: 50)

Central to this notion of 'appearance' is the sense of committing to the process of 'beginning', of being willing to initiate action in such a way as to make such appearance possible. In a musical sense, this might mean to practice one's instrument, or to learn song lyrics in order to perform more confidently, for example. Moreover, to 'appear' is always to do so as a 'beginner' – one who begins and is witnessed in their 'beginning' – alongside many other such 'beginners', all committing to be seen and heard in public.

> Just as we strive to bring our beginnings into the world, others strive to bring their beginnings into the world as well. And it is only when our beginnings are taken up by others – others who are capable of their own actions – that we come into the world.
>
> (Biesta 2006: 48)

To 'appear' in this way – as a citizen within and before a community – is always therefore to do so in the context of plurality and difference, at least to some degree, recognizing that one's own 'beginnings' are tempered or even changed by the 'beginnings' of others, all striving to 'appear' among their fellows as unique and singular individuals. The notion of 'appearance' is therefore a dialogic and negotiated affair between individuals and groups, and central to the long-term existential goals of actualization:

> The life span of man running toward death would inevitably carry everything human to ruin and destruction if it were not for the faculty of interrupting it and beginning something new, a faculty which is inherent in action like an ever-present reminder that men, though they must die, are not born in order to die but in order to begin.
>
> (Arendt 1958: 246)

Hence, a school music concert, a CM event or a public sharing by a 'health music' group become important sites for identity work, where participants/performers are able to explore and express a public-facing *and social* version of themselves which others bear witness to:

> Music represents a remarkable meeting point of intimate and social realms. It provides a basis of self-identity (this is who I am, this is who I'm not) and collective identity (this is who we are, this is who we're not), often in the same moment.
>
> (Hesmondhalgh 2013: 2)

This call on participatory music practices to 'appear' in public requires them to account for the different quality standards which come into play as the practice is drawn along the dialogic continuum towards the aesthetic dimension where 'listeners' will make judgements about the quality of what they hear. As a community musician, I may start off working with a group of participants asking questions about how to facilitate participation – who's in the room? How do we work together? and so on. However, once that same group is called upon to perform in public, the questions turn increasingly towards the aesthetic quality of the sounds to be produced for a listening audience – how do we blend voices and entrain to each other more strongly? Involve more dynamics? Maintain pitch? Communicate more expressively?

The quality of experience for all involved – participants and listeners alike – is enhanced the more effectively the 'public' presentation of music addresses the quality standards of the aesthetic dimension. Crucially, however, it is the extent to which the aesthetic and participatory dimensions are held in creative tension with each other which really determines the overall quality of the experience. Once it no longer matters 'who' is performing but only 'what' and 'how' it is performed, the power of individual 'appearance' wanes. It is these shifting territories between the aesthetic and participatory dimensions which bring music's complexity more vividly into our awareness.

In summary, accounting for the 'aesthetic' dimension of music means accounting for the quality of music that is produced in performance, while accounting for the 'participatory' dimension of music means accounting for the people involved (or not involved), and structuring musical opportunities to maximize access, inclusion and participation (Camlin 2016a, 2016b). Unless instances of musicing are located very firmly within either 'presentational' or 'participatory' traditions, attempting to understand quality by reference to the standards of either dimension *on its own* proves problematic. What constitutes quality in more fluid or dialogic instances of socially engaged musical performance is complex, and above all, contingent on the situation itself. See Chapter 7 for some examples of musical projects which situate themselves in a creative tension between presentational and participatory dimensions.

Paramusical dimension

In exploring the aesthetic and participatory dimensions, we have focused so far on what we might think of as the intrinsically 'musical' dimensions of musicing. Next, we turn to the 'paramusical' dimension, where 'active engagement with music impacts beyond the development of musical skills' (Hallam 2015: 1). While the first two 'musical' dimensions describe the dialogic relationship between presentational and participatory forms of music, the third dimension – the 'paramusical' – accounts for the benefits that arise from musicing, including all of the things outlined in Chapter 3, from improvements in an individual's physical and psychological health, confidence, self-esteem, self-expression and identity, through to increased social cohesion, social capital and group identity. The choice of the term 'paramusical' is a careful one made by its originators:

> We are going to suggest an alternative to the phrase 'extra-musical', as this gives the wrong impression that things are either 'totally musical' or extra- (that is, 'outside') musical. Instead, what we want to understand is the kind of relationship between those phenomena that we perceive as specifically 'musical' and all of those actions and activities which 'go-with' these. We will use the term 'para-musical' for this latter 'go-with' class of phenomena – paramusical meaning the 'more-than-musical' phenomena [...] which are often justified as [...] therapeutic outcomes [...] – be these individual, relational, social, or political phenomena.
>
> (Stige et al. 2013: 298)

The introduction of a third 'dimension' to the model further emphasizes the complexity of musical situations, whilst at the same time, unifying the other two dimensions in a more 'dialogic' relationship, thereby further preventing discourse from falling back into a more dichotomized argument about the relative merits of music for listening to vs. music for doing, or the other stale dichotomies of musical quality mentioned earlier.

Aesthetic traditions facilitate the communication of emotions through the performance of musical works, while participatory traditions facilitate the expression of human relationships, but both traditions do so in ways which are intrinsically musical, in that there is no other way in which these specific works and/or particular relationships could be expressed: music expresses these works and relationships uniquely. By contrast, the benefits and effects of the paramusical dimension are not exclusive to music; positive health and well-being, social cohesion and human flourishing in general – are achievable through many different and non-musical routes, as well as musical ones.

The paramusical dimension itself contains at least four sub-categories through which some kind of positive impact or benefit might be activated through musicing, and we can think of these as broadly individual, relational/social, cultural and economic. The comprehensive and complex nature of the individual and relational/social benefits of musicing – especially in relation to health and well-being – can be seen clearly in the 600+ mechanisms outlined by Fancourt et al. (2021) and discussed extensively in Chapter 3.

Additionally, there is also a cultural aspect of the paramusical – being musical is never just about being generally musical but is always about being musical in a specific way, using the instruments, heritage and expressions of particular sociocultural traditions, either by adhering to those traditions or by transgressing or combining them. Cross and Woodruff (2009) identify this quality of music as 'culturally enactive' in that the act of musicing invokes an 'experience of meaning [...] which derives from the particularities of the cultural contexts in which we develop and come to play a part' (Cross and Woodruff 2009: 7). In short, at least some of the impact of musicing occurs as a result of 'active participation in, and engagement with, the dynamics and specificities of particular cultural contexts and processes, as well as of individual life histories' (7). Music – and perhaps especially songs – take on meaning not just from the sounds which constitute them or our (neuro-)biological responses to them, but from the socio-cultural situations we associate them with, whether that's a football terrace, a concert hall, a family or community event, a memory of such an event, an artefact or a playlist. Music is never a culturally neutral medium.

It is also worth remembering that some of music's paramusical value can be expressed in hard economic terms. As discussed in Chapter 1, it is perhaps little surprise that the value of music is often expressed by national Capitalist governments in terms of its contribution to GDP rather than any intrinsic – or other extrinsic – value. In current political discourse, music's value can also be expressed as an economic 'proxy' – a cost–benefit analysis of inputs vs. outcomes, with little regard for its intrinsic artistic value: 'social prescription reduces over subscription of drugs. It can lead to the same or better outcomes for patients without popping pills. And it saves the NHS money, because many of these social cures are cheaper or free' (Hancock 2018).

Herein lies a caution – too much emphasis on the paramusical effects of music – on what music *does* – can draw discussion of its value further from what music intrinsically *is*, and how it achieves those effects in the first place. Hence, a dialogic relationship between the paramusical and the musical (aesthetic and participatory) dimensions of musicing helps to keep this relationship in balance. A further caution is in remembering that – as discussed in Chapter 3 – no act of musicing can 'cause' any intended social impact to actually occur – such impact can only be 'planned for' or 'enabled' (Matarasso 2014). Additionally, we need to be mindful not to allow agendas of advocacy – 'Music is brilliant! At everything! Let's just do more music!' to overtake more critical interrogation of what music is particularly good *for*, and under what circumstances.

Assumptions

Orienting ourselves to the paramusical dimension, we find a further set of underlying assumptions, principle among which is the belief that there *are* positive impacts which 'go along with' the music and which benefit individuals and groups in complex and intra-active ways, including (but not limited to) improved psychological well-being, confidence, self-esteem, empathy, physical health, as well as facilitating increases in social cohesion and social capital. Music shifts our mood, thereby helping us to face life's difficulties and challenges more effectively. It also helps us to develop attitudes of cooperation which in turn enhance our social networks. While we cannot 'make' these impacts happen, we can set about to create the conditions where they may be more likely to occur, which is a matter of carefully thinking about the activities we are party to and how they are structured.

Reflective questions

Examples of the kinds of reflective questions that a musician might therefore ask themselves, if oriented towards the paramusical dimension, could include:

- What do I hope will be the impact of this? Why do I think that?
- What difference do I imagine the activity will make to people's health and/or well-being? How will people benefit from this?
- How will I know if/when we achieve that?
- What change in society do I imagine/hope this will contribute to? Why? How?
- Why is music a good way of doing this? Why not [insert other activity here]?

Holistic

So far, we have considered the model of 'music in three dimensions' by examining each of its three dimensions. It is important to reiterate that in highlighting the characteristics of each dimension, I am in no way suggesting that music can be separated or categorized into falling more exclusively into any of them. The point of the model as dimensions of musicing existing in a dialogic 'creative tension' with each other is rather to make the point that *all* of these dimensions are active in all music, to a great or lesser extent.

In a holistic sense, any musical practice will be stronger the more it attends to the qualities and creative 'pulls' of all three dimensions, especially those which are perhaps habitually more neglected. In a diffractive sense, this means attending to the 'differences that matter' (Barad 2007: 46) in any given situation but being willing to look beyond a more fixed orthodoxy of which dimensions have *customarily* come to matter in more fixed musical traditions. A participatory experience will be more powerful if the musical quality of what is produced through such participation is greater, and if the participants experience positive impacts on their mood, well-being and sense of social connection. Similarly, a 'presentational' performance culture can be enhanced and transformed by thinking more critically about how to broaden participation and foster the 'performance' of relationships among its various communities of producers and consumers, leading to more transformational experiences for more diverse populations, especially for those who do not share the same cultural backgrounds. And a 'health musicking' intervention will be stronger if both of the musical dimensions – attending to musical quality in the 'performance' of relationships – are more actively engaged.

Thinking of music in this way is to extend Stern's notion of music as a gestalt of vitality still further, 'to frame the object of study in a different way – to perceive music in all of its manifestations' (Cross and Morley 2010: 66). This holistic model of music is certainly not complete, but very much a work-in-progress. There may well be other dimensions to account, or subtleties to explore, but what I hope it does is open our conception of music into a more 'dialogic' frame, where we are called on to consider music from the perspective of the pluralistic, complex, contested and often 'messy' ways in which it comes to be a meaningful activity. As a model, it also provides a useful jumping-off point for thinking about music more diffractively. The various dimensions are often less apparent when musicing is undertaken from a more fixed position within any one of them, and hence bringing all three dimensions into our awareness as musicians is an important way of leading us out of more habitual ways of doing and thinking about music.

Holistic assumptions

Viewing music from a holistic perspective means attending to the call of *each* of its dimensions simultaneously, albeit to greater or lesser extents. Of course, some traditions of musicing have evolved to sit more naturally within one or other dimension, and the model does not suggest that all musicing needs to sit in the centre. Rather, all musicing needs to at least be aware of the call of the other dimensions which may be less present, and to make a choice about what – if anything – to do about it, by asking ourselves pertinent questions which bring those other dimensions more fully into our awareness. This in itself is a conscious act of imagination, by calling up perspectives which invite us to into different ways of thinking about why we do what we do. Attending to less present dimensions of our musical practice in order to enlarge our thinking about music might be likened to the Arendtian notion of 'going visiting' (Arendt 1989: 43), bringing unfamiliar or unexplored perspectives into our conscious awareness. When it comes to civic imagination, such a move is likely to prove invaluable, as I shall discuss. Thinking holistically about music also means thinking about music as a form of vitality – as discussed in Chapter 3 – and how that manifests in practice. In particular, it might mean attending to how and why music's capacity for both self-transcendence and attachment – and hence love – are activated.

Reflective questions

Examples of the kinds of reflective questions that a musician might therefore ask themselves, if thinking about music holistically, could include:

- What difference do I make in the world as a musician? How do I put my musical skills and knowledge to service? And why?
- What's the purpose? What am I hoping to achieve?
- Is the music I'm involved with any good? Do I know what it's good *for*? How can I improve it?
- What kinds of musicing are most familiar/comfortable to me? Which the least? And how do I step outside of my comfort zone? How do I 'go visiting' other traditions? What are the ethical considerations?
- Which dimension/s am I naturally inclined/oriented towards? How do I strengthen the other/s?
- What am I good at? What are my skills best suited for?
- What wouldn't I do? Why don't I do that?
- Who else do I want to work with on this? Whose perspective/skills/insight would be useful?
- What boundaries define what I do? Where do they lie? When and how do I cross / reinforce them? Why? Why not?
- How is love – the aesthetic of relationship – manifest in my work?

Implications

There are a number of implications of the model of 'music in three dimensions': not only does it provide a means of discussing music as a CAS, where musical quality needs to be understood as 'contingent'; it also highlights the value of dialogue, dissensus and diffraction as important epistemological concepts for understanding such complexity, and the ways in which theory and practice might combine to form an ethical praxis for the education of musicians.

Holistic philosophy of music

First, the holistic philosophy of 'music in three dimensions' recognizes the full 'adaptive' complexity of musical situations and also helps to resolve some of the philosophical tensions contained in the long-standing 'aesthetic vs. praxial' debate, by recognizing that both dimensions are equally necessary – if not essential – to an understanding of musical experience. The interplay – or 'dialogic space' (Wegerif 2012: 158) – between them helps to create a richer context of musical meaning, especially when understood in relation to the 'paramusical' dimension of music, which helps embed that meaning deeply within people's lived experience of music. If the various traditions of musicing have tended to be studied from an ethnomusicological perspective – understanding isolated musical practices and what makes them distinctive, rather than what unites them with other traditions – then a holistic understanding of music as a CAS goes some way to filling some of these gaps between perspectives, and begin the process of articulating musical experience as a 'polyphonic truth' (Camlin 2016c).

Quality is contingent

Another important implication of the model is that fixed ideas about quality do not help provide the most useful insights into the experience of music. If all music might be said to exist in different kinds of relationships with aesthetic, participatory and paramusical dimensions – especially when those relationships may be constantly changing and evolving – any understanding of quality is always situated within that dynamic. In other words, the quality of any given instance of musicing is always contingent on (a) its situation, (b) any intended outcomes within that situation and (c) the extent to which those intentions are realized in practice, alongside (d) any unintended outcomes which might also arise (Camlin

2014). Indeed, within some participatory traditions, quality is already implicit within the act of participation itself:

> Since an African musical performance is so much a part of its social setting, we can recognise African critical standards by what happens in the situation itself. In such a context, everything one does becomes an act of 'criticism': people express their opinions by participating. They make a contribution to the success of the occasion, and they behave with the understanding that what they do is an act of artistic participation as well.
>
> (Chernoff 1979: 153)

Therefore, in order to understand whether any given instance of musical performance is any good, we first need to be clear what it is intended to be good *for:*

> Art's importance stems from the effectiveness with which it is 'put to work' in the realization of a variety of overlapping and interwoven human values or 'goods'. The value of art, like all value, is a function of what it is good for, the uses to which it is put.
>
> (Elliott et al. 2016: 6)

From a holistic perspective, it is the transformative 'paramusical' dimension of musicing which helps to unify what might otherwise be more separate concerns. Whether listening to, or making music, surely all musicians hope that the instances of music they create, facilitate or participate in will have a deep emotional connection with the hearts and minds of listeners and/or participants, ultimately leading to life-affirming – or even life-changing – 'strong' experiences (Gabrielsson 2011).

Dialogue

A further implication which follows from the notion that quality is contingent is the way in which a 'dialogic' understanding of musical experience can help to make sense of its complexity. By dialogic, I simply mean an assumption that 'that there is always more than one voice, [and that] meaning is never singular but always emerges in the play of different voices in dialogue together' (Wegerif 2012: 3). Because music 'means' in so many differently situated ways, our understanding of music as a CAS needs to start with reference to those many unique situations. This dialogical stance also helps us to understand how individuals can take up positions in relation to these different dimensions of music's potential. Dialogue is an important concept in this regard, as it is about amplifying less audible 'voices' and perspectives in order to raise music and musicing as a polyphonic discourse.

I started using a 'dialogic' frame within my doctoral studies, to understand the complexity of situations represented in but one set of musical practices, that of CM, which tend to appear towards the 'participatory' and 'paramusical' dimensions of the 'music in three dimensions' model. As a community of practice (Lave and Wenger 1991), CM has traditionally voiced concern at the lack of consensus or agreement surrounding what constitutes CM practice (Brown et al. 2014; Deane and Mullen 2013; Higgins 2012; Kelly 1983; McKay and Higham 2012). Even though the practices of CM are complex, fluid and emergent, the CM community seemed to want conceptions of those same practices which were simple and fixed, so that those unfamiliar with the practices – in particular, funders – might grasp them more easily. However, this is to do the diversity and complexity of the practices themselves a disservice. Rather than seeing this historical lack of consensus as a fundamental weakness of the community, as some imply (Kertz-Welzel 2016) – I suggest that we might view the diversity of CM practice – and the disagreements surrounding such practice – as one of CM's defining characteristics (Camlin 2016c, 2017b). Rather than simpler conceptions of CM practice which reduce its considerable and characteristic diversity, we need more sophisticated ones which help to communicate its full richness, as a way of understanding it as a situational response to the needs and aspirations of its participants, and its situations. While this book may advocate for a more 'diffractive' understanding of music, and the complex ways in which its many dimensions intra-act and are experienced in practice, there remains a value for me in a dialogic perspective as it highlights the need to actively seek out heterodox views which counter one's way of customarily thinking about music and to include them in discourse as a way of expanding such thinking.

Broadening this discussion out from CM, if music is about anything, it is surely about how it facilitates the manifestation of individual 'truths' – about ourselves, our communities, our beliefs, our values, our passions and our purpose – but of course, all of these truths are personally held. Conceiving of music as a 'dialogic space' (Wegerif 2012: 143–45) is in effect asking all who participate in it to respond to the invitation that Nye Bevan was wont to make at the conclusion of his speeches, 'this is my truth, tell me yours' (Foot 1974), and is an invitation which extends to its practitioners as much as to its participants (Camlin 2015a).

As already noted, thinking about musicing in dialogic and/or diffractive terms helps to render obsolete many of the dichotomies which have traditionally raised divisions between different musical traditions. Dichotomized positions – e.g., access vs. excellence, product vs. process, aesthetic vs. participatory and so on – become transformed from opposing monologies into dynamic forces which widen dialogic space, when seen from within the ongoing dialogue about music and music education. When we understand them as forces which exist in a dialogic 'creative tension' (Adorno 1973: 153; Wegerif 2012: 4) with each other, we start to build a better understanding of how and why instances of musicing can be so similar and so different all over the world.

Dissensus

Another implication of a dialogic perspective is that the many perspectives in a complex field like music do not have to actually agree with each other, or reach a consensus, in order to reach an understanding. It is the collective power of 'a plurality of independent and unmerged voices and consciousnesses, a genuine polyphony of fully valid voices' (Bakhtin 1984: 6) which constitutes meaning in the fullest sense. This kind of 'dissensus' is 'not a conflict of interests, opinions or values; it is a division inserted in "common sense": a dispute over what is given and about the frame within which we see something as given' (Ranciere 2003: 69).

When I first started writing about dissensus in relation to music (Camlin 2016c, 2017b), I was referring specifically to CM, and the need to challenge the orthodoxy of 'consensus' as a necessary turn to communicate CM practices. However, the notion of 'dissensus' extends to the fullest conception of what music is and what it does, suggesting that *any* position in relation to music's three dimensions is potentially valid, based simply on the degree to which it is an authentic experience of a musical situation. This notion of dissensus is fundamentally dialogic in its essence. Each voice in a dialogue is unique and worth listening to; each has something to contribute. If dissensus emphasizes difference, then dialogue emphasizes the common sense of purpose that emerges when different – and perhaps dissenting – views are given equal space to be heard and accounted. The act of dissensus helps to create this 'dialogic space' i.e. 'the gap between perspectives in a dialogue' (Wegerif 2012: 4) where truth and meaning are ultimately to be found:

> Truth is not found in a single utterance but always in a dialogue. Different positions held together in a dialogue do not take away from the truth; they enable truth: not truth as a proposition but what Bakhtin refers to as 'polyphonic truth', truth in action which is found through and across a number of different voices.
>
> (114)

In such a dissensual context, to be a musician is therefore to refuse to be categorized as any particular kind of musician, but rather to be *this* musician, making music in *this* situation with *these* people and *these* materials, within *these* cultures and traditions. Dissensus is thus an important concept for an understanding of musicing as a holistic praxis. As well as providing a rich territory in which different ideas about music can be engaged in a common discourse, it helps to make space for new or unheard voices which widen not just discourse but also the potential community of practitioners and practice. If CM is about Derridan notions of 'acts of hospitality' (Higgins 2012: 133), this can surely be extended from welcoming participants into a space we create, to welcoming different views into our broader discourse which have the potential to change it. If we are to foster inclusion and access in our practices, all of our borders should be open, and all of our boundaries should be permeable, including our conceptual ones.

Epistemology

In turn, viewing musical experience from a perspective of contingency, dialogue and dissensus raises important questions about the kind of knowledge it represents, and how it can be 'known'. As discussed in Chapter 3, limiting our knowledge of musical experience only to those phenomena which can be isolated and measured is to miss an awful lot about what gives music its vitality, and the way that all of the various mechanisms implicated in musicing might intra-act. As Fancourt et al. (2021) highlight, 'no leisure activity will activate just one causal mechanism, and applying simple models of mechanisms to complex leisure activities risks overstating the causal contribution of individual mechanisms' (333). The fullest knowledge of musical experience comes from understanding it in its totality – as a vitality – and as each such experience might be unique, there is a corresponding phenomenological imperative to 'reposition first-hand, individual experience of arts and culture at the heart of enquiry into cultural value' (Crossick and Kaszynska 2016: 7).

Critics of a more phenomenological approach to questions of cultural value might highlight the problem of 'generalizability' – that people's individual experiences do not provide a sufficient warrant to infer the effectiveness of a given practice across different situations. However, the point about cultural experience generally is that it is *not* generalizable. It is not a simple matter of cause and effect, with guaranteed outcomes. Or to put it another way, perhaps the only thing that *is* generalizable about cultural experience is its lack of generalizability – its contingency, and the dialogic and dissensual nature of its practices. Any effective cultural practice is always a case of *what is effective, for who and under what circumstances*. Understanding musicing as a complex set of intra-actions between traditions, repertoire, instruments, sounds, relationships and groups of unique individuals and their (neuro-)biological hardware requires us to examine such apparatus and the way they combine to create unique musical experiences.

Praxis

A further implication of the way this model has evolved, is in recognizing how this kind of knowledge development is an outcome of situating HE provision inside 'real-world' musical practices which, almost by definition, have evolved in more practical ways without necessarily being grounded in academic knowledge. When we are required to articulate 'real-world' practices in academic terms, it is perhaps inevitable that new knowledge will result, as we discover new ways of conceiving and discussing those practices. We might therefore view the situating of HE study within cultural practices as a useful methodology for transforming the 'productive knowledge' (Bowman 2005: 52) of the diversity of Arts practices into a richer 'imbrication' of theory and practice, or 'praxis' (Nelson 2013: 62). There are clear benefits to students as they not only learn about the musical practices which they are involved in but also contribute to an ongoing process of articulating those practices, introducing them directly to the kind of epistemological developments (ways of knowing) which can occur within an action research context. It would be reasonable to expect that applying a similar principle of using 'real-world' situations to site undergraduate learning would result in similar epistemological developments, which might in turn contribute to stronger arguments about the value of the Arts in society.

One final implication of this holistic philosophy of music is what it means for the education of musicians. In an industry where the traditional boundaries between the fields of music performance and music education have become increasingly porous, musicians require an understanding of music that goes well beyond just being able to play their instrument well, encompassing a range of pedagogical knowledge and skills for working with a wide range of individuals and groups in a multitude of different, changing situations, including those where music may be used as a vehicle for bringing about social change, or increased levels of individual self-expression and actualisation. I discuss some of these implications in Chapter 8.

Conclusion

To conclude, the 'music in three dimensions' model provides a dialogic way of conceiving of musical practices, recognizing the importance and inter-play between three complementary, integrated dimensions of music: the aesthetic/presentational; the praxial/participatory; and the paramusical. It enables a more sophisticated discussion of what constitutes 'quality' in these practices, by recognizing that any such discussion needs to be grounded in a clear contextual understanding of musical situations, which are of course always subject to change. Assessing the quality of a musical experience solely on the basis of more one-dimensional ideas about music is insufficient; the dialogic inter-relation of these complementary dimensions all need to be accounted, and in proportion to the demands of the situation.

If we seek a 'consensus' in terms of understanding musical experience – and musicing in particular – there are a number of risks. First, we risk limiting our understanding of music only to those situations where such a consensus already exists. This is a problem of what we might call the 'rational community' of music, which I discuss in more detail in Chapter 5, where existing privilege might be used to perpetuate inequality of access to public resources. Also, in seeking a clear consensus of the value of music, we are likely to find answers which 'reduce' music to a few of its elements and ignore both its adaptive complexity, and the many profoundly different ways in which it might be a meaningful activity. We also run the risk of perpetuating the same circular arguments about deciding what *counts* in musical experience, when we could instead be illustrating a fuller picture of what music *does* by broadening and deepening practical dialogues about it as a polyphonic truth. Failing to do so means failing to build a richer critical understanding of music by not actively promoting a 'dialogic space' in academia for dissenting perspectives to be heard.

In other words, diverse practices of musicing need to constitute the overall apparatus for understanding what music is, and what it does. Using aesthetic traditions as the primary, or exclusive, lens through which to view musical phenomena will always produce particular habits of thinking, which in turn are likely to reproduce those traditions, because the apparatus of understanding is configured to focus on issues of most pertinence *to* those traditions. Conversely, a dissensual approach to understanding music will introduce more lenses, and a greater diversity of lenses, to be able to view musical phenomena differently, and develop broader insights. From this perspective, dissensus is clearly not a position of weakness – as some critics of CM's diverse practices imply (Kertz-Welzel 2016: 119); it is in fact a position of strength, and reflective of the complex processes inherent in musical practices. The real power of music can only be understood through the sheer diversity of its practices, and its many dissenting voices. If we want that full power to be heard and felt, we have to recognize and celebrate the dissensual nature of its practices, and bring its many dissenting voices clamourously into discourse as a polyphonic truth; a dialogue that must be heard and enjoined.

5

Music, Politics and Society

FIGURE 5.1: Solfest Stage View 2013. Photographer: Dave Camlin.

Honourable and dishonourable traditions

In this chapter, I consider some of the issues which surround what we *do* with music, once we have begun to think about it in more holistic terms. In particular, I consider what national governments are interested in what music can do – both in terms of strengthening national identity and in terms of supporting the health and well-being of its citizens. The power of music – to animate musical works which captivate and inspire; to bring disparate people together in a spirit of common purpose and unity; to bring about powerful paramusical effects on people and society – has a long and chequered intellectual and political history.

Music is generally considered to bring about social 'goods', part of a widely held 'belief in the power of the arts to transform lives for the better' (Belfiore and Bennett 2008: 3), an advocacy position which is often critically unchallenged. However, across the musical spectrum, music is also implicated in the production of harm. The values of aesthetic traditions have been 'extensively critiqued from various postmodern perspectives as a historical relic, intimately associated with outdated forms of Eurocentric power, privilege and patronage' (10). Within the participatory dimension too, 'the very idea that the arts can produce changes in the consciousness of the collective is forever bound up with the experiments in social engineering pursued so relentlessly by the Nazi, Fascist and Communist states' (10). The call to 'be musical' may exclude as many as it includes, and the ways that music and musicing are used to bring about desired political outcomes can reinforce the same inequalities which are claimed to be addressed through musical 'interventions'. In the way that music comes to impact on people's lives, music therefore has an undeniable political dimension.

In this chapter, I therefore explore some of the complex ways in which music's role in political life is mobilized, from the way that it can reinforce more partisan identities as well as imagining alternative ones, through to how it might be seen to make a positive impact on people's lives whilst simultaneously being implicated in political structures which perpetuate inequality and injustice. Understanding how music is mobilized as a *trick of the imagination* to support the development of political–biographical identities beyond one's immediate social group provides crucial insights into how it might also be mobilized in the development of more global (terrapolitan) political–biographical identities. Similarly, understanding how music might be implicated in the reinforcement of structural inequalities provides a valuable caution about the risk of advocacy agendas and a 'deficit' culture when it comes to thinking about music as an act of civic imagination. Musicing is potentially a powerful medium for fostering human kinship affiliation, but not a neutral one; without strong ethical underpinning, it carries with it the risk of being used to realize unethical ends – reinforcing and reproducing structural inequalities, or rallying around oppressive causes.

The 'polis'

To say that music has a political dimension to it is to say that it has a function in the 'polis', by which we might mean the way that humans express their affiliations and obligations, principally to other humans. We might think of the 'polis' as broadly the sphere of public life, as distinguished from the private life of the family. As an idea, it is very much associated with its origins in ancient Greece, where to be political – to be part of the 'polis' – is to be 'someone who acts as a citizen, a fully functioning member of a Greek polis or city-state within a participatory democratic system' (Wiles 2016: 23). I am turning to Alasdair Macintyre for a broader definition of the term to mean 'the relationships of free [people] to each other [, where] the free self is simultaneously political subject and political sovereign' (MacIntyre 1981: 185).

In terms of human political association, the ancient history of the nation-state – or indeed the ancient Greek city state – are relatively *recent* developments in the long history of human evolution, and humans have developed and maintained political relations across much smaller affiliations for a much longer period. Such political affiliations can still be seen in the way that 'traditional societies' – e.g. indigenous communities without formal political structures – manage relationships both within and across communities (Diamond 2013). Turning again to Macintrye, we might therefore expand our ethical notion of the 'polis' to mean 'a community whose shared aim is the realization of the human good' (MacIntyre 1981: 182). Agreement within that community on which goods and virtues are to determine the way that the community operates 'makes possible the kind of bond between citizens which constitutes polis' (182).

Bonding and bridging social capital

We might see these agreements within the community – either formally written down as legal constitutions or informally negotiated in response to the vicissitudes of everyday life – as forms of 'symbolic capital'; they come to symbolize attitudes and behaviours in relation to others within or outside of the community which confer status 'in the form of recognition from the other players in the field' (Söderman et al. 2015: 6). Moreover, these agreements are profoundly social, as they express ways of being in relationship with others, so we can think of them as 'social capital'.

Robert Putnam (2001) distinguishes between two kinds of social capital, which he refers to as 'bonding' and 'bridging' forms of social capital. At its simplest, 'bonding social capital constitutes a kind of sociological superglue, whereas bridging social capital provides a sociological WD-40' (Putnam 2001: 23). It is this crucial distinction between the different ways that humans build social capital which is at the heart of our discussion: 'bonding' social capital unites people in a common purpose which creates a boundary between those inside the group and those outside of it, whereas 'bridging' social capital reaches across social divisions to establish alliances which are mutually beneficial. Music is capable of both, and the honourable and dishonourable history of music as a social force is bound up in this complexity.

Feeling felt

As discussed in Chapter 3, at the heart of music's potential as a form of social capital is its affordance for communication of emotional states, shared intentions and exchanges of vitality, in other words, how it supports the fine-grained quality of human interaction. This inculcation of vitality forms starts in early childhood, as a way of socializing the infant into the complexity of human relationships:

> The matching/mismatching of vitality forms can shape what the infant does and how he feels about doing it. it is like sculpting his mind from the inside out. It is a powerful tool in the parent's ongoing socialisation of the infant into the family and wider culture. It has another advantage. It is well suited for negotiations. It is not a set of rules. It opens the door to the diplomatic dealings that characterise the compromises about what you can and cannot do, and where are the real limits to be set in different contexts. These negotiations are essential for learning some degree of subtleness in ordinary dealings with others. Vitality forms play a large part in all of this.
>
> (Stern 2010: 115)

The means through which this matching/mismatching of vitality forms occurs is profoundly inter-personal, in that it relies on both parties attuning to each other in an ongoing kind of unspoken dialogue, leading to what Dan Siegel refers to as the sense of 'feeling felt', where we 'allow our own internal state to shift, to come to resonate with the inner world of another' (Siegel 2011: 27). Stern highlights the importance of this attuned communication to the work undertaken in music therapy:

> As the therapist and patient enter the same dynamic flow created by the music, there will emerge moments of 'mutual recognition' when they both realise, at the same time, that they are sharing a common experience. This is brought about through affect attunement, joint attention, and mutual confirmation. Such shared moments then act much as do 'moments of meeting' in changing the relationship and moving it to a deeper level of intersubjectivity.
>
> (Stern 2010: 140)

To reiterate the point made earlier in Chapter 3, this is how the affordances of communicative musicality – the attuned musical communication between an infant and a primary care-giver – can extend far beyond the mother–infant dyad. Viewed in this way, we can trace a musical dimension to the business of building political affiliations, from the family unit right through to the nation-state, and possibly further. In agential realist terms, it is the memory of the particular configuration of the 'apparatus' of communicative musicality – the way in which attunement is felt through patterns of diffraction – which drives the musical imagination.

Musical citizens

Throughout history, music has been mobilized as a key means of expressing political affiliation, by which I mean the way in which music facilitates the 'performance' of kinship relations, from a small group of intimate family members through to whole societies of unknown strangers. In the following section, I discuss some of these affiliations as they relate to an anthropological understanding of human social and political evolution. For some time, anthropologists have characterised the division of human societies into 'four categories of increasing population size, political centralization, and social stratification: band, tribe, chiefdom, and state' (Diamond 2013: 14). These terms more specifically describe social relations within 'traditional societies' (7–9) – i.e. societies which are *not* western, educated, industrialized, rich and democratic (or WEIRD for short). This orthodoxy has recently been challenged on the basis that 'what actually seems to have happened ... defies all such assumptions' (Graeber and Wengrow 2022: 451). Drawing on the archeolgical record, Graeber and Wengrow suggest that far from a linear evolution toward greater political and bureaucratic complexity, it appears more likely that for much of human history, political affiliations have been more flexible and temporary arrangements than previously imagined. Nevertheless, there is an important distinction to be made between forms of kinship between people we know in person, and those we form only imaginary connections with. I will therefore use social approximations of the anthropological terms (family, community, people, country) both for ease of explanation, and to avoid becoming enmired in an ongoing anthropological debate.

The first two of these affiliations – family and community – are also what we might term 'social' identities in that they are 'generated through roles and relationships between people, and the wider social and cultural context' (Government Office for Science 2013: 10). Social identities represent our networks of close relationships – immediate family, friends, relations, neighbours – those people whose social lives intra-act with our own on a regular basis. The other two affiliations – to people and country – are what we might term 'biographical' identities in that they are 'are more "standalone" identities which individuals might use to describe themselves to another or how they perceive themselves' (10). Other kinds of affiliations – e.g., 'gender, age, race, occupation, gangs, socioeconomic status, ethnicity, class, nation states or regional territory' (Bamberg 2010: 4) as well as religion and/or sexual orientation – might also be mobilized in the formation of 'biographical' identities, many of which intersect in the overall construction of identity. As I shall discuss, musical culture may be an important means of extending and ultimately transcending more partisan identities that might otherwise present limits (social, psychological and biological) on the extent of human cooperation.

Music and the family

Although not strictly the 'polis' as such, the foundation of all subsequent political affiliations is the family, as this is literally where the most vulnerable in society – its infants – are cared for and nurtured to prepare them for civic life. 'The smallest and simplest type of society consists of just a few dozen individuals, many of them belonging to one or several extended families' (Diamond 2013: 14). Especially within 'traditional' societies, music – in the form of communicative musicality – lies at the heart of this family relationship, helping to establish and maintain bonds of trust and affection between infant and care-giver but also extending to other family members as a way of 'performing' the kinship relations which unite them as a group. Steven Mithen (2007) suggests that this communicative musicality would have been at the heart of human communication as a pre-cursor to the development of language and may also therefore be inferred as being at the heart of all hominid communication more generally. The 'vocal grooming' hypothesis (Aiello and Dunbar 1993: 187) – that communicative musicality is a uniquely human intangible form of the more physical grooming found in many mammals and especially our nearest primate relatives, bonobos and chimps – provides important insights into how intimate family connections can be maintained over both distance and time.

Music and the community

For humans, this fundamental capacity to use music's communicative capacity to build bonds of kinship extends beyond the immediate family. At the level of 'tribe' or community, 'a local group of hundreds of individuals' (Diamond 2013:

15) might be able to sustain bonds of kindship based on a mutual interest in a prosperous local environment and the resulting distribution of resources arising from those shared interests. In such circumstances, music might be an important way in which groups of people are able to express their commitment and obligations to the group, a way of signalling their honourable social intent, through the exchange not just of emotional states but also vitality effects and interpersonal attunement. We might consider such exchanges as performances of 'honest signals', in other words, 'signals that are either so costly to make or so difficult to suppress that they are reliable in signalling intention' (Pentland 2008: 2). Musical expression is a potent way of doing this because it reveals to a listener 'qualities of the music's producer that are necessarily concomitant on the nature of the signal' (Cross and Woodruff 2009: 4).

It should come as no surprise then, that 'among modern humans, those groups who are dependent upon each other are particularly prone to make music together' (Mithen 2007: 207). However, the roots of such musical kinship might be much older. Mithen conjures up a vivid picture of how musical communication might have mediated social cohesion in a hominid community at the archaeological site FxJj50 in the Koobi Fora region of East Africa 1.6 million years ago, inviting us to imagine the particular sound world which might have characterized such a gathering:

> Emanating from the site would have been a variety of calls, reflecting the diversity of activities, how these changed through the day, and the varying emotional states of individuals and the group as a whole. One might have heard predator alarm calls; calls relating to food availability and requests for help with butchery; mother–infant communications; the sounds of pairs and small groups maintaining their social bonds by communicating with melodic calls; and the vocalizations of individuals expressing particular emotions and seeking to induce them in others. Finally, at dusk, one should perhaps imagine synchronized vocalizations – a communal song – that induced calm emotions in all individuals and faded away into silence as night fell and the hominids went to sleep in the trees.
>
> (Mithen 2007: 137–38)

Having a repertoire of shared cultural resources – including music – helps to affirm membership of a particular 'tribe' or 'community' – 'this is the song we sing when we need to bring a tree from the forest together; when we all get together at Christmas; when we're sharing a family car journey' – and so on. We might also recognize these local repertoires in the folk traditions of particular communities – in the United Kingdom, the songs which we sing in *this* Sheffield pub in the run-up to Christmas, the 'signature' tune of the town band, the local wassailing song and so on. What is performed in such instances is not just the repertoire, and not just the people performing them either, but the accompanying forms of vitality which carry the sense of trust, mutuality and kinship:

> The traces of vitality forms that were experienced in the past are carried in memory. They are connected with the other aspects of remembered experience. When the vitality forms of the experience can be evoked, a whole experience can tumble out.
> (Stern 2010: 127)

The animation and re-animation of these bonds of kinship creates a world where boundaries of safety and security can be clearly established, dividing the world up into three basic groups of people: friends, enemies and strangers. From the perspective of 'traditional' societies, friends are 'the members of your own band or village, and of those neighbouring bands and villages with which your band happens to be on peaceful terms at the moment' (Diamond 2013: 49), while 'enemies' are 'members of neighbouring bands and villages with which your band happens to be on hostile terms at the moment' (49). In such societies, music and group singing can be seen as a vital part of maintaining social cohesion, something which has been largely lost in technologically advanced (WEIRD) societies, where music has become something people listen to for individual pleasure or benefit rather than something they make, play or do within their communities. Nevertheless, it is important to recognize where the foundations of musical communication as a form of kinship have come from, as these experiences lie at the heart of music's potential for social connection.

Limits of human cooperation

Evolutionary theory suggests that the 'social' identity of tribe/community ought to represent the limit of human cooperation, according to a neural theory developed by Robin Dunbar, which suggests that:

> Group size is limited by the number of relationships that an individual animal can successfully monitor and that this in turn is limited by the relative size of its neocortex. The best predictor of group size turns out to be the neocortex ratio (defined as the ratio of neocortex volume to the volume of the rest of the brain).
> (Aiello and Dunbar 1993: 185)

For anatomically modern humans, a group size of 148 is the result of this prediction, also referred to as 'Dunbar's Number' of *c.*150 (Dunbar 2011). The 'vocal grooming' hypothesis (Aiello and Dunbar 1993: 187) explains in part how bonds of kinships can be maintained across such a large number of individuals. However, clearly humans are able to form social alliances which extend beyond this. When it comes to 'biographical' identities – my people, my country – how do humans circumvent the apparent biological limits of cooperation in order to foster bonds of kinship beyond one's immediate social circle, with people who one hasn't met? And what role does music play?

Music and the people

To understand how music may be instrumental in the formation of 'biographical' identities – including national identities – means first understanding how music might mediate the social problem of the 'stranger', or those 'who do not fit the cognitive, moral, or aesthetic map of the world' (Bauman 1995: 200), what Lingis (1994) terms 'the nomad, the guerrilla, the enemy' (9) – the stranger, the other. In 'traditional' societies, strangers are simply 'unknown individuals belonging to distant bands with which your band has little or no contact' (Diamond 2013: 49). Because we do not know the intentions of the stranger, they pose a potential threat to the security of the group:

> One widespread rule is to beware of strangers: routinely to attempt to kill or drive off a stranger detected on your territory, because the stranger may have come to scout out your territory or to kill a member of your tribe.
>
> (Diamond 2013: 290)

However, within the more biographical identity of 'chiefdom' or 'people', where we are in a loose alliance with people we do not know, we need other ways of establishing trust and kinship with strangers despite the fact that we may never have exchanged our emotional state or our vitality flow with them: 'Strangers in a chiefdom must be able to meet each other, to recognize each other as fellow but individually unfamiliar members of the same chiefdom, and to avoid bristling at territorial trespass and getting into a fight' (Diamond 2013: 16).

Diamond shares a wonderful example of the complex ways in which an individual from a traditional society who unexpectedly encounters a stranger from another community whilst out hunting or foraging might go through an elaborate process of biographical story-telling to establish whether a kinship relationship exists between them which will remove the need for them to physically attack each other. If no such bonds are established through the exchange (which might last for many hours), the other must be considered at best a 'stranger' or at worst an 'enemy' and attacked or driven off (50).

Getting along with the stranger – rather than fighting with them or driving them off your territory – means either establishing that there is, in fact, a social identity which unites you, or by appealing to characteristics which transcend 'social' identities, which might be more partisan such as a common culture – traditions, practices, appearances, behaviours which are recognizably similar to your own. In musical terms, this might be a common repertoire – musical works with which everyone is familiar. More broadly, demonstrating a mutual capacity through musicing to exchange emotional states and vitality effects with strangers is a short cut to forming bonds of kinship, as anyone who has joined in a musical exchange with people they didn't know previously will attest.

I can think of many examples from my own experience when language barriers have prevented a close connection from developing with strangers, but as soon as we started musicing together, the barriers disappeared, and bonds of kinship were quickly established. Campfire singing is a good case in point. As a young man travelling on my own through Europe, I always took a guitar with me. Having pitched tent for the night on some municipal campsite, I'd get my guitar out and start singing Beatles songs, and within ten minutes or so would have drawn other young travellers into an impromptu session which would last for the evening, during which time new friendships were established. More recently, while in artistic residence in Brazil with vocal quartet Mouthful, I met the wonderful musician Rico Branco who was leading choirs of homeless people in Rio de Janeiro. We spent a couple of days in each other's awareness, unable to have more than a cursory conversation because of our lack of a common language, but once we sat down for the evening with guitars and traded Radiohead songs, we became kin – 'now you are my brother' Rico told me. 'Finding your tribe' is often literally about identifying the cultural referents which establish a bond of kinship.

At a deeper level, musicing might also be an appeal to the recognition due to strangers simply 'by virtue of our shared humanity' (Appiah 2007: 176). Being able to 'tune in' to a musical opportunity and join in with it is a way of evidencing not only one's uniquely human capacity to do so but also to lay one's honourable intentions bare, by exposing one's own vitality as a co-constitutive element in the music. Hence why so much participatory music is geared up around facilitating participation (Turino 2008: 36–49) – the easier something is to join in with, the more people can and will do so, and the quicker bonds of trust and kinship can be established. Musicing is a medium for performing our humanity because it permits us to communicate through the exchange of emotional states and vitality flow rather than through the more precise yet emotionally slippery medium of language. What I *say* are my intentions and what my intentions really *are* can be inconsistent, because I can use language to hide my true intentions. However, a musical exchange where I can tune in to someone's emotional state, or their vitality flow, can provide a more reliable short cut to mutuality and trust. As I shall discuss, musicing can also be an encounter where particularly human values – love, reciprocity, justice – can also be enacted and enjoined. Furthermore, it can do so quickly, as a mediator of 'fast social bonding' (Pearce et al. 2015).

Music may therefore have an important role to play in the formation and maintenance of socio-political alliances and allegiances. The association of particular musical – or other cultural – repertoire with particular sets of beliefs and values is a way of affirming bonds of mutuality and trust which extend beyond the limits of those in my immediate social circle. Such association also enables us to deploy a *trick of the imagination* to establish a kinship relationship with other people who appear to think and feel like I do, even though I may have never met them. In this way, musical communication is about *actual* exchanges of vitality dynamics and also *imagined* exchanges of vitality dynamics with other individuals not present and who we may not know individually. The 'we' that is created through musical communication therefore includes those present in the actual musical moment as well as others whose presence is implicit and invoked through the imagination.

Religious belief is a potent example of this. I can imagine that the same bonds of kinship which unite the people I associate with in my place of worship extend to all people everywhere who congregate in similar places of worship organized around the same religious beliefs, and even singing the same songs. Reified into print, song books can even become emblematic of the cultural identity of a religious group, or any group for that matter with a shared set of beliefs and values. The singing of a particular song from this common repertoire at a particular occasion can become a way of mobilizing and affirming a collective identity among groups of people who are largely unacquainted, whether this is in a place of worship, a football stadium, or a political rally. *These* musical people, in *this* place, performing music from *these* cultures and traditions with *these* materials.

Music and the nation-state

While the role of music in establishing bonds of kinship at the level of tribe/people is complex enough, this complexity increases exponentially when we consider the relationship between music and the state. In the rest of this chapter, I consider some of this complexity, by examining the ways in which music might contribute to both outward-facing national identity as well as inward-facing political concerns for citizens' health and well-being. I then go on to discuss some of the challenges which have historically arisen from the practical materialization of these discourses, and their tendency to lead to the mobilization of more partisan identities – 'rational communities' which increase structural inequalities. Learning the lessons of how culture (and music specifically) may have historically contributed to structural inequalities at both a national and global level is important if we are to invoke it in imagining a more sustainable future.

We may think of the nation-state as the basic unit of political identity – after all, most of what we do is mediated through our identity (or not) as citizens of a particular country, from our obligations through taxation or the licence granted to us via a passport to travel outside of the country, right through to the certificates issued by the state to confirm when we are born and when we die. However, the evolution of the state is relatively recent. As Jared Diamond says, in terms of human evolution, it is something which occurred 'yesterday' i.e. only 'within the last 11,000 years, in just certain areas of the world, measured against a time scale of the 6,000,000 years of human evolution' (Diamond 2013: 12) as well as against the more specific 230,000 year history of the species Homo Sapiens (Vidal et al. 2022). Graeber and Wengrow (2022) challenge a more linear conception of the evolution of the state, suggesting that the modern state may represent a particular interdependence between 'sovereignty, bureaucracy and a competitive political field' (367), but that these state characteristics have been present in many human societies in different combinations over a longer period. Nevertheless, whatever the circumstances of the evolution of the state, for most humans alive today the country on our passport is the de facto category of our political affiliation.

In a global society, states contain many 'peoples' and 'tribes', from diverse ethnicities and religious backgrounds, with varying dis/abilities, of all ages and states of health, from different starting positions in terms of wealth and privilege, performing different functions within society, with a great variety of local cultures and traditions. Unifying such a diverse cross-section of people into a single, coherent national identity is complex, problematic and often unstable, as the changing political map of the world reveals.

Music and national identity

Music serves at least two principal functions in a state system: helping to articulate a state's national identity, and as a cultural resource for the health and well-being of its citizens. In the following section, I consider some of the tensions implicit in these relations. Rather than ways of resolving conflicts where everyone knows – and is perhaps related to – each other and where mutual cooperation is a prerequisite for community cohesion, states require institutions to guarantee such peaceful co-existence: 'police and laws and moral commandments to be nice to strangers' (Diamond 2013: 11). A state also needs to mobilize culture as a way of expressing expectations about the common characteristics and underpinning values of its citizens, and the cultural factors which make the state uniquely itself. Unless we live in a very small country, we cannot possibly hope to meet every other citizen of that country, yet it is still possible to maintain a sense of national identity – the sense that other citizens of the same country are our 'kin' by dint of a shared political identity – and music is again instrumental in this. In terms of music and national political affiliations, it is possible to see that the same *trick of the imagination* used to form bonds of attachment at the level of tribe/people can be deployed to imagine a kinship relationship with millions of others within a national boundary, by performing cultural behaviours – singing the same songs, for example – which we imagine as common to all citizens within a country.

Perhaps the most obvious musical example of such mobilization of culture for national political identity is a country's national anthem, the song which it is expected each of a country's citizens will be able to join in with and which is performed at state occasions and international sports competitions as well as at local events, to reinforce a sense of national identity through the expression of espoused values (Clarke et al. 2010: 3–5) held to be universal to all citizens of that country. Similarly, national song books or singing initiatives might also be seen as ways in which particular cultural repertoire can be promoted by state education systems to emphasize desired qualities of nationhood and citizenship. The choices of particular repertoire which accompany significant cultural events – the music played at Olympic ceremonies, other international sporting or cultural events, or state funerals, for example – are intended to focus and synchronize the emotions of all in attendance – and those watching – on expressions of national sentiment. International music competitions like the Eurovision Song Contest might be seen to be fostering trans-national identities, but they do so by expecting competing nations to represent themselves with musical performances which celebrate a uniquely national identity.

Estonian singing revolution

A good example of the way in which music has been mobilized as a resource in the negotiation of national political identity is in the movement now referred to as the 'singing revolution' (Tusty and Castle Tusty no date) in Estonia towards the end of the 1980s. Over a period of a few years, non-violent protest in the form of public singing of songs with particular national resonance for Estonian citizens was instrumental in resisting and ultimately rejecting 'russification' (Kaskla 1992: 175) and achieving national independence 'through a careful and peaceful strategy that balanced national aspirations and geopolitical realities' (167). As a clear act of 'dissensus' (Ranciere 2003), simply gathering in civic spaces and singing anthems which spoke of Estonia as a sovereign state, Estonians were able to establish the idea of independence which was denied to them as a territory of the Soviet Union. The idea was expressed so clearly and so forcefully through mass group singing that Estonian independence from Russia – so the story goes – became an inevitability which ultimately became a reality in 1991, without any loss of life. While the impact of the singing alone on the political outcome of Estonia's independence may be over-stated, its symbolic contribution to the country's independence movement is without question. Estonians were literally 'singing the rights [they] did not possess' (Camlin 2017b) as a means of achieving those same rights, to self-determination and national identity. We might recognize similar impulses in the musical behaviours of beleaguered Ukrainians under Russian invasion as I write; whole cities are being destroyed and millions displaced, but the singing of patriotic songs is a way of emphasizing – and even re-building – a national identity which cannot be silenced by bombs.

We might therefore see that when it comes to 'biographical' identities, there is a much greater fluidity of political affiliation than at a social level. Beyond my immediate community, I can conceive of myself as affiliated to a range of possible biographical identities, some of which do not contradict each other (being Estonian and musical, for example), and some of which clearly do (being Estonian and Russian in the late 1980s). States clearly have significant influence on the political identities of their citizens, but they cannot entirely determine them, as the case of the Estonian Singing Revolution testifies. Contemporary Hong Kong activist Nathan Law suggests that the affiliation to Hong Kong as a political identity is manifest in the expression of particular values which cannot be dictated by the state, and which in fact can only be properly understood in their application within everyday life: 'Just as the Nazis could not define what was German, neither can any political party do the same today. Our culture, values and identity are defined by the people' (Law and Fowler 2021: 95).

Furthermore, we can see that these acts of political affiliation – at the biographical level – are fundamentally acts of civic imagination. If I imagine myself to be Estonian rather than Russian, then behaving as if it were true – even if my passport says otherwise – by singing the songs that only Estonians could know is one way of making the impossible possible, of literally verifying my preferred identity. If I express my imagined Hong Kong citizenship by participating in the singing of Glory to Hong Kong in public (BBC News 2019), then I am asserting that political identity even though it is denied to me. In a similar fashion, DBC Pierre attributes the enduring power of 'the relentless poetic songs of the people' being mobilized as 'potent anti-occupation propaganda' (Pierre 2021: 43) as being instrumental in the swift return to power by the Taliban in Afghanistan in 2021. In each case, musicing is instrumental in how these accounts of political affiliation are negotiated and played out, helping us to glimpse the potential of musicing as a resource for civic imagination. In the following chapter, I consider how similar acts of civic imagination might relate to a biographical identity at a level above the state, namely a global/planetary identity. First, however, it is important to my argument to explore the role of music *within* national political affiliations, and some of the complexities which characterize such discourse.

Music as a national political resource

As well as being implicated in the formation and 'performance' of political affiliations, music is further mobilized – especially in national discourse – as a resource for improving the quality of life of a nation's citizens. In the second half of this chapter, I explore the complexities of this connection between art and national politics, and its somewhat troubled political history. Art has been championed by national governments over many decades as a resource for social change, and yet intractable social problems remain. Some of the reason for this, I suggest, is due to a lack of 'vigilance' on the part of cultural institutions, often acting with the best intentions. The so-called 'deficit model' of culture has seen significant amounts of public resource invested in the 'rational communities' of cultural institutions to democratize their practices, and yet such initiatives have sometimes perpetuated and even extended inequalities rather than lessened them. This is important for my argument as it strikes a note of caution about idealistic approaches to bringing about meaningful social change and highlights the need for more democratic and 'just' approaches to developing cultural policy, an idea that is already becoming mainstream, at least in the United Kingdom (Arts Council England). If musicing might be considered a resource of civic imagination, it matters *who* is doing the imagining. I also suggest that the civic imagination itself is constrained by national discourse, as it restricts the kinds of biographical identities which citizens can mobilize in their lives; developing a more planetary identity means thinking beyond the political orthodoxy of national interests and its grip on cultural policy.

In recent years, a significant part of the value of music to people and society has been articulated in terms of how it might contribute to the alleviation of some of the symptoms of living in this period of human history – for example rising inequality and increased mental illness or all of the challenges associated with the nexus of challenges outline in Chapter 1 – exponential global population expansion, climate change, displacement and of course zoonotic diseases and so on. From the late 1990s in the United Kingdom, this was expressed in terms of how music might demonstrate a 'social impact' – e.g., reduce inequality and increase social mobility – and more recently, it is expressed in terms of how music might make a positive contribution to people's health and well-being. Despite the fact that 'it is rarely a question of arts and culture effecting direct changes', arts-based interventions in social outcomes persist because they are perceived to 'creat[e] conditions for change through a myriad of spillover effects' (Crossick and Kaszynska 2016: 58).

To state the obvious, these are political aims in that they have been established through policies created largely by national governments to support the health and well-being of a nation's citizens. In the United Kingdom, a raft of funding from the new socialist administration in 1997 gave rise to a burgeoning Arts education, including initiatives like Creative Partnerships (McLellan et al. 2012), Youth Music Action Zones (YMAZ) (Youth Music: n.d.), Musical Futures (Hallam et al. 2011), Sing Up (Sing Up: n.d.), Music Hubs, In Harmony and many others. More recently, initiatives like the All-Party Parliamentary Group (APPG) on Arts, Health and Wellbeing (All-Party Parliamentary Group on Arts, Health and Wellbeing 2017), the Culture Health and Wellbeing Alliance (CHWA: n.d.), and MARCH network (MARCH Network: n.d.) have all explored the potential of the Arts in addressing persistent health inequalities, while the Social Impact of Music-Making (SIMM) research network (Pairon and Sloboda: n.d.) explores social impact in a global context.

All of these initiatives are political attempts to solve what are fundamentally ideological – rather than purely social – problems. As Phelan (2008) suggests, the power of musicing to achieve its full effects is necessarily limited when it is bolted on to political agendas in this way: 'the ideological appropriation of music-making activities by ideologies as diverse as Nazism, communism or capitalism [suggests] that music called to completely embody a known, conceptual ideology, is necessarily constrained in its ability to generate meaning' (150). What is often unspoken in the discourse about the value of the Arts – and music in particular – is the political and ideological foundations of intractable social problems. We might see many of the social problems that nation-states need to address to support the health and well-being of their citizens – structural inequalities and the accompanying increases in physical and mental ill health – as symptomatic of simply living in the times we live in, where a neoliberal ideology is able to free states from their ethical responsibility to deal fairly not just with their own citizens, but with the competing interests of other nation-states, other of earth's creatures, and the earth's natural resources, which are unable to speak for themselves.

Neoliberal ideology calls for freedom – of financial markets, principally – to operate with minimum regulation, leading to a general inability to directly address the world's most pressing problems – the human population explosion since industrialization in particular, and its devastating effect on the earth's environment in numerous complex ways. The ongoing centrality of the nation-state as the default unit of political affiliation – and all of the implications of 'state interests' – in a globally connected world means that dealing with global problems is inefficient, as evidenced by the recent failure at Cop26 to limit the human destruction of vital ecosystems (KCLID 2021). Paradoxically, the lack of regulation implicit within a neoliberal ideology might also be an underlying cause of some of the social problems that arts activities are intended to be interventions *in*. In other words, such interventions might be seen to arise from a particular set of political circumstances, namely the widening inequalities which occur within a liberally deregulated political system.

Injustice and the difference principle

Viewed in this way, the injustices which arts activities are intended to address might be seen as symptomatic of a political system which has largely been liberated from the need to be 'just'. At this point in my argument, it is therefore worth a brief discussion of what I mean by the term 'justice', as it is one of those words whose virtue is almost self-evident and which very few people would be inclined to reject as a principle. Indeed, the notion of justice is often invoked at precisely those moments where injustices are perpetuated. As I shall discuss, without a careful consideration of what we mean by 'justice', it is possible to implement cultural policies which simply do not realize their ambitions for broader cultural participation. More specifically, without attendant 'vigilance' (Bourdieu et al. 1991: 87) in accounting for the material circumstances which mediate cultural participation, cultural policies intended to widen participation can instead merely widen the *gaps* in participation.

For philosopher John Rawls, principles of justice-as-fairness refer to 'the principles that free and rational persons concerned to further their own interests would accept in an initial position of equality as defining the fundamental terms of their association' (Rawls 1999: 11). In other words, principles of justice-as-fairness are what we would apply to a situation if our own starting position within that situation were hidden to us behind a 'veil of ignorance' (12). However, what this does not imply is a completely equal system; a key part of Rawls' theory is the introduction of some level of difference within society, such that there are incentives for people to work hard in order to improve their situation. However, this 'difference principle' is not without limits. Any difference in material circumstances is only justifiable 'if the difference in expectation is to the advantage of the [party] who is worse off' (78). If this difference in starting positions is allowed to grow too wide, it becomes unjust as it represents a material disadvantage that no-one behind a 'veil of ignorance' would tolerate, in case it happened to be them who started from a position of significant deficit to the other parties. No-one would be likely to agree to participate in a 100 m running race if one of the runners got to start only 10 m from the finish line, unless you were fairly certain that you were going to be the lucky runner.

Rawlsian notions of justice are invoked by politicians across the political spectrum, from the 'levelling up' and 'trickle down' agendas of the current UK government through to the burgeoning equal opportunities movement, although in both cases, very little is made of the restrictions on freedom implied by the 'difference principle'. Libertarian views of justice rely on the notion of mutual benefit being distributed throughout the system when left unregulated – the principles of 'trickle down' economics – while equal opportunities on their own might be insufficient to tackle injustice (106). In the running race example above, everyone having the equal opportunity to compete in the race is unlikely to make much of a difference to the outcome, as long as some of the runners maintain a material advantage in terms of starting positions. Equality of opportunity within a context of structural inequality still leads to further inequality – especially if the reward for winning the race is further improving the starting positions of your children – unless the question of starting positions itself is addressed.

Vigilance

This is what we might term an issue to do with a lack of 'vigilance' or an insufficient attention paid to the structural causes of inequality (Bourdieu et al. 1991: 87). According to this model, there are three degrees of 'vigilance'[1] which describe an increasing awareness of the complex underpinning of cultural participation. 'First-degree monitoring' consists of simply 'waiting for the expected or even alertness to the unexpected' (87). In relation to the question of cultural participation, simply creating 'equal opportunities' for access to cultural resources does not necessarily result in an equal distribution of those resources, because of the structural inequalities which mediate access.

Similarly, 'second-degree' vigilance only goes so far in terms of addressing cultural inequalities. While it may presuppose 'spelling out one's methods and adopting the methodic vigilance that is essential for the methodical application of methods' (87), this position can also lead to a reinforcement of cultural inequalities, as it also presupposes which practices, approaches or traditions 'count' as having cultural value and that people outside of those 'cultures that count' are somehow in 'deficit' because of their non-participation. The emphasis then becomes on 'democratising' culture i.e., making pre-determined cultural experiences more accessible or inclusive, an approach to addressing cultural deficit which, after twenty years or so in the United Kingdom, has unceremonially 'reached a dead end' (Gross et al. 2017: 19). Second-degree vigilance is very much the position of the cultural evangelist, who believes that their particular form of cultural expression is intrinsically more valuable than others, and the problem is simply that not enough people are able to access it. Paradoxically, well-meaning, second-degree vigilance or the 'methodical application of methods' (87) to the problem of cultural participation can ultimately result in *more* resources being controlled by those who set cultural agendas, thereby reinforcing the structural inequalities which limit cultural participation (Hesmondhalgh 2013: 140).

By contrast, the third degree of 'vigilance' is about recognising how one's own cultural perspective may colour one's perceptions, and the need therefore to 'break free from [...] the false absolutes of the traditional culture which may still be at work in second-degree vigilance' (87). In other words, 'the polemical action of scientific reason cannot be given its full force [without] an analysis of the social conditions in which sociological works are produced' (3). What Bourdieu et al. mean by this 'third degree' of 'vigilance' is the necessity to take an 'epistemological break' from one's view of the world, to understand the world as it is experienced by others who may not share one's perspective or background.

Without such 'vigilance', an enduring and central paradox surrounding the use of the arts in addressing social and health inequalities is that the arts themselves may be one of the ways in which such inequalities are reproduced, or even extended. As a case in point, the UK Warwick Commission in 2015 found that 'the wealthiest, better educated and least ethnically diverse 8% of the population [account] for 44% of attendances to [publicly-funded] live music' (Neelands et al. 2015: 33). This is a stark reminder of how far the gap between the most and least privileged in society has grown in relation to public cultural resources, despite – or perhaps even because of – explicitly addressing those inequalities over a number of decades.

Rational communities of music

The problem appears to be that without clear principles for a 'just' distribution of resources, it is easy for more privileged groups to determine how those resources are allocated, reinforcing particular – and apparently very rational – world views about what counts in terms of cultural value. These rational arguments about cultural value in turn give rise to a situation we might characterize as the problem of the 'rational' community, where cultural inequalities are perpetuated, often unintentionally and even – ironically – as attempts to democratize cultural access. In the following section, I examine how such 'rational communities' in relation to cultural participation may have led to widening inequalities of access to cultural resources, before returning to the question of how such inequalities might be more effectively addressed.

According to Alfonso Lingis, a 'rational community' is one where 'rational discourse is implicated in the statements put forth by anyone who endeavors to think rationally. Each one speaks as a representative of the common discourse' (Lingis 1994: 3). In a 'rational community', there is general agreement over what counts as a 'rational' perspective, in other words, that there are commonly held beliefs, values, traditions and assumptions which are so rational that they are pretty much taken for granted as self-evident truths: 'In our rational collective enterprises we find, in principle, nothing alien to us, foreign, and impervious to our understanding; we find only ourselves' (6).

Doxa

Within a 'rational community', the individual voices of community members are interchangeable, so long as what is uttered is consistent with the consensus of the community as to what is legitimate to express. Over time, these ways of being in the world become so familiar that they become invisible to the members of a 'rational community' and are simply an unquestioned orthodoxy, a way of expressing 'how we do things round here', a 'set of core values and discourses which a field articulate[s] as its fundamental principles and which tend to be viewed as inherently true and necessary' (Burnard and Trulsson 2015: 231). In short, they become a 'habitus', or 'those particular dispositions and attitudes towards practice which a person acquires, unaware of their constitution according to particular rules, in the sense that such dispositions seem natural' (200). This process makes it very difficult for the originating beliefs, values and assumptions to be interrogated or examined:

> When habitus encounters a social world of which it is the product, it is like a 'fish in water': it does not feel the weight of the water, and it takes the world about itself for granted'. [...] It is because this world has produced me, because it has produced the categories of thought that I apply to it, that it appears to me as self-evident.
>
> (Bourdieu and Wacquant 1992: 127)

Any musicing tradition which occupies a more static position in relation to the three dimensions of music outlined in Chapter 4 might become a 'rational community' over time, where a consensus over what counts as valid within those particular traditions becomes more fixed. The practices of any given tradition of music are at least loosely determined by a consensus within that 'rational community' about which practices have legitimacy. Aesthetic music traditions like WAM are perhaps more susceptible to becoming 'rational communities', because what is most important in such communities is not *who* is performing per se, but rather *what* is being performed, the expression of the musical works themselves. If I am organizing an orchestral concert and one of the musicians falls ill, they can be replaced in the concert with another player without unduly affecting the audience's experience of the musical work.

However, the privileging of any cultural practice over any other is fundamentally a 'misrecognition of arbitrariness' or a belief in an 'absolute form of recognition of legitimacy [which is] unaware of the very question of legitimacy' (Deer 2008). A consensus within a 'rational community' such as WAM about what counts as legitimate expression – often relating to particular culturally sensitive performances of particular selected works which have been 'canonized' over time through accumulative acts of 'distinction' (Bourdieu 1979) – can lead to a very narrow understanding of culture. In turn, this can lead to a situation where are all those outside of a 'rational community' of culture – because they do not have the means of expressing their membership of such a community – are considered to be in a cultural deficit. If the consensus of such a 'rational community' is that its own forms of cultural expression are the best there could possibly be – as evidenced by its own impeccable standards – then clearly everyone else is missing out.

Intervention

This blindness to the experiences of those outside of the 'rational community' is suggestive of a further lack of vigilance, but it has not prevented successive governments of all political stripes to continue funding such communities to address the problem of cultural deficiency, often expressed in terms of promoting cultural access and inclusion in order to intervene in people's lives for the better. The problem with such interventions is that someone has to be the one (more actively) intervening and someone has to be the (more passive) beneficiary of such intervention. Because of this, the risk with the term is that it can come to mean the objectification of other people i.e., someone (usually someone in a more privileged socioeconomic position) gets to decide whose lives need 'intervening' in, and how (Camlin 2018b).

Even if it is borne out of good intentions, this process of 'othering' is one of the ways in which the 'rational community' maintains its hegemonic grip on the means of cultural production. Because the term 'intervention' reinforces a world view where this separation between the 'haves' and the 'have nots' is taken for granted, it also reinforces the very thing cultural institutions say they're trying to diffuse, namely the boundary between the 'rational community' and those outside of it. If cultural policies are 'intervening' in people's lives, there is a risk of turning those people into 'objects', emphasizing not only their exclusion from the activities they are seeking to be included in, but perhaps more significantly, emphasizing the status of the 'rational community' which defines the terms of such exclusion. Simply going about the business of using music to make the world a better place may be an act of 'symbolic violence' (Bourdieu and Passeron 1977) against those who are unable to participate in that ideal. This lack of attention to the complex sociocultural conditions which mediate cultural participation is what Bourdieu and Wacquant (1992) term a 'misrecognition [...] a violence which is wielded precisely inasmuch as one does not perceive it as such' (Bourdieu and Wacquant 1992: 168). Developing greater 'vigilance' in ensuring that this is not the case is therefore imperative when it comes to cultural participation, by understanding the material sociocultural conditions which mediate such involvement. In other words, by being able to look beyond the boundaries of the 'rational community' to understand how culture manifests among those whose cultural practices seem 'strange'.

The community of those who have nothing in common

Of course, what exists outside of any 'rational community' is far from a cultural wasteland. From inside a 'rational community', those outside of it may be seen as 'strangers' – involved in cultural practices which are unfamiliar and which seem to have less intrinsic value than those practiced within one's own community. However, those outside of a 'rational community' may not be that interested in what goes on inside of it, unless being part of it would provide a means of leveraging some kind of capital – symbolic or otherwise. By definition, to be outside of a 'rational community' of culture is to not have enough in common with those who are part of such a community to qualify as a member oneself. However, this doesn't mean that non-membership is experienced as a deficit at all – people simply express their cultural identities in other ways. The unfamiliarity of complex cultural practices and traditions may simply present too many 'opportunities to feel incompetent' (Symonds et al. 2017: 521) for people to want to be part of a 'rational community' of music. To paraphrase Pink Floyd, 'they don't need no intervention', especially as outside of such 'rational' communities a whole other set of opportunities for cultural participation present themselves, even though the 'strangeness' of their practices may not attract the same level of political funding that their more 'rational' counterparts enjoy.

It is therefore precisely in such situations where a deeper understanding of cultural participation can be fostered. Lingis characterizes the encounter between people outside of a 'rational community' as a 'community of those who have nothing in common' (Lingis 1994), where kinship is established not through having the same cultural references and experiences but rather through being unique and singular human beings:

> In the rational community our voice is a representative voice, while it is only in the other community that we speak in our own, unique and unprecedented way. This in turn means that it is only in and through our engagement with the other community, that is, in and through the way we expose ourselves to what is strange and other, that we come into the world as unique and singular beings – and not as instances of some more general 'form' of what it is to be human.
>
> (Biesta 2006: 67)

In other words, within the rational community, what matters is *what* is said rather than *who* is saying it. In the 'community of those who have nothing in common', it is the other way round – what matters is *who* is speaking rather than *what* is said. Emerging from the discourse of a 'rational community' to encounter those outside of it is not about replacing one set of cultural norms for another but rather letting go of those norms altogether, and instead engaging with *who* one is encountering. Such encounters are encounters with the strange, and the 'stranger': 'Beneath the rational community is another community, the community that demands that the one who has his own communal identity, who produces his own nature, expose himself to the one with whom he has nothing in common, the stranger' (Lingis 1994: 9).

What Lingis implies is an encounter with individuals whose practices may be unfamiliar, unrecognizable, which may not make sense, or which seem odd and confusing. Haraway characterizes this as our approach to making 'oddkin': 'Staying with the trouble requires making oddkin; that is, we require each other in unexpected collaborations and combinations, in hot compost piles. We become – with each other or not at all [...] mortal earthlings in thick copresence' (Haraway 2016: 4).

Crucially, such encounters – where we meet one another outside of the protective cultural carapace of the 'rational community' of our familiar cultural experiences – are discursive sites where we are called on to find a common way of communicating with strangers. Above all, they are profoundly ethical encounters which provide opportunities for what bell hooks refers to as an ethic of love: 'living ethically ensures that relationships in our lives, including encounters with strangers, nurture our spiritual growth' (hooks 2000: 120).

When such an ethical encounter is a musical one, music truly becomes about the 'performance' of relationships. However, while music might be an 'intimate orientation to strangers' (Dueck 2017: 395), the kinds of 'strangers' we are likely to encounter in our day-to-day musical practices may often simply be other representatives of our 'rational community' who we haven't met yet. To encounter people from outside of our 'rational communities', we have to be prepared to 'go visiting', sometimes literally, to places where we wouldn't usually find ourselves, among people we wouldn't usually encounter. For students that I have taught, musical encounters with people outside of one's own 'rational community' can be exciting and liberating experiences, where greater emphasis is placed on the 'relational dimensions of musical communication' (Camlin 2022: 21) simply because they have to work harder to *establish* relationship, and where they are required to 'think differently about music in order to make sense of and participate authentically' (21) in unfamiliar musical/cultural traditions and practices.

Having opportunities to engage in such encounters also becomes a vital part of how musicians can develop greater 'vigilance', because it exposes them to other cultural and musical traditions from elsewhere along music's complementary dimensions and provides them with invaluable opportunities to 'confront their own and others' musical beliefs and assumptions and, thereby, to develop a disposition to consider that what may seem natural, common, and universal about music, is not' (Elliott 1990: 162). As discussed in Chapter 4, exploring musical practices from different positions along the aesthetic-participatory continuum can inspire a more holistic understanding of music, and is something I discuss further in Chapter 8.

Addressing cultural inequalities

Addressing cultural inequalities in a meaningful way is therefore about how to engage with ways of 'knowing' and 'doing' culture which do not resemble – or which even challenge and threaten – our own. It has become clear that the 'deficit' approach to the democratization of culture as an 'intervention' in people's lives to change/improve them has already 'reached a dead end' (Gross et al. 2017: 19). The uncritical consumption of public cultural resources by a minority elite is at worst an act of symbolic violence against the majority who do not benefit from such consumption. It reinforces the sense of privilege and status enjoyed by those within the rational community of publicly subsidized music, and perpetuates inequalities of access. Which is not to say that there is no value in the cultural consumption of 'the 8%' (Neelands et al. 2015: 33). However, a more critical consumption of public cultural resources recognizes the need to ensure that those resources are used to provide *all* citizens with similar opportunities to enjoy a creative and fulfilling cultural life, something reflected in changes to the artistic priorities of Arts Council England in their current 'Let's Create' strategy (Arts Council England: n.d.).

Application of knowledge

In practice, this means applying the knowledge of music as a complex adaptive system (CAS) (see Chapter 3) in the production of social 'goods', through as diverse and inclusive a process as possible. In recent years, there has been a blossoming of policy initiatives responding to criticism of the apparently 'elitist' nature of the sector of Arts and culture (Elliott et al. 2016; Hunter et al. 2016; Gross et al. 2017), with the sector characterized in terms of a lack of 'vigilance' in the use of public funds to develop accessible and inclusive activities for the broadest benefit to people and society (Neelands et al. 2015). Increasingly, such approaches sidestep the intrinsic/instrumental dichotomy by arguing that the desired social 'goods' arise from the intrinsic value of participating in authentic artistic practices. Rather than addressing cultural 'deficits', they focus instead on building cultural 'capabilities', in other words 'being able to use imagination and thought in connection with experiencing and producing works and events of one's own choice' (Nussbaum 2007b), so that 'people have the substantive social freedom to make versions of culture' (Gross et al. 2017: 3), and where culture is 'not something that people have, it is something that people do' (Elliott 1990: 147).

This is not to sacrifice the 'rational community' of the aesthetic traditions of musicing in favour of its participatory counterpart. Rather it is acknowledging the dialogical sense of, 'when faced with a choice, do both' (Eno and Schmidt 1979). We need both – preserving the riches of the aesthetic tradition whilst democratizing cultural participation so that every citizen can be an artist, and fully enjoy their human right 'freely to participate in the cultural life of the community, and to enjoy the arts' (United Nations 1948).

Whilst the current resurgence of initiatives to redress inequalities of cultural participation are to be welcomed, we also need to be vigilant to the risk that they become hijacked by the 'rational community' of art and culture as simply a further means of maintaining cultural inequality, especially – and paradoxically – whilst *championing* cultural democracy. New philosophies of cultural practice and new directions in cultural policy can only be considered effective if they bring about structural changes in the way that cultural resources are distributed and accessed. They need to account for, and be critically aware of, the trade-offs and limitations of particular practices, who (or what) is excluded by them, and which particular configurations of the cultural apparatus lead to which results. Otherwise, they may simply become another way for those within the 'rational community' to justify their position of privilege, and maintain an unequal distribution of resources.

The word 'cope' and the word 'change'

So far, my argument has focused on how nation-states can invoke music in the formation of both outward-facing national identities and also in the general coherence of the lives of a nation's citizens in terms of their health and well-being, notwithstanding the complex ways in which such attempts to foster cultural participation are often lacking in 'vigilance'. However, while these various attempts at mobilizing music as a resource to facilitate national political objectives like improving individual health and well-being – or the myriad other ways that music might be conceived to have 'social impact' – there is also a sense in which these attempts also fall short. If music is 'implicated in the construction of the self as an aesthetic agent' (DeNora 2000), the choices available to us about how we construct such an identity are limited by social norms and political realities. Developing greater coherence between our various social and biographical identities can lead to a more satisfactory state of existence but which are nonetheless constrained by the overarching ideologies which mediate all social life.

Neoliberal consumerism calls us to assert our individual tastes and style in an increasingly pluralist world. In western society, we are expected to demonstrate our 'individuality' through the conspicuous consumption of a near-infinite range of pre-determined cultural choices – the clothes we wear, the 'stuff' we put in our houses, our vehicles and our holidays, the data we constantly upload and download, and of course the music we 'consume'. It is through this conspicuous consumption of 'stuff' that we mediate our 'appearance' in the (consumerist) world in the Arendtian sense. Paradoxically, in our materialization as citizens within a 'rational community' of consumption where 'advanced capitalism is a spinning machine that actively produces differences for the sake of commodification' (Braidotti 2013: 58), we reject the 'other' community described by Lingis and Biesta – where we actually exist as unique and singular human beings – in exchange for a world of consumption where we merely *resemble* someone from this 'other' community of uniqueness and singularity. Our identities as 'consumers' may really amount to little more than permutations drawn from an ever-expanding set of pre-determined cultural stereotypes within the 'rational' community of capitalism.

Viewed in this way, our musical selves may not really be that different from the selves we express as 'indebted subjects' (Žižek 2014: 43), brought about through our conspicuous consumption of ourselves in the myriad ways capitalism permeates our choices in everyday life, including the music we mobilize as a soundtrack to our lives as consumers. As well as a potential resource for strengthening our mental health, is there also a sense in which cultural participation can therefore contribute to a weakening of our mental health as well, through a reinforcement of the neoliberal idea of individual freedom as the centre of WEIRD human experience?

However, musicing – *active* participation in music-making – might provide a means of liberating us from this miasma, providing an alternative social reality to the one we customarily experience in our everyday lives. Yes, we can see musicing as a way of intervening in the right of every human being 'to participate in the cultural life of the community' and 'to enjoy the arts.' (United Nations 1948). However, we might also see it as a more political kind of intervention i.e., one of the few ways we have of being able to intervene in the ideological conditions of global capitalism which permeate our everyday lives, precisely because it affords us the opportunity to experience our fellow citizens in an alternative relationship of equality and mutuality. Viewing musicing as an intervention in the political – not just the social – lives of citizens gives it the potential to be more than just an intervention in how people experience their current social reality. It can also provide a window on alternative mutual and compassionate ways of 'being' with our fellow humans, a politicized way of rejecting the inequality implicit in the neoliberal social contract altogether. It can help everyone involved raise important questions about the *social* nature of the call to participate in global capitalism.

The question of arts participation is problematized by some theorists as a cost-effective means of justifying public expenditure whilst diverting attention away from more structurally complex social problems (Bishop [ed.] 2006; Bishop 2006; Roche 2006; Jackson 2011). In the words of Arrested Development, 'the word "cope", and the word "change", are directly opposite, not the same' (Arrested Development 1992). It is for this reason that I prefer to talk about 'dissensus' rather than interventions. While 'intervention' might provide a way for citizens to cope better with the impact that global capital has on their everyday lives, 'dissensus' provides a frame for rejecting the nature of the social contract under global capitalism altogether. To 'dissent' is then more than just to make minor adjustments in the allocation of public resources for cultural participation, but to raise more fundamental questions about cultural value, and the various 'frames' through which we come to see particular cultural activities as having value and being worthy of public support in the form of government subsidy in the first place. This kind of 'dissensus' also carries with it the imperative to do something about the unequal and undemocratic distribution of resources to facilitate cultural participation.

Rejecting the false dichotomy of 'excellence – inclusion' is an important step in this regard, as it means a rejection of the orthodox 'frame' wherein we have come to view cultural participation: 'we don't want X, but we also don't want its inherent negation, the opposition to it that remains within the same field' (Žižek 2014: 66). The discursive practices of cultural excellence haven't altered the reality of many people's cultural experience but neither have the discursive practices of inclusion, because they both come from the same world, and co-constitute it. Progress means rejecting both, and instead being willing to make an 'epistemological break' (Bourdieu et al. 1991) from our cultural histories and traditions in order to make space for a more democratic paradigm of cultural participation.

At the present moment in human history, we stand at a curious impasse. Rapid advances in technology call us into a globally connected civilization, yet our political structures remain resolutely oriented around the nation-state, leading to countless frictions between individual countries and an emerging global order. It is perhaps difficult for governments to see that treating the symptoms of a world in distress – existential threats to human and animal habitats, declining mental health and dissatisfaction – is not the same as addressing the causes of that distress, which may have more to do with the way that the current political order of nation-states is bashing up against a burgeoning global political awareness, with the movement of people and ideas across the world creating significant moments of tension and friction, and outbreaks of conflict. In the following chapter, I explore what it might mean to imagine alternative ways of addressing these tensions, and especially how music might become a key part of this re-imagining of civic space.

NOTE

1. Which I explore in more detail elsewhere (Camlin 2021a: 90–93).

6

Music Making and Civic Imagination

FIGURE 6.1: Earthsong Loweswater 2022. Photographer: Jonathan McMeekin.

> *But today, the Rock cries out to us, clearly, forcefully,*
> *Come, you may stand upon my*
> *Back and face your distant destiny,*
> *But seek no haven in my shadow.*
> *I will give you no hiding place down here.*
>
> (Angelou 1993: 267–73)

My argument thus far has been about establishing a number of premises about music, and therefore musicing:

1. that music is a complex adaptive system whose effects transcend sociocultural specificities and is experienced as a vitality,

2. that musicing is about both the performance of musical 'works' and the 'performance' of human relationships – in the pursuit of paramusical outcomes – whose efficacy is grounded in the uniquely human phenomenon of musical entrainment and communicative musicality,
3. that fostering such musicality is about the development of individual capabilities to participate in socioculturally specific instances of musicing,[1]
4. that music and musicing are implicated in the formation and sustenance of both social and biographical identities, including national identity,
5. that the cultural and social value of music and musicing is contingent – music can both address *and* reproduce/reinforce cultural and other structural inequalities.

In this chapter, I illustrate how these premises about musicing might intra-act to provide insights into the main argument of this book, that musicing can be a resource for imagining – and beginning – a means of sustainable human planetary existence, in the face of multiple existential threats arising from the 'Great Acceleration' (Anthropocene Working Group 2019) of global population growth over the last few hundred years, and the industrialization required to support such growth. My argument will address issues to do with post-nationalism, cosmopolitanism or what we might more properly refer to as 'terrapolitanism' (to illustrate the inseparability of human existence and all other life on earth), and how musicing might facilitate the formation and sustenance of terrapolitan identities in the same way that it has facilitated the formation and sustenance of national identities over recent human history. A fundamental problem of sustainable development is that 'without some invocation of collective will, based on an idea of "ordinary" shared experience beyond the privileged confines of the wealthy and powerful, it is hard to imagine any possibility of making the world better' (Hesmondhalgh 2013: 164). What I hope to illustrate is that musicing might be one such invocation of our collective imagination.

Citizens of the planet

First, it is important to outline what might be meant by a 'planetary' identity, alongside the other social and biographical identities discussed in the previous chapter. Identifying as a 'citizen of the planet' is a relatively recent development, and perhaps only something which has become conceptually possible in the last hundred years or so, emerging only once travel off-planet became possible, and the interconnected nature of global systems became empirically viewable. First-hand experience of the earth in its entirety – a holistic sense of human existence as being inextricably bound to the earth – is still only possible for astronauts and billionaires, but a second-hand understanding of this phenomenon is possible through recordings. Perhaps the most significant moment in the history of global identity is the phenomenon referred to as 'Earthrise', the moment in 1968 when astronauts orbiting our planet were able to see the earth in its totality for the first time, as a blue globe in the vast darkness of space, a moment beamed around the world at the time, and which subsequently has become an iconic image. There can be no more powerful reminder of how all life on earth is inextricably intra-active.

Political maps of the world show the world as a patchwork of nation-states spread out across a globe, whereas Earthrise revealed no such political distinctions, a powerful reminder of the planet as a totality rather than as separate nations. Being able to conceive of oneself as an inhabitant of this blue ball floating in space introduced a shift in human identity which is arguably still playing out, and will do for some time. The price of such a vision – the technological and industrial developments of national and global capital necessary to power such missions of space exploration – is ironically threatening the fragile ecosystems which only technology could reveal to us.

Cosmopolitanism

However recent the possibilities for literally viewing the world as a totality, cosmopolitanism itself (literally, to be a citizen of the 'cosmos') has a long history dating back to the Cynics of the fourth-century BC who coined the term. As an idea, cosmopolitanism was originally intended to signify a kind of paradoxical 'dissensus' – 'a rejection of the conventional view that every civilized person belonged to a community among communities' (Appiah 2007: 12), the 'cosmos' signifying everywhere outside of the 'polis', rather than the more astronomical associations the term carries today (Miller and Ury 2010: 340). In the eighteenth century, Christoph Wieland defined cosmopolitanism in the following way:

> Cosmopolitans regard all the peoples of the earth as so many branches of a single family, and the universe as a state, of which they, with innumerable other rational beings, are citizens, promoting together under the general laws of nature the perfection of the whole, while each in his own fashion is busy about his own well-being.
> (Weiland 1788, cited in Appiah 2007: 12)

Immanuel Kant relied on notions of cosmopolitanism to develop ideas about global politics which were published as Perpetual Peace, containing the proposal for 'an international legal order in which sovereign republican states are voluntarily organised into a "league of nations" that protects the rights of all human beings – citizens and foreigners alike' (Kant 1795, cited in Miller and Ury 2010: 340).

Critics of cosmopolitanism

The ideals of cosmopolitanism appear laudable, especially in terms of promoting peaceful cooperation between nations: 'cosmopolitanism begins with the simple idea that in the human community, as in national communities, we need to develop habits of coexistence' (Appiah 2007: 17). However, there are a number of inconsistencies in the philosophy which are important to highlight. First, cosmopolitanism has come to be associated with interests which operate outside of national interests, and thus are not bound by them, leading to a Marxist critique of cosmopolitanism as little more than 'capitalist expansion beyond the confines of the national state' (Miller and Ury 2010: 341). Within the Kantian conception, cosmopolitanism only comes to exist in relation to the established order of national interests:

> For Kant, cosmopolitanism was predicated on the existence of free, sovereign states that granted individual rights to their own citizens, and thereby provided a legal basis for membership in the 'league of nations'. In other words, Kant's cosmopolitanism transcended national categories, but, at the same time, it was fully cognisant of and dependent upon them.
>
> (Miller and Ury 2010: 341)

Paradoxically, in reinforcing the political orthodoxy of nation-states which it is also attempting to transcend, this kind of 'national' cosmopolitanism creates spaces outside of the purview of national interests, where individuals and organizations might be liberated from their obligations to the state (to pay appropriate taxes, for example). The way that some individuals and multinational corporations are able to evade state tax liabilities – or are able to 'off-shore' their wealth – by being citizens of everywhere and nowhere simultaneously – leads not to a general emancipation of the human condition, but rather to increasing wealth inequalities, suggesting a 'moral and ethical incompatibility' (Miller and Ury 2010: 347) of cosmopolitanism with national interests.

Furthermore, the Kantian view of cosmopolitanism is bound up in the collective rights of human dominion over the earth's resources:

> Kant's proposal rested on the assumption that all human beings share the 'right to communal possession of the earth's surface' and, as such, they are subject to a

> 'cosmopolitan law' (*ius cosmopoliticum*) that regards all individuals as citizens of a universal state of humankind.
>
> (Miller and Ury 2010: 340)

We can see that this view of the 'communal possession of the earth's surface' has become problematic, in that the exploitation of this right – especially by the more industrialized nations over the last few hundred years – is significantly responsible for many of the ecological challenges which currently face all life on earth (Anthropocene Working Group 2019). The industrial revolution accelerated human population growth, leading to a degradation of the natural environment simply to power such growth, as well as the concomitant loss of species referred to as the Holocene Extinction or the 'sixth mass extinction' (Begum 2021). For theorists like Braidotti, 'a negative sort of cosmopolitan interconnection is therefore established through a pan-human bond of vulnerability' (Braidotti 2013: 63). In other words, all life on earth is united through its precarity, and yet nation-states seem particularly badly placed to address the issues in a coherent way.

Post-nationalism

Problematizing the idea of the nation-state as the *de facto* unit of political organization is complex, not least because national identity *is* the primary identity of political affiliation, as represented in the universal system of national registration of births, deaths and marriages as well as state passports to indicate rights and entitlements which arise from being citizens of a particular country. As an alternative to cosmopolitanism, the idea of 'post-nationalism' is characterized by 'ideas that concern how nation-states and national identities lose their significance relative to transnational and global configurations' (Knudsen 2011: 78), although such discourse is still constrained by the practicalities for citizens of having to go about their daily lives as citizens (or not) of particular countries, which itself can be a fraught business owing to the large numbers of displaced people around the world. Post-national thinking moves beyond the orthodoxy of the nation-state in radical ways:

> The post-national may also have an ideological dimension based on recognizing national boundaries and distinctions as arbitrary and unreasonable, thus promoting a mode of thought in which all people are seen as global citizens rather than citizens of a given nation. An imagined post-national world could be conceptualized as a political structure based on equality, with no national or ethnic boundaries governing social inclusion or exclusion.
>
> (Knudsen 2011: 78)

Terrapolitanism

However, a planetary identity which goes beyond the orthodoxy of the nation-state also brings with it a myriad of new complexities to grapple with, not least of which is the relationship of humans to the planet and the impact of such a relationship. The historically prevalent attitude of human dominion over the earth (which is not necessarily extinguished in post-national thinking) discounts the impact that such an attitude towards the earth (and its other co-habitants) has on the material conditions of life on earth. Viewing the earth's natural resources as something to be exploited at the expense of environmental degradation is the attitude which has brought us to the current nexus of crises. The assumption of privilege of human interests above all others – an anthropocentric assumption of human 'exceptionalism' – might therefore be considered a key factor underpinning the various challenges humans currently face. An interdisciplinary research group of scientists recognize the extent of this impact by suggesting we are already in a new epoch entirely – the Anthropocene – where the impacts of human existence are evident in the disruption to natural systems, including:

> Global warming, sea-level rise, ocean acidification and spreading oceanic 'dead zones'; rapid changes in the biosphere both on land and in the sea, as a result of habitat loss, predation, explosion of domestic animal populations and species invasions; and the proliferation and global dispersion of many new 'minerals' and 'rocks' including concrete, fly ash and plastics, and the myriad 'technofossils' produced from these and other materials.
>
> (Anthropocene Working Group 2019: n.pag.)

Others suggest that the Anthropocene is more evidence of anthropocentric exceptionalist arrogance, and should be considered merely a geological 'event' in the geological history of the earth rather than a new epoch entirely (Brannen 2019; Bauer et al. 2021); what *follows* the period of the 'Great Acceleration' of the last few hundred years of human existence will be of more material significance, making what humans do during this transition all the more critical. Recognizing humanity as existing within a complex web of existence which is to a great extent dependent on all other forms of animal and plant life for a sustainable future is to view the relationship between humans and the earth from a position of humility. It is what Donna Haraway refers to as an attitude of the 'Chthulucene',[2] an epoch yet to come, characterized by a human attitude of 'becoming-with' (Haraway 2016: 168) the earth and its diverse life forms rather than striving for dominion over it. In this context, Haraway concurs in regarding the Anthropocene as a 'boundary event' between the current Holocene epoch (the *c.*12,000 years since the last Ice Age) and the Chthulucene, and might be more accurately referred to as the Capitalocene:

> If we could only have one word for these [...] times, surely it must be the Capitalocene. Coal and the steam engine did not determine the story [...] One has to at least include the great market and commodity reworldings of the long sixteenth and seventeenth centuries of the current era [...] One must surely tell of the networks of sugar, precious metals, plantations, indigenous genocides, and slavery, with their labor innovations and relocations and recompositions of critters and things sweeping up both human and nonhuman workers of all kinds.
>
> (Haraway 2016: 47)

However, if we think of the impact of the 'Great Acceleration', clearly such development is unsustainable, as the current nexus of global existential crises indicates. However, in attempting to address such global issues, human political identity has become resolutely 'stuck' (Graeber & Wengrow 2022: 114) at the point of national identity, largely in order to preserve the conditions for continued growth – anticipated yet never materializing – even at the expense of the planet's habitability. The biggest conceptual stumbling block to being able to 'think global' in order to 'act local' may well be the current political orthodoxy of the nation-state. To break the current cycle of degradation, an attitudinal shift is required, to be able to mobilize resources more effectively to address global challenges. As Maya Angelo's poem implies, it is the earth itself which calls upon us to mobilize a new global identity which recognizes the destructive capability of unrestricted capital growth and seeks more sustainable ways of coexisting. Cosmopolitanism is unable to address this need as it implies a global identity still wedded to the orthodoxy of the nation-state as the basic unit of political affiliation, for cosmopolitans to exist outside of. Post-nationalism too recognizes that primary political identities tend to be both social and localized:

> In accordance with post-national thinking, it may very well be possible to speak of a global consciousness – cultivating the feeling of being part of a larger transnational cultural movement, but still, globality is not something people belong to, the globe is not 'home'. 'Belonging', understood as individual processes of identification, requires personal relationships, obligations, proximity, and generally, also certain conceptions of territorial fixity.
>
> (Knudsen 2011: 89)

To resolve these contradictions and tensions requires ideas about global identity which (a) emphasize local identities and (b) recognize the interdependence of human existence with all other life on the planet. 'New Materialist' philosophies speak directly to this need, to 'challenge longstanding assumptions about humans and the non- or other-than-human material world' (Gamble et al. 2019: 111). In particular, the 'performative' (Barad 2007: 36) type of materialism proposed by Karen Barad and Donna Haraway among others 'calls into question the givenness of the differential categories of human and nonhuman, examining the practices through which these differential boundaries are stabilized and destabilized' (79). In terms of political identity, 'terrapolitanism' becomes a natural result of such ways of thinking. Rather than citizens of the 'cosmos', citizens of the earth – of 'terra firma' – might be seen to be citizens who recognize their ethical responsibilities and obligations extend not just to all human life on earth, but to *all* life on earth, as well as to the *conditions for* ongoing life on earth.

For Haraway, 'Terrapolis' is a 'fictional integral equation, a speculative fabulation, an *n*-dimensional niche space for multispecies becoming-with' (Haraway 2016: 11). Rather than seeing the expansion of the 'polis' to include only other human entities, terrapolitanism is a recognition of the earth's call to us to look beyond our anthropocentric view of the world. It is a call to address issues of inequality and injustice, and the ways in which human industrial development has impacted negatively not just on the indigenous human cultures it encounters but also on the natural non-human entities – other animals through to entire ecosystems – which have been sacrificed or compromised in the name of human progress. Mobilizing a planetary identity means developing a position of humility in order to foster a more sustainable and just way of living with the earth, at least partially in the hope that mobilizing such an identity will also foster an attitude of humility and justice towards each other as well, as fellow citizens of the same Terrapolis.

It is into this imagined Terrapolis that musicing – as one of our oldest means of sociopolitical organization – may be of service in the transformation of human planetary identity. Just as music has been instrumental in helping to forge and sustain national identities over centuries, so too we might look to it now to help us imagine – and also begin to inhabit – a world beyond the political orthodoxy of the nation-state, an earth beyond the one degraded by the 'Great Acceleration' of human population growth and attendant industrialization and structural inequalities.

What is civic imagination?

The arts have an established history as a site of civic engagement. Stern and Seifert (2009) summarize this relationship in terms of three complementary approaches which they term didactic, discursive and ecologic theories of action. Didactic theories focus on 'the ability of the arts and culture to instruct or persuade the population' (15) while discursive approaches focus on 'the use of the arts to provide settings in which people can discuss issues, form connections, and take action' (15). Ecologic theories meanwhile 'view all cultural participation as a form of civic engagement and assert that the arts generate a variety of spillover effects that increase social capital and community capacity' (15). Civic imagination is a recent development in thinking about civic engagement which transcends these approaches in order to understand how people address the complexities, contradictions and inconsistencies of living in the conditions of late capitalism, and the increasing failure of existing political structures to be able to address those challenges:

> As people envision a future that goes beyond what they see as the contemporary problems of politics, they develop and modify working theories of civic life. These cognitive roadmaps or moral compasses help people make sense of their place in the political world.
>
> (Baiocchi et al. 2015: 3)

In other words, civic imagination describes 'the capacity to imagine alternatives to current cultural, social, political, or economic conditions' (Jenkins et al. 2020: 5). Of course, the central paradox of imagination is that it is difficult *to* imagine things which do not yet exist. Imaginative acts are always performed from within an existing order, and as such are prone to leading to simply new configurations of the same problems. While acts of imagination might highlight potential approaches to addressing more structural inequalities, they can also simply be ways of doing something differently whilst remaining within the constraints of the existing system, thereby ultimately preserving those same structural inequalities. Imagining alternative ways of addressing the nexus of existential crises facing human civilization and planetary ecosystems is particularly challenging, precisely because any such imagined futures are shaped by the current geopolitical realities which condition such imaginings. Addressing global challenges therefore means navigating the tensions surrounding national/cosmopolitan identities, to imagine ways of coexisting globally which transcend those identities.

Dialects of civic imagination

Imagination in this context is an active commitment to do something, not mere 'armchair revolution' (Freire 1970: 48). To constitute 'praxis' – or 'action and reflection upon [the] world in order to transform it' (60) – acts of civic imagination are not merely reflective; they require a corresponding materialization of the ideas called into being through the act of imagining: 'imagining is never enough if it does not inspire action' (Jenkins et al. 2020: 30). The original authors of *The Civic Imagination* (Baiocchi et al. 2015) characterize it in terms of three complementary discourses or 'dialects' of action, which are about (i) redistributing power and privilege; (ii) building community solidarity and (iii) solving problems. Figure 6.2 illustrates the dialogic, intra-active relationship between these dialects/dimensions, which may be present to a greater or lesser degree in any appeal to civic imagination.

The dialect of *Redistributing Power and Privilege* is focused on 'working for social change' and tends to adopt 'more confrontational tactics, including nonviolent direct action' (Baiocchi et al. 2015: 60). Such a perspective 'sees fighting power and advocating for greater equality as central to the role of civil society'. Action associated with this dimension of civic imagination is characterized by the following traits: 'Connecting local problems to larger systems, accepting conflict as part of working for social change, believing direct action is necessary to address structural problems, privileging the voices of marginalized populations, and questioning elite and expert sources of knowledge' (61).

In contrast, the dialect of *Building Community Solidarity* starts from a premise that 'under conditions of solidarity, people are more likely to work together, to solve problems together, and to create positive change in their communities' (Baiocchi et al. 2015: 62). Action associated with this dimension is therefore characterized by 'calls for people to come together, in organizations that support community identity and collective culture, and in efforts to strengthen shared spaces' (62), in turn emphasizing 'the centrality of solidarity, fellowship, and feelings of togetherness in underpinning efforts to solve social problems' (63).

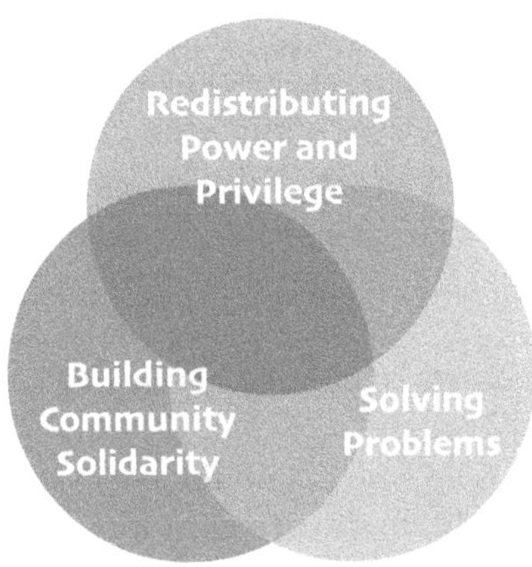

FIGURE 6.2: Dialects of civic imagination.

The third dialect of civic imagination – *Solving Problems* – is about 'bringing people together – and giving them the right tools, information, and means of communication – [to] create solutions to even the most complicated social problems' (Baiocchi et al. 2015: 64). Within this dimension of civic imagination, the emphasis is on intellectual engagement with the issues, and other kinds of divergent thinking 'not only to build solidarity but also to spur creativity and generate new ideas' (64).

Each of the different dialects of civic imagination has its own 'trade-offs and blind spots' (Baiocchi et al. 2015: 69–74), in terms of how its focus on a particular approach might overlook key aspects of an issue, or make other options less visible (69). Therefore, an effective application of civic imagination to a particular social issue is likely to involve one, two or all three dialects – in varying degrees and at different times – in response to the complex and changing sociocultural specifics of the situation. Where direct action might lead to alienation of other citizens from the cause – for example roadblocks which impede other citizens from going about their daily business – an appeal to the dialect of 'solving problems' might help to restore or activate community solidarity. Whereas when civic dialogue and problem-solving fail to deliver change because of 'deeply entrenched structure and privilege, and the limited reach of new technologies' (73), the call to direct action articulated through the dialect of 'redistributing power and privilege' might be made more strongly.

Similarly, questions of 'community solidarity' can have a blind spot when it comes to questions of representation between those more actively involved in acts of civic imagination and the wider population:

> The contradictions between a stated commitment to 'multiculturalism' and practices that promote exclusivity are partially the result of an imagination that centers on solidarity. Seeing the world in this way can magnify the commonalities between some neighbors and downplay the discrepancies in privilege that divide them from the rest of the community. There is an assumption that everyone can be part of the 'we', without much attention to who is absent and why. Individuals and groups focused on solidarity may imagine their community in a way that does not correspond with demographic reality, and their actions may reinforce existing divides by being exclusive of less visible groups.
>
> (Baiocchi et al. 2015: 73)

This is perhaps especially true where music is used as a medium for building community solidarity, owing to its capacity for building strong bonds of social capital which are simultaneously inclusionary and exclusionary. As discussed in the previous chapter, without a high (third) degree of 'vigilance' as to the material (sociocultural) conditions which mediate participation, well-meaning attempts to use music as an instrument for bringing about social change can merely reinforce and even amplify existing structural inequalities.

Disavowal of politics

Underpinning all of these intra-active dialects of civic imagination is a unifying theme, that of a fundamental disavowal of existing political processes to be able to fully address the issues requiring imaginative civic solutions (Baiocchi et al. 2015: 37–47). At the heart of civic imagination is therefore a fundamental paradox that political action arises from this disavowal of politics itself, a further example of Rancière's notion of 'dissensus', of rejecting the frame of available political discourse as an essential turn towards civic action, and ultimately political transformation, where 'people's disavowal of the political [is] their attempt to rescue what they feel is good and valuable in democracy' (Baiocchi et al. 2015: 40).

If civic imagination is a political act within civil society – inasmuch as it is a disavowal of politics and the political options available to address *social* problems – we can also apply the same principles of civic imagination at a *global* level, through a similar process of disavowal of national political action to address global issues. This is in fact the stance currently taken by many environmental activists – that national governments are only ever managing to *think* about solving global problems when really more direct and urgent action is needed to prevent ecological disaster. In such instances, the dialect of redistributing power and privilege is mobilized in order to inspire citizens to take direct action themselves, which in turn puts pressure on politicians also to act.

However, to make the conceptual leap from civic imagination as a means of intervening in local or even national politics, to a means of imagining future sociopolitical realities which do not yet exist, is to question political orthodoxy itself, and requires corresponding imaginative frames within which civic imagination might be reconstituted. Active involvement in artistic and cultural activities provides one means of making such imaginative leaps, where 'there is a crucial link between cultural engagement and an ability to act as a global citizen in a democratic system' (Crossick and Kaszynska 2016: 58). Jenkins et al. (2020) approach this by exploring how popular culture can mobilize civic imaginations 'as a provocation for civic engagement rather than as escapism' (7), where fans of particular popular cultures can invoke ethical values of 'empathic imagination [to] better understand and respond to others' suffering' (11) as a resource of inspiration for facing the challenges of everyday life. Online and virtual worlds – where biographical identities like nationality, ethnicity, gender, age, dis/ability and so on can be disguised or their significance reduced – can become interstitial spaces outside of everyday life where gamers can bring to life imagined versions of themselves, their relationships and their ethical obligations to others.

Haraway addresses the same issue through her use of the term *SF* to mean a multiplicity of perspectives which are inextricably entangled with each other:

> SF is a sign for science fiction, speculative feminism, science fantasy, speculative fabulation, science fact, and also, string figures. Playing games of string figures is about giving and receiving patterns, dropping threads and failing but sometimes finding something that works, something consequential and maybe even beautiful, that wasn't there before, of relaying connections that matter, of telling stories in hand upon hand, digit upon digit, attachment site upon attachment site, to craft conditions for finite flourishing on terra, on earth.
>
> (Haraway 2016: 10)

Integral to Haraway's vision is the sense of improvisation in the process of 'becoming', rather than 'being'. It is this speculative nature of what she refers to as a 'web' of 'worlding' – a subjunctive frame of curiosity and experiment – which drives civic imagination beyond the familiar. Worlds which do not yet exist can be brought into vivid life through the way we allow our creative imaginations to play with the materials which call us to become entangled with them. In terms of developing identities, we might think of it as a sort of 'negative dialectics' where the 'consistent consciousness of non-identity' (Adorno 1973: 4) enables us to inhabit spaces where new identities can tentatively appear. Rather than resolving the contradictions and inconsistencies which emerge when we turn our attention away from political orthodoxy, we might rather allow ourselves to inhabit the resulting interstitial space, 'multiplying difference while preserving resemblances rather than assimilating them through identification' (Crotty 1998: 133). Haraway (2016) calls it 'staying with the trouble'.

Sovereignty of the states

As human civilization has evolved, forms of political organization have morphed and changed too, settling into the present geographical orthodoxy of the world divided into a collection of nation-states. Until very recently, the evolution of the state was believed to be a response to the technological advances in agriculture which brought about fundamental changes in the means of production and division of labour, from subsistence farming to collectivization. David Graeber and David Wengrow bust that particular myth – along with many others – in their radical re-working of anthropology *The Dawn of Everything* (2022), where they suggest that the presumed linear progression from bands to tribes to chiefdoms to states is really founded on a number of mistaken assumptions. They present robust archeological evidence to suggest that humans have 'played with' many different forms of political affiliation over our history, 'assembling and dismantling hierarchies on a regular basis' (114) – especially when they foster inequality – and moving quite freely between more dispersed and more collectivist or state-like social arrangements in response to changing circumstances, often on a seasonal basis. However, somewhere in the last few thousand years 'we lost the ability freely to recreate ourselves by recreating our relations with one another' (514), and became 'stuck' in 'one single mode... of social arrangement' (114), the nation-state. Despite the recent seismic changes in information technology which bring us into an ever-closer relationship with our fellow humans across the globe, our political structures continue to reinforce the idea of us as citizens of a particular geographical location, rather than anything more terrapolitan.

Human culture in general serves to reinforce this paradigm of the pinnacle of human civilization as a collection of independent states, each with its own values, songs, stories, games, religions, language and traditions which make it unique, despite the rather obvious large-scale international conflicts between nations and groups of nations which have erupted over the globe in the last few hundred years as a result. Human culture, therefore, reinforces not just the cultures of particular nation-states but also the *idea* of the nation-state as the ideal unit for political organization. The integrity of national boundaries – or any political boundary for that matter – is founded on the idea that it is safer, more secure and more beneficial for citizens to exist within those boundaries, and this in turn relies on there being external threats to that integrity which need defending against, as these external threats – real or imagined – help to demarcate the boundary. One only needs to look at the expansionist policies of aggressive countries that predicate their aggression on perceived threats from beyond their borders for confirmation of this approach.

At one level, the major conflicts of the twentieth century – as well as being clear about the defence of democratic principles in the face of inhuman despotism and unbridled nationalism – can also be seen as a defence of the orthodoxy of national interests in the face of 'rootless cosmopolitanism' (Appiah 2007: 113), addressing the threat of globalization to national interests by reinforcing those interests, and in some instances re-drawing the national boundaries which contained them. On the other hand, peace – at whatever level – is generally the result of a realization that ongoing conflict will ultimately only lead to destruction, and often to the destruction of one's own self and/or society. Recognizing the things we have in common, rather than those which make us different to each other, is what has historically enabled people from different cultural and political backgrounds to get along.

European project as civic imagination

We might see these kinds of political affiliations as more pragmatic than virtuous:

> From an Aristotelian point of view a modern liberal political society can appear only as a collection of citizens of nowhere who have banded together for their common protection. They possess at best that inferior form of friendship which is founded on mutual advantage.
>
> (MacIntyre 1981: 183)

However, even in western traditions there are some imaginative political movements which have been founded on more than mere pragmatism. The European project which emerged from the ashes of two world wars was one such act of civic imagination. Rather than maintaining only national identities, the European project called into being the transnational identity of 'Europe' which transcended the more partisan national identities which seemed to be in perpetual conflict. While this of course can be seen as a pragmatic response to conflict, the European slogan of 'united in diversity' points to a desire to affiliate to a higher political order, in much the same way that the United States of America or the United Kingdom have been clearly more able to leverage a global position through a similar political affiliation to a transnational identity which has withstood numerous internal civil and cultural conflicts.

An anxiety surrounding the European project has always centred on the issue of sovereignty as if citizens are required to choose between being *either* a national citizen *or* a European one. However, the idea that people can only have one level of political affiliation is itself contestable – we move quite freely between affiliations to our family, community, people and country, and draw on each of them in different ways to express different ways of being in the world: 'identities are multiple, in that individuals develop and perform multiple identities dependent on the social and cultural settings in which they find themselves and the socio-cultural categories available to them' (Barrett 2017: 109). In fact, when presented with a political identity as a choice of only one, many citizens of the United Kingdom prefer to express their identity as one level below that of being British – being Scottish, or Irish, or Welsh or a Northerner, for example. Being part of Europe meant that citizens of Northern Ireland had to worry less about whether they were part of the United Kingdom or the Republic of Ireland, and was a key part of the

Good Friday Agreement. In this instance, a European identity became a means of stepping over the complexities of more partisan national identities, tensions which have naturally recurred following the United Kingdom's departure from the European Union. In the United Kingdom as a whole, requiring citizens to affiliate at the level of national identity through the ongoing Brexit saga rather than anything more terrapolitan has led to complex and bitter rivalries which are still playing out, and will do for some time.

Bruno Latour amplifies this point, in an essay entitled, 'L'Europe est seule, mais seule l'Europe peut nous sauver' (Europe is alone, but only Europe can save us):

> What made it possible for the United Europe, the most formidable institutional invention to go beyond the limits of the sovereignty of the States, not to burst, was because it participated, with the United States, in the construction of a world order that exceeded it. With America, European states were other than states. Without it, they are no more than states – disagree on everything.
>
> (Latour 2017: n.pag.)

Imagining a more cosmopolitan European identity may not entail a rejection of a national one, but it does threaten national identity in another sense. Affiliating to a higher level of political affiliation might be seen as a disavowal of national politics altogether, a rejection of the orthodoxy of nation-states, especially when it comes to addressing global issues most effectively. The burgeoning global environmental movement is very much a disavowal of national political orthodoxy by predominantly young people, expressing a view that national governments are now an obstacle in taking action to reduce carbon emissions and limit global warming, characterized by Greta Thunberg as 'blah blah blah' (BBC News 2021). This is very much a dissensus in the sense of 'a dispute over what is given and about the frame within which we see something as given' (Ranciere 2003: 69), where the 'frame' in question is the orthodoxy of the nation-state as the *de facto* unit of political affiliation, especially when it comes to addressing thorny global issues.

As Braidotti cautions, 'developing a new kind of post-nationalist nomadic European identity is certainly challenging in that it requires dis-identification from established, nation-bound identities' (Braidotti 2013: 53). However, perhaps the only way out of intractable issues of national sovereignty is to move beyond them, and to allow for planetary identity as the highest form of political affiliation currently possible, a move which is almost certain to meet with considerable resistance by the vested interests of nation-states themselves and the cosmopolitan, transnational entities which capitalize on the profits to be made outside of national interests, for example 'off-shoring' businesses to evade tax liability.

Music making and civic imagination

How does music fit into this complex picture of imagining a planetary identity? First, it is important to recognize musicing as part of a broader tradition in which participation in the arts in general can 'provide spaces within which alternative ways of thinking, imagining and acting may take shape' (Crossick and Kaszynska 2016: 63):

> The value of art and culture in relation to politics rests in the fact that they can give rise to new forms of imaginaries – sets of beliefs, customs and institutions which could present an alternative to a current system, and fuel political imagination more broadly.
>
> (Crossick and Kaszynska 2016: 64)

It is important to recognize that civic space is fundamentally a space of collaboration and dialogue, where citizens can communicate, dis/agree and negotiate with one another about issues that matter to them, especially where conventional political solutions appear to fall short of achieving satisfactory outcomes. Civic imagination is therefore a discursive/dialogic practice, not something individuals can do alone. It requires a collaborative effort, and an attitudinal shift towards the kind of 'communalism' espoused by political theorists like Murray Bookchin (2005, 2015). The arts lend themselves well to this kind of enterprise as they engender 'non-hierarchical' communities of engagement, 'a valuable model of the responsiveness and interactivity that a good democracy will also foster in its political processes' (Nussbaum 2007a: 39). Moreover, as a form of 'ritual play', the Arts have a historical provenance as 'a site of social experimentation – even, in some ways, as an encyclopaedia of social possibilities' (Graeber and Wengrow 2022: 501). Graeber andWengrow (2022) suggest that forms of ritual play are where people can experiment with alternative social arrangements to the ones they happen to find themselves in, and indeed such acts provide opportunities for humans to imagine and enact ways of being with each other beyond those conceptual constraints. According to them, this use of ritual play to imagine alternative social relations represents 'the flexibility and freedom that seems once to have characterized our social arrangements' (140) throughout our entire history right up to the current moment where we appear to have become 'stuck in permanent relations of dominance and subordination' (140) in the sovereignty of the states.

Music and the dialects of civic imagination

As a communicative medium, music can therefore contribute in particularly useful ways to such discourse, albeit in a different way to language. While the precision of language might be better able to communicate within the problem-solving dialect of civic imagination more directly and clearly, music's emotional qualities and its capacity for social bonding might lend themselves to the other dialects of civic imagination – protesting and building solidarity – in unique ways which may complement linguistic approaches, or even do a better job, following the maxim, 'where words fail, music speaks'.

When it comes to matters of redistributing power and privilege, music as a form of protest has a long history of association. Making a point more assertively – on a demonstration march, for example – is an important way not just of communicating ideas more forcefully and clearly, but attaching those ideas to an emotional expression, and purposing them with vitality. Musicing in this context therefore functions as an amplifier, to articulate issues of inequality and injustice more powerfully, and with a more emotional heft as a way of (literally) demonstrating the strength and depth of feeling that protestors have about a particular issue.

Building community solidarity is an important dialect of civic imagination for complementary reasons, depending on whether any proposed solutions are either known (and advocated) or uncertain, and hence in need of discovery. In the first instance, when a solution to a particular issue of inequality or injustice has been proposed and is seeking to attract support, bringing diverse groups of people together in solidarity is a way of focusing the collective consciousness on proposed solutions as a way of increasing agency around implementing those solutions. In the second instance, when solutions to thorny issues are elusive or uncertain, bringing people together can help not just to bring more views and perspectives into dialogue with one another in order to crystallize or even generate possible hitherto-unidentified solutions, but to do so in ways which emphasize a 'just' way of addressing the issues which do not result in a solution for some at the expense of others. In other words, bringing people together in solidarity at the level of common humanity – in the belief that such an emphasis will in turn lead to insights and possible solutions to a given issue – can highlight the need for any solutions to be developed in ways which are consonant with the mutual interests of all parties.

Clearly, we can see musicing mobilized in relation to both these instances of community solidarity building around the world, from rallies and marches to artistic movements. However, as Hesmondhalgh (2013) argues, music's value as a political resource may tend towards less direct materializations of civic imagination:

> Music's most significant effects on the world are not directly political, in the sense of contributing to forms of publicness that involve deliberation, or that advance political struggle, but instead relate to the sustenance of a public sociability, which keeps alive feelings of solidarity and community. In this and in other ways too, musical culture develops values and identities that feed into deliberation, democracy, and politics in substantial but rather indirect ways.
>
> (Hesmondhalgh 2013: 10)

Rather than seeing this aspect of music's contribution to civic imagination as incidental to more direct action, Hesmondhalgh suggests that it is precisely music's 'rich ordinariness' (111) which underpins its potency as a resource in such circumstances: 'The claim that music's most important and valuable relationship to collective flourishing is via its contribution to political struggle is wrong because music makes much stronger contributions to collective flourishing through sociable publicness than through deliberative publicness' (Hesmondhalgh 2013: 144).

As Jenkins et al. (2020) suggest, 'before you can change the world, you need a vision of what a better world might look like – this is the primary function of the civic imagination' (31). Musicing – as a 'performance' of relationships which emphasizes the humanistic values to support such a vision-mobilizes the human *qualities* necessary to underpin an imagined future which is better than the world being sought to be changed. Although by no means a given – for reasons I will elaborate on shortly – it is possible to imagine these same humanistic values extending to parties whose voices are not present in the dialogue, including non-human entities and the natural world more generally. We might therefore view musicing as one of the means by which 'a transversal relational ethics to counteract the inhuman(e) aspects of the posthuman predicament' (Braidotti 2013: 115) can be materialized.

Disavowal of politics through artistic expression

If the various dialects of civic imagination are all underpinned by a disavowal of the political status quo, one of the means available to citizens in such a disavowal is through the arts, where values can be expressed and shared through the exchange of forms of vitality: 'Civil society thrives because every member can speak out and truly represent themselves through art and other forms. If this avenue is closed, the vitality of a civil society is compromised and the circulation of ideas is curtailed' (Law 2021). The context of Nathan Law's comments – the contemporary resistance movement in Hong Kong – is of particular significance to our discussion, as it provides a good example of how music can be instrumental in mobilizing the various dialects of civic imagination to address how solutions might be found for the complex problems of political identity.

Following the return of Hong Kong by the United Kingdom to Chinese governance in 1997, a period of profound dissensus has increasingly accompanied the Hong Kong people's resistance to their political situation, taking the position that to be a citizen of Hong Kong is to be neither Chinese nor British, despite these being the only choices of national identity available to Hong Kong citizens. Compared with the Estonians and their singing revolution of a few decades earlier, citizens of Hong Kong already enjoyed a cosmopolitan identity by dint of Hong Kong's position as an international centre of global finance built up during its period as a British colony. Additionally, capitalizing on their close political ties with both China and the United Kingdom, citizens of Hong Kong had been able to mobilize an international identity which transcended the other identities available – a sub-region of China or a former British colony – neither of which capture fully the unique identity of the people of Hong Kong. Imagining a society which is neither a vassal state of the United Kingdom nor a 'special administrative region' of China is a powerful act of imagination because in the orthodoxy of nation-states, it is a political impossibility. It only becomes possible in a world which has moved beyond such an orthodoxy into a new global political order where citizens of anywhere can mobilize a more cosmopolitan identity *alongside* a more local or national one.

Bringing people together to protest this paradox, through acts of non-violent singing, was a key means of building community solidarity. In this context the singing of Glory to Hong Kong (BBC News 2019) – an anthem which expressed a Hong Kong identity – became a means of singing the rights as citizens (to a cosmopolitan Hong Kong identity) which were not available under the prevailing political system. The singing of this particular song expressed a political identity which was much harder to express in words, because the only legal identities available to be expressed in words – Chinese citizen, UK citizen – could not encapsulate the identity. Rather, the singing of Glory to Hong Kong called a new identity – a politically impossible identity – into existence, thereby rendering such an identity possible, while rejecting the system which prevented it. The song's literal meaning was complemented both by the emotional content underpinning the song's public 'appearances', and at a deeper level by the values which were conveyed through the vitality dynamics underpinning such appearances.

This 'process of becoming' (Lam 2022) is precisely what Rancière terms a 'dissensus': 'a paradoxical world that puts together two separate worlds' (Ranciere 2003: 39). As an example of political dissent, it highlights how musicing might be seen as not just a metaphor for civic imagination, but more literally as an 'interstice' – a civic space where alternative social realities to the 'zones of communication that are forced upon us in everyday life' (Bourriaud 1998: 16) can be encountered and enjoined.

The broader lesson that a history of music in human evolution teaches us (see Chapters 3 and 5 in particular) is that it is possible to mobilize the social identities of kinship formed and sustained literally through in-person musicing to invoke more imaginary biographical identities of kinship with others not directly involved in the musicing. Music is therefore instrumental in the development of political identities of kinship, a way of performing the relationships which constitute an affiliation to one's family, community, people or country. Singing along with a national anthem can reinforce a national identity just as singing along with a particular pop song can reinforce a particular 'tribal' identity. The example of musical protest in Hong Kong – and the suggestion of this book – is simply that musicing can be mobilized in exactly the same way to imagine – and activate – a planetary identity, even though such an identity is not currently possible within the constraints of Latour's 'sovereignty of the states'. Musicing presents itself as a potential resource for civic imagination not just because of the paramusical benefits associated with it (see Chapter 4), but as an 'interstice' in everyday life – 'another world of virtual time' (Blacking 1974: 27) – where civic imagination can be practically encountered and explored as a different way of enacting civic responsibilities and identities. Musicing – as a relational and interpersonal activity – can overcome cultural or other barriers to establish a kinship connection (Rawls 1999: 90) founded on common humanity, an attitudinal prerequisite for working together more closely as a species (Hawking 2016).

Vigilance as qualifier

Of course – as alluded to in Chapter 5 vis 'rational communities' – even solidarity has an 'inside' and an 'outside' to it – standing in solidarity is usually taken to mean unifying against a mutual threat, most often the interests of a group or force outside of the boundaries of such solidarity – exploitative working practices, oppressive ideologies, prejudice of many kinds and so on. In such circumstances, emphasizing solidarity can be a means of finding commonalities *in order to* position oneself and/or one's people in a more advantageous position to be able to leverage more resources. Such leveraging of resources might be done at the expense of those in positions of power – as a means of *addressing* structural inequalities – but they might equally be about positioning oneself and/or one's people against other groups in similar positions of disadvantage. Or worse, they might be about reinforcing existing privilege against perceived threats to such privilege, directly *contributing to* the hardening and widening of structural inequalities.

From a sociocultural perspective, we might think of this as relating to the three degrees of 'vigilance' (Bourdieu et al. 1991: 87; Camlin 2021a) – the need to attend to the material conditions which mediate cultural participation – in order to ensure that any cultural practice does not become an act of 'symbolic violence' against those unable or unwilling to participate in it (third-degree vigilance). It is important that musical attempts at civic imagination resist both evangelical attempts to advocate that music is a panacea for all social and political problems (first-degree vigilance), and also attempts to address perceived cultural 'deficits' by objectifying non-participants as in need of somehow 'saving' through their participation in the cultural practices of a more privileged group (second-degree vigilance).

Within the literature of civic imagination, the complexities of these issues are highlighted as 'trade-offs and blind spots' (Baiocchi et al. 2015: 89–94), which include the exclusion of marginalized groups from activities (90); 'glossing over issues of inequality and privilege' (97); speaking euphemistically rather than directly about issues of inequality (101–03); not openly naming one's own privileges (104); allowing more homogenous group identities to develop over time (106).

> In sum, community builders and problem solvers often exclude certain populations, limit their outreach tactics, and forget to question the boundaries they create between themselves and others. Just as the omission of inequality in a conversation suggests that the speaker might not be tuned in to issues of inequality, a group's failure to consider how activities or projects potentially alleviate or exacerbate inequality has significant consequences.
>
> (Baiocchi et al. 2015: 107)

In the development of terrapolitan identities, some of these challenges may be alleviated by the fact that a terrapolitan identity does not represent a *competition* for resources where solidarity functions as a way of mobilizing particular biographical identities in order to improve one's individual position, but rather is about 'thinking globally, acting locally' – working together to develop ways for everyone to consume less of the earth's finite resources. However, all acts of civic imagination carry the risk of being ways of 'signalling' virtue whilst behaving in ways which further limit justice and increase inequality. Therefore, any emancipatory power of civic imagination hinges on ethical questions of both vigilance on the one hand, and intention on the other.

Music's floating intentionality

We can think of intentions as 'mental expressions of directional forces getting ready, even straining to "move," or already started but still unfolding. Like a musical phrase, they lean forward subjectively' (Stern 2010: 21). Until musicing is purposed with a specific intention, its 'proto-musical behaviours' – the various constituents of musical communication – contain what Ian Cross describes as a 'floating intentionality', or 'a multiplicity of "aboutnesses" that would facilitate the use of proto-musical behaviours as foci of social interactions' (Cross 1999: 22). In other words, it is the ambiguous nature of musical meaning which makes it a valuable resource for identity development, as it is a material which can be shaped to suit an intended purpose:

> Music both entrains movement and experience, and allows each participant to interpret its significance for him or herself, independently, without the integrity of the collective musical behaviour being undermined. Music's ambiguity – its 'floating intentionality' – in the self and for or with others, may thus be highly advantageous for groups, serving as a medium for participation and contributing to the maintenance of social flexibility.
>
> (Cross and Morley 2010: 70)

Returning to the example of music in Hong Kong's resistance movement, because of music's floating intentionality, the song 'Glory to Hong Kong' was able to be charged with a particular meaning – through its mixing of language, emotion and vitality – which resonated with Hong Kong citizens as well a wider international audience.

Mobilization of terrapolitan identity

Music as a 'performative' act – in the fullest sense to account for both the performance of musical works and the performance of human relationships – is always a performance of multiple identities. I am performing 'I' as a personal identity which is also about 'performing' the things that make me unique – that only 'I' could 'perform'. It is also about the performance of a social identity – the 'we' involved in the performance – as well as more biographical – geographical, political or cultural – identities. It may also be about the performance of an identity which transcends my other identities, e.g. a religious or spiritual identity. Moreover, it may be all of them at once, and as such they all intra-act with the other identities during such a 'performance'.

The concept of 'floating intentionality' is especially pertinent here. In the 'performative' act of musicing, music's 'floating intentionality' can be deployed to emphasize particular identities, and de-emphasize others. The mobilization of any particular political affiliation – to family, community, people, nation or planet – does not *necessarily* mean sacrificing any of those identities in the realization of any of them more exclusively. It is possible for me to maintain an affiliation to my family, my community and my people – however, I choose to identify them – whilst simultaneously identifying as a citizen of a particular nation-state and behaving in a way which demonstrates my commitment to its collective values – principally not only by following its laws but also by demonstrating a practical understanding of its language/s, culture, customs, traditions and values. There is no inconsistency in identity which arises by maintaining these different identities simultaneously. As Folkestad suggests, 'an individual can have more than one cultural identity, and it might be that the global multicultural person of today is characterized by having the possibility of and ability to choose and change between several cultural identities' (Folkestad 2002: 154).

Furthermore, I can conceive of my political identity in ways which privilege any of these identities to a greater or lesser extent. I can imagine myself as first and foremost a family member or as one of a circle of friends, or through my professional or cultural allegiances or as a citizen of the country whose passport I hold, or as all of those affiliations and many more. The difference lies in our intention, and musicing can help us to blur those distinctions, or to emphasize some identities while de-emphasizing others: 'even when appropriated as part of nation-building projects, it seems that music can consistently provide hints, or perhaps better, reminders, of more complex notions of identity and belonging' (Hesmondhalgh 2013: 164).

Intertextuality

Intertextuality is 'a general prerequisite for the connection or link between something already known and something new, a fundamental process in all musical activities, including in the formation of musical identity' (Folkestad 2017: 125). We might see each of these affiliations (to family, community people, nation and planet) as different sociopolitical 'texts' to be understood through the complex interplay between them. Over time, different sociopolitical texts come to resonate more or less with human experience. Identifying as cosmopolitan – or terrapolitan – is simply another way of expressing a political identity, but in this instance, the political unit is the planet, rather than any of the more partisan identities which constitute political identity – family, community, people and nation. Introducing the idea of civic imagination in music is to allow for the possibility of musicing as a 'performative' act connecting with a planetary identity. And mobilizing music's 'floating intentionality' to establish such an identity is not done at the expense of any other identity – rather, it is to extend the range of possible identities which can be mobilized through musicing: 'musical imagination and creation involves acting in a global intertextual musical arena in which national or ethnic backgrounds are negotiated and reconfigured in new cultural surroundings' (Folkestad 2017: 122). In such circumstances, identifying as a citizen of the planet simply becomes a decision 'to assign higher priority to affiliations and allegiances with humankind than to particular nation-states' (Bowman 2016: 63).

Terrapolitanism is not a competition

More partisan identities can be – and often are – mobilized to position the members of a group more favourably in relation to the interests of other groups competing for the same resources – e.g. food, fuel, medicines and capital – almost inevitably resulting in conflicts for those resources (Appiah 2016). Music can be instrumental in reinforcing such identities:

> The idea of national identity in music, meaning that the music itself carries basic inherent national values and ideas to which immigrants and new citizens should be assimilated, is today still emphasized by political groups, in opposition to the view of the formation of new national identities based on a multitude of ethnic and cultural identities.
>
> (Folkestad 2017: 122)

Music has been clearly implicated in such conflicts – as a way of amplifying cultural differences in order to position partisan identities more favourably, or indeed as a means of forming strong social bonds in order to commit atrocities such as the uses of music in Nazi Germany (Turino 2008: 190–210) or its 'troubling' links to nationalism and inter-national conflicts more generally (Hesmondhalgh 2013: 156). Musicing with the intention of preserving and reinforcing national, cultural, religious, biological or other more partisan identities might therefore be implicated in some of the problems we currently face as a species, part of the 'dishonourable intellectual history' (Belfiore and Bennett 2008: 11) of the social impact of the arts, strengthening those sociopolitical identities which are crucial in the formation of elites, and widening inequalities.

In contrast, mobilizing a planetary identity is a recognition of the devastation which such more partisan conflicts and inequalities produce. Crucially, unlike each of the preceding categories of political affiliation, mobilizing a planetary identity is not undertaken as a means of competing for limited resources, but rather of distributing them more justly. There is no other planet with which we are competing with for resources, and there are no resources worth having off the planet. All of the resources that humans – and all life on earth – require in order to sustain life are to be found on the planet, and it is therefore in the interests of all life on the planet that the earth's resources are distributed equally and justly. Music can be instrumental in the formation of such identities precisely because of its ambiguous nature:

> Acting in the global intertextual musical arena of today implies the formation of new musical identities on both individual and collective levels: identities in which the national, ethnic and cultural identities blend into the artistic identity of the individuals involved in the musical activities as well as of the artistic product – the music itself.
>
> (Folkestad 2017: 135)

In the same way that we can use music as a *trick of the imagination*, using music's 'floating intentionality' to imagine a kinship relationship with other people we have not met, at the level of 'my people' or indeed 'my country', we can deploy the same cognitive trick to imagine a kinship relationship with other people (and perhaps also other non-human entities) we have not met, at the level of 'my planet'. Planetary identity is the highest form of political identity currently possible for humans, and for some theorists including Karen Barad, it implies a kind of 'post-human' thinking which excludes nothing living, 'taking issue with human exceptionalism while being accountable for the role we play in the differential constitution and differential positioning of the human among other creatures (both living and non-living)' (Barad 2007). In the fullest sense of planetary identity, this attitude of kinship extends to all life on the planet, and the planet itself.

The act of musicing is fundamentally an act of cooperation: what one does with the music after it has been made is a different matter. The musical work can be co-opted as a resource for the mobilization of multiple identities – honourable and dishonourable – but the process of making music together, of musicing *with ethical intent*, requires sensitivity, trust, attunement and an attention to the expression of others. Furthermore, when such cooperation involves people whose backgrounds and experiences are different to our own, musical cooperation leads to intercultural understanding, empathy/copathy and humility. These attitudes are precisely the attitudes required to facilitate a sense of global 'kinship'. Musicing with the intention of mobilizing a global identity therefore becomes a way of 'staying with the trouble' (Haraway 2016: 1) of how to develop a more sustainable future for all life on earth, by emphasizing – and literally performing – these attitudes, and a corresponding set of underpinning values.

The performance of values

In the following section, I consider what these underpinning values might be, and how they 'appear' in public through their 'performance' within acts of musicing. First, it is important to recognize that the Arts in general have a powerful role to play in how values are materialized. All of the Arts are ways of 'performing' values:

> Folktales, drama, opera, novels, short stories; biographies, histories, ethnographies; fiction or nonfiction; painting, music, sculpture, and dance: every human civilization has ways to reveal to us values we had not previously recognized or undermine our commitment to values that we had settled into.
>
> (Appiah 2007: 30)

Art making in general is a site where values are expressed, reinforced, illuminated or championed, and also a site where such values can be questioned, contested, challenged and replaced. There is therefore a general sense in which Arts practices are fundamental to acts of imagining alternative ways of thinking and being. Artistic expression is often a way of expressing values which might elude linguistic expression, or which question existing orthodoxies, by expressing paradoxes and highlighting alternative ways of 'seeing', calling up alternative visions of political existence which stimulate civic imagination. In other words, Art uses metaphors to inspire people to think differently about their reality, an essential step in mobilizing civic imagination:

> As people envision a future that goes beyond what they see as the contemporary problems of politics, they develop and modify working theories of civic life. These cognitive roadmaps or moral compasses help people make sense of their place in the political world.
>
> (Baiocchi et al. 2015: 3)

However, musicing is not just a metaphor for imagining alternative ways of relating to one another, but more literally a site where such relationships can be enacted. As Helen Phelan suggests, during musicing 'performative choices become strategies towards the realization of values, not primarily by embracing these values conceptually, but by embodying them musically' (Phelan 2008: 148). Furthermore, the materialization of such values in and through musicing can be a way of experiencing the kind of kinship which has been eroded over time by the requirement to participate as citizens in the current economic order of consumerism, and its attendant emphasis on individual freedom:

> Participatory music making and dance are among a variety of activities that can be potent resources for social change and provide alternative models for citizenship

> precisely because they operate according to values and practices diametrically opposed to a capitalist ethos.
>
> (Turino 2016: 298)

Nationalist/capitalist values

This capitalist ethos is inextricably bound up in the neoliberal 'sovereignty of the states', where national values *are* capitalist values, which permit certain types of freedom and limit others. Billionaires are able to express their freedom to go about their business outside of ethically and morally constrained sociopolitical arrangements because that is what their wealth affords them. Their behaviour represents a kind of cosmopolitanism, but a cosmopolitanism detached from any ethical *imperative* to behave virtuously – even though they may act with apparently charitable intentions from time to time. The ultimate freedom in a capitalist system is to build up sufficient capital to have the freedom to do whatever you will, without constraint. The 'performance' of national values is therefore also about a 'performance' of the political orthodoxy of the 'sovereignty of the states', and an ongoing commitment to the principles of global capital, as the only means of preserving individual and collective liberty.

However, this 'freedom to' is a fundamentally different kind of freedom to the universal freedoms which arise from the recognition of human rights (United Nations 1948), which are chiefly 'freedom from' disease, poverty, abuse, exploitation and so on (Harvey 2007: 36). Clearly, these different kinds of freedom – 'freedom to' and 'freedom from' – are in ideological competition with each other. If the freedom to exploit labour and resources in order to increase profits conflicts with appeals for workers to be free from such exploitation, in a capitalist system it has historically been the interests of the former freedom (to) which are privileged, leading to the increases in inequality which are characteristic of modern society (Wilkinson and Pickett 2010; Dabla-Norris et al. 2015; OECD 2015).

Humanist values

Conversely, humanist values express the mutual obligations and responsibilities to our human 'kin', to those who are like us by dint of sharing a (neuro-)biological identity as members of the same species. Such obligations and responsibilities limit individual freedoms (freedom 'to') by appealing instead to the mutual interest of universal themes such as rights which extend to all members of the species. These attitudes – 'the reassertion of the need for new universal values in the sense of interconnectedness among humans, on a worldwide scale' (Braidotti 2013: 48) – limit the extent to which inequalities can multiply, and therefore represent a more sustainable way of developing human interests. Nussbaum (2007) suggests that the arts in general are a good way of developing common interests because they 'generat[e] vital spaces for sympathetic and reasoned debate, helping to build democracies that are able to overcome fear and suspicion and, ultimately, creating a world that is worth living in' (40). As I shall discuss, recognizing the similar ways in which other animals can also foster similar kinds of attachment and attunement both within and across species is a way of fostering attitudes of multispecies copathy.

As a collaborative exercise in group imagination, musicing might therefore be seen as a way of materializing values which underpin a more sustainable future, based as they are on ethical principles of kinship, mutuality and trust. As Hesmondhalgh notes, 'musical culture develops values and identities that sustain the ideal of living well together, and this can contribute in important ways to political life too' (Hesmondhalgh 2013: 171). As a performative act, there are three sets of humanist values which I suggest are particularly evoked through musicing, because of the literal nature of their evocation. There may be other values which can be evoked symbolically or metaphorically through musicing, but the three I outline here – love, reciprocity and justice – are the ones which are inextricably bound up in the act of musicing itself.

Performing love

As discussed in Chapter 3, as a 'performance' of love, exchanging vitality dynamics and experiencing neurobiological attunement through a musical exchange is a profound way of feeling connected to one another, and invokes the same sense of 'feeling felt' (Siegel 2011) and 'unconditional positive regard' (Rogers 1961) which lie at the heart of our experiences of love. In a recent paper (Camlin et al. 2020), we suggest that musicing might therefore be seen to create a space where boundaries of intimacy can be individually negotiated, through the degree to which one gives oneself over to the music and the interpersonal entanglement of vitality effects at play in the musical moment; as one of the therapeutic practitioners in the study suggested, a form of psychological 'safe danger' (11). As a 'performance' of love, musicing establishes the conditions for interpersonal intimacy whereby individuals are able to mediate the degree of such intimacy based on their own levels of comfort in the exchange of vitality effects, moving in and out of a vitality 'flow' with others at their own discretion, and with some degree of control.

Performing reciprocity

In a similar fashion, these experiences of mutuality during musicing might also be seen to be a 'performance' of reciprocity – again, not just attitudinally, but in a more literal sense. Barenboim's view of musicing as a simultaneous dialogue between voices – 'each one expressing itself to the fullest while at the same time listening to the other' (Barenboim 2009: 20) highlights the mutual simultaneous communication required to achieve a satisfactory musical result. If you're going to make music, you cannot be silent: you have to express yourself. Moreover, you must also listen. We might say then, that the creation of music together represents 'a shared concern for goods which are the goods of both and therefore exclusively of neither' (MacIntyre 1981: 185), which MacIntyre identifies as the most genuine kind of friendship, and moreover 'which provides the paradigm for the relationship between husband and wife in the household as well as for that between citizen and citizen in the polis' (185).

Working together in a mutually supportive way to achieve a common musical goal requires trust and sensitivity in attending to both the capabilities and expressions of the 'other'. In 'performing' reciprocity, 'musicians' come to experience what it means to be involved in reciprocal exchanges where the 'goods' which are created could not be achieved in isolation, or by competing for them. Musicing, therefore, represents an experience of the mutual benefits of transacting within a 'gift' economy (Hyde 2012) where exchanges of vitality – given mutually and intra-actively – give rise to tangible mutual benefits. This principle of reciprocity – of not just refraining from causing harm to the other but actively supporting their actualization in and through the actualization of oneself – is a foundation of all ethical traditions (Appiah 2007: 60). As Turino (2016) notes, these kinds of exchanges also represent a fundamentally different way of being in relationship with one's fellows – ways which are 'diametrically opposed' to the forms of capital exchange which characterize civic relationships within a neoliberal capitalist society (298).

Performing justice

In the particular materialization of such exchanges, we can also find evidence of underpinning values of Rawlsian 'justice-as-fairness'; in particular, a physical materialization of Rawls' 'difference principle', that 'the higher expectations of those better situated are just if and only if they work as part of a scheme which improves the expectations of the least advantaged' (Rawls 1999: 75). Turino suggests that within participatory traditions, the division of responsibilities between participants is done along lines of 'core' and 'elaboration' musical roles. While these roles are not necessarily determined by levels of experience, such a division of musical responsibility facilitates the inclusion of 'people with a wide range of abilities within the same performance [which] is important for inspiring participation' (Turino 2008: 31). If something appears too complex to be able to join in with, it will deter others from doing so, or make it more difficult for them. Conversely, if something is too easy and predictable, it is easy for everyone involved – 'musicians' and audience alike – to get bored or apathetic.

Having different roles – which are all essential to the realization of the music, but which differ in terms of their complexity – ensures that the most accomplished and the least experienced play an equally integral part in the resulting music. In turn, this ensures that the musical experience provides opportunities for all parties involved to develop their skills and increase their confidence. If the difference between these roles grows too wide, the music ceases to work as music, so it is in everyone's interests to keep the principle of difference wide enough to keep the music exciting and engaging, but not so wide that the music becomes unstable. In this way, we might see that musicing – especially without an audition – might therefore be seen as an exercise in democratic equality (Rawls 1999: 75–89), where the collective ambition of the group cannot be realized at the expense of the development of its least musically accomplished participant.

Performance of virtue

Although these values – of love, reciprocity and justice – are mobilized through the act of musicing, they are not domain-specific, and they do not exist solely for the duration of the musical moment. Instead, we might see the inculcation of these values through musicing as an attitudinal resource which participants can carry with them beyond the musical exchange. Just as 'we become just or courageous by performing just or courageous acts' (MacIntyre 1981: 180), so we develop values of love, reciprocity and justice through their 'performance', and 'performing' them in music is to materialize them in people's experience of others. In practice, it can take a good degree of patience and humility in equal measure to stay with the process of musicing where there is a wide range of musical ability – especially if you imagine yourself at either end of the capability continuum – but this in itself also teaches a valuable lesson about the long-term benefits of doing so. Restraining egocentric arrogance (e.g. 'I'm better than this lot') or gently challenging self-limiting beliefs (e.g. 'I can't sing') in order to produce a satisfactory musical outcome are both ways of maintaining a healthy principle of difference in the production of the greater good.

In all of these examples of values-in-performance through music, I should emphasize that this is in relation to music *making* (musicing), not just music *per se*.

It is the *act* of musicing which establishes these values because to make music effectively requires interpersonal attunement, attendance to voices and perspectives which are different or even dissonant to one's own, and an ethical commitment to collectively maximize the contribution of all participants.

Problems of humanism

The materialization of humanist values of love, reciprocity and justice through musicing sounds like it can only be a good thing, but there are some further complexities which disturb this utopian ideal of musicing. As discussed in Chapter 5, music has an 'honourable and dishonourable' tradition in terms of its social utility, in that the values which are inculcated within a musical group can help form strong bonds of trust and attachment within the group which are simultaneously inclusionary and exclusionary. As discussed previously, it is the *ethical* intention which lies behind musical motivations which can shape attitudes of cooperation or competition, both within the group and reaching beyond it.

Furthermore, appealing to our common humanity in the performance of humanist values through musicing might also be seen to reinforce an anthropocentric view of the world which ultimately limits the development of a sustainable future. Human exceptionalism – despite the considerable inequalities which persist across the human species – is one of the key drivers of environmental degradation, the idea that the earth is a resource for humans to exploit. The 'Great Acceleration' of industrialization and environmental degradation brought about by the human population explosion is evidence of how human exceptionalism can destabilize the planet, and therefore any practice which celebrates and privileges the 'exceptional' capabilities of the human species needs handling with care. Simply uniting all humans to cooperate more peacefully for a common purpose to exploit the earth's natural resources more efficiently in a Kantian 'league of nations' would be a profound failure of civic imagination. Indeed, some environmental activists would suggest that it is precisely such a status quo which is now a significant barrier to addressing the most pressing environmental challenges.

Musicing in a post-human world

Looking beyond human interests in the ongoing flourishing of life on the planet means invoking the 'post-human', although we should be careful what we mean by such a term. The question of post-humanism is a complex one, with multiple schools of contrasting thought pointing in quite different directions. On the one hand, there are post-human theories which are about what happens 'after' the human – as simply a carrier of information – has been ultimately supplanted by artificial intelligence (Hayles 1999; Mason 2019). For writers like Mason and countless authors of science fiction, the dystopic 'post-human' vision is itself part of the problem, relinquishing human ethical responsibility to machine logic and divesting ourselves of any ethical obligation to the planet and its other life forms. The flipside of this dystopic vision of the post-human is a utopian euphoria of the opportunities for human development which arise from technological advances. As a result, 'in mainstream public debates the posthuman is usually coated in anxiety about the excesses of technological intervention and the threat of climate change, or by elation about the potential for human enhancement' (Braidotti 2013: 57).

There are also post-human theories which look 'beyond' the anthropocentrism of human experience to account for non-human experience in humans' ethical treatment of the world (Barad 2007; Braidotti 2013; Haraway 2016). Moving beyond an anthropocentric view of the world is an essentially ethical step in recognizing the claim of all life on earth to be able to sustain, especially in light of the destruction wrought by hundreds of years of industrial growth and the associated explosion of population in the name of human development. It is this kind of 'ethical' post-humanism which is invoked here, rather than its more 'dystopian' or 'utopian' counterparts. Barad's post-humanism is 'a thoroughgoing critical naturalism, an approach that understands humans as part of nature and practices of knowing as natural processes of engagement with and as part of the world' (Barad 2007: 366).

Braidotti is right to be worried that there are 'limitations of an uncritical reassertion of Humanism as the binding factor of this reactively assumed notion of a pan-human bond' (Braidotti 2013: 87). Hence, ethical post-humanist values might still include love, reciprocity and justice, but rather than extending 'merely' to all humanity (itself quite a conceptual leap), they need to extend further transversally, to include all of the natural worlds, through what Braidotti terms 'the process of becoming-earth' (66), a recognition that all human and non-human materials are similarly implicated in their commodification within capitalist strictures. The values themselves – and the experience of them through musicing – are still fundamentally the same, but they can come to mean quite different things in their intention and in their application. Invoking post-humanist values is to emphasize a terrapolitan political identity alongside other biographical identities, a means of actively dissenting in the 'sovereignty of the states', and opening up new avenues of discursive practice which re-imagine the relationship between the human and the planet:

> To be posthuman does not mean to be indifferent to the humans, or to be de-humanized. On the contrary, it rather implies a new way of combining ethical values with the

> well-being of an enlarged sense of community, which includes one's territorial or environmental inter-connections.
>
> (Braidotti 2013: 190)

As previously discussed, it is possible to hold multiple social and biographical identities simultaneously, and musicing provides a literal as well as a metaphorical space where such identities – and values – can be 'performed', as materializations of mutual responsibilities and obligations. If such 'performances' are undertaken with an ethical intent to act according to those values – in whatever political context that defines our appearance as a citizen – to our community, our people, our country or our planet – then musicing indeed becomes a potent form of civic imagination.

Of course, there is a certain paradox implicit in what we might call 'post-human' thinking – of thinking in ways which decentralize human experience – in that *all* theories are human theories, even those which disavow anthropocentrism, *because* they are theories made by humans. No matter how much one might seek to escape the orbit of human intellectual exceptionalism, articulating such a position requires us to deploy the same intellectual devices of reason which formally constitute the practices we seek to question. As Donna Haraway cautions, 'it matters what thought think thoughts' (Haraway 2016: 12).

Musical citizens of the planet

Of course, we do not yet know precisely *how* an ethical post-human attitude will materialize within human society more generally because at this point in history we cannot say with any certainty *whether* such a general attitude *will* fully materialize or not. In terms of the future, there are no guarantees, only possibilities. As discussed in Chapter 5, cosmopolitan identities have been contested for hundreds of years, and the 'sovereignty of the states' is unlikely to simply disappear overnight. However, for Haraway, what follows the Anthropocene – as a boundary event marking the end of the Holocene epoch rather than a new epoch in itself – is an optimistic vision (the Chthulucene epoch) of humans in a state of 'becoming-with' all other life on the planet. Her 'Terrapolis' is 'rich in world, inoculated against posthumanism but rich in com-post, inoculated against human exceptionalism but rich in humus, ripe for multispecies story-telling' (Haraway 2016: 11).

In such a world, musicing may be a means of 'performing' the values necessary to coexist with 'companion species' in sustainable ways, not least in developing notions of multispecies understanding. Again, it is important to differentiate between a more general ethical attitude towards other species, and some of the ways in which our musicality might furnish a more literal understanding of multispecies empathy and 'copathy' (Koelsch 2013: 206). As discussed in Chapter 3, it is an affordance of the limbic brain that 'permits [all] mammals to sing to their children. Vocal communication between a mammal and its offspring is universal. And mammals can play with one another, an activity unique to animals possessing limbic hardware' (Lewis et al. 2001: 26). While the qualities of mammalian vocal communication may be very different across species, the underlying neural hardware may be more similar than we imagine, providing a very direct neurobiological relationship to other of Terra's 'critters'. While no other animals may be able to entrain to each other musically in the way that humans can, we can recognize prototypical versions of such musical communication in the ways that mammalian bonds of attachment are often expressed through vocal exchanges, from whale song to the bleatings of livestock to re-establish maternal connections. If crude anthropomorphizing of animal behaviour may lead to highly romanticized notions of animal existence, recognizing the similar neural structures which underpin all mammalian experience can help to develop multispecies copathy. Furthermore, once such copathic attitudes are founded on a neurobiological basis, the limits of human exceptionalism are highlighted, in turn making it more likely that such copathy can extend even further into non-human realms.

Music and the universe next door

What makes music distinctive in terms of civic imagination is that when humans make music together, because of the specific ways that the act of musicing entangles human neurobiology at an interpersonal level in order to communicate musically, the resulting phenomena are perceived to be more or less a shared experience, such that there emerges a collective understanding of the ways in which music facilitates kinship. We might therefore view communicative musicality as a social resource for the development of higher-level biographical identities – for example to tribe, people, nation and planet – as well as a means of providing psychological and physiological reassurance of safety – a 'secure base' – during the disruptions associated with the development of such pluralistic and often contradictory identities.

The sound produced by a musical group is a literal manifestation of the relationships which constitute the group's identity, as represented by the resulting patterns of diffraction/interference. These patterns of soundings and feelings are subtly different each time they are collectively produced, a sonic and embodied reminder of the power of relationships to shape a collective identity. This group sound is emergent and diffractive – constantly changing and evolving as different voices in the musical exchange react and respond to all of the other voices, in real time. It is also polyphonic in nature, the interplay of multiple voices representing a myriad number of ways in which individuals can attune to a collective identity through the human capacity to entrain one's own expression to that of the group.

Such materializations of creative imagination are never neutral; they are always charged with intention, and if such intention is ethically charged, they are infused with values of love, reciprocity and justice. Musicing is therefore another way of 'staying with the trouble' – this time of staying with the trouble of how kinship relations with other human (and non-human) entities are formed and sustain over time, an ongoing effort to 'tune in' to each other's internal world and find collective expression through such musical and neurobiological entrainment. In that sense, musicing presents itself to us as a resource for experiencing multiple social and biographical identities, without any inherent contradiction or negation in their simultaneous materialization, because of music's 'floating intentionality'. It enables us to inhabit multiple realities simultaneously, where we can experience a 'universe next door' alongside the one we physically exist in, by collectively conjuring up patterns of diffraction and superimposing them onto the fabric of our everyday lives. If the big questions of anthropology are to do with 'how did we find ourselves stuck in just one form of social reality, and how did relations based ultimately on violence and domination come to be normalized within it?' (Graeber and Wengrow 2022: 519) then musicing might provide one avenue to explore to help us become 'unstuck'.

Above all, while a group sound is only temporary, lasting only so long as the sonic patterns of diffraction created by the group continue to resonate in the air, the feeling of group identity mobilized in the process of musicing endures. In that sense we *are* the music, not just 'while the music lasts' (Eliot 1942), but long after the sounds themselves have decayed to silence. We carry this feeling with us, and it can be a potent reminder of our collective humanity – of what it means to feel fully alive, through our appearance in the world as part of a complex fabric of collective meaning. The temporary republics of harmony that we build when we make music together – and the memory of them – are materials with which we can begin to *construct* Terrapolis; in fact, we may view them as a key part of the civic grammar of that mythical future world. If we engage in musicing as an act of civic imagination, it can remind us of our ethical responsibilities and obligations to the wider world, by materializing the necessary attitudes to lead us towards more sustainable ways of coexisting with all life on the planet. Barad (2007) suggests that 'intra-acting responsibly as part of the world means taking account of the entangled phenomena that are intrinsic to the world's vitality and being responsive to the possibilities that might help us flourish' (438). Musicing is a practical way of engaging with these responsibilities as citizens of the earth – a way of repeatedly materializing the values of love, reciprocity and justice which are essential as we journey to Terrapolis.

Practical applications

In this final section of the book, I discuss two issues which arise from the previous section, namely (i) the implications of musical 'praxis' as a highly situated and pluralistic phenomenon, and (ii) how musician education needs to evolve to account for such complexity, especially in the context of recovery from a global pandemic and the call to view musicing as a resource for developing more sustainable ways of living harmoniously on and with the planet.

NOTES

1. There may be some potential for transfer of some of those capabilities to other socioculturally specific instances of musicing, but these cannot be assumed.
2. From the Greek chthonios, meaning 'of, in, or under the earth and the seas' (Haraway 2016: 52).

PART 3

PRACTICAL APPLICATIONS

7

This Musician

FIGURE 7.1: Fellowship of Hill and Wind and Sunshine Choir on Thorneythwaite Fell 2018. Photographer: Nick Landells.

In Chapter 2, I briefly outlined some of the material circumstances which have underpinned the development of the ideas in this book. In this chapter, what I hope to show is how those ideas have further developed within the specific contexts where they have materialized, in my own 'praxis' as a musician over the last decade or so. In showing how those ideas have emerged, I thereby also hope to illuminate how the specific configurations of people, places and musical practices are *constitutive of* those ideas. This chapter is really an acknowledgement of everything I have learned from participating – often in a leadership role – with other people in and through music. It is an acknowledgement of thanks to all of the students and participants I have worked with over the last ten years or so, as these ideas have developed. It is also an acknowledgement of my suggestion that I – like every musician – can only ever be *this* musician, making music in *this* situation with *these* people and *these* materials, within *these* cultures and traditions.

The specific configuration of my ideas is intimately bound up in my practices as a musician – are constituted intra-actively with such practices as a 'praxis' of 'mindful doing' (Bowman 2005: 69) – and it is therefore in the spirit of enquiry to lay some of those practices bare, the better to be able to view these intra-active constitutions of theory and practice. By praxis in this context what I mean is the particular ways that (i) practices and (ii) ideas about those practices intra-act and evolve over time. The perspective of Artistic Citizenship further highlights the ethical responsibilities of praxis:

> Praxis is a multidimensional concept that includes active reflection and critically reflective action guided by an informed ethical disposition to act rightly, with continuous concern for protecting and advancing the well-being of others. It is action dedicated to personal and collective flourishing, grounded in commitments to transform and enrich people's everyday lives.
>
> (Elliott et al. 2016: 6)

In terms of where ideas come from, even the music in three dimensions model – which has become the central concept in how I think about music – did not emerge fully formed from my own imagination, but instead came about through dialogue with other musicians – peers, students and participants. It was in fact a direct challenge to my own assumptions that led me towards dialogics as a way of making sense of complexity. The earliest version of the model positioned the 'paramusical' dimension on the same plane as the aesthetic and the participatory dimensions, but to the right of the participatory, as an extension of it, suggesting that the paramusical benefits of music arose exclusively through participation – through the 'doing' of music. The model did not withstand much critical interrogation. In a discussion with undergraduate students at Sage Gateshead, one of them[1] pointed out – kindly, I should add – that the paramusical benefits of music can be activated just as strongly through an engagement with its aesthetic elements in performance, an observation so blindingly obvious which highlighted my own advocative bias about the power of musicing. In response to this critique, shifting one small part of the conceptual apparatus just a short distance – moving the paramusical dimension of the model from the end of a continuum to form a triangle of dimensions constituting a dialogic space between the aesthetic, the participatory and the paramusical – changed my whole way of thinking about music.

Of course, because my ideas about music have emerged through my practice as a musician, it may be that these ideas only really help *me* to understand *my* practice. However, even if that were the case, what I hope a discussion of them highlights is the importance of recognizing the specific and situated ways in which musical practices are configured. If we allow that music is a 'discursive practice' (Foucault 2002), then the grounds of such discourse are endlessly situated. As David Elliott notes, 'there is no such thing as "music" in the general sense, unless by "music" we mean a universe of specific musical worlds, domains, or microworlds' (Elliott 1990: 156). Either within a 'rational community' or outside of one entirely, it is the specific configuration of musical practice – the individuals, repertoire, traditions, relationships and associated discourse of *any* musical practice – that gives it potency. In laying my own praxis bare, what I hope to encourage is others to do the same, to recognize the specific ways in which our unique praxis as musicians – our individual handling of ideas and their application in practice – takes shape in response to the situations we find ourselves in, such that they 'systematically form the objects of which they speak' (Foucault 2002: 51). In the context of civic imagination, what I hope this approach highlights is the importance of our 'locality' in shaping ideas about – and responses to – questions of sustainability and human connection.

Therefore, in this chapter, I highlight some of the ways in which my ideas have developed through various professional opportunities over the last decade or so, firstly through working with students at both Sage Gateshead and the Royal College of Music in my capacity as lecturer, before turning to some of the ways in which those ideas have also developed from my practice as a researcher and a community musician. Of course, that is not to suggest that these experiences have been the only influences on my musical praxis; my experience of musical performance and the various insights I have developed through collaboration with the inspiring musicians I consider myself fortunate to be associated with would be a considerable omission in that regard. Also, it is not to suggest that my praxis only commenced at the point of postgraduate study. Far from it, prior to undertaking a doctorate, I had always considered myself to be a 'reflective practitioner' (Schön 1984), learning from my experiences and formulating new ideas as a result. Postgraduate study, however, marks the point at which my reflections on practice were made through peer-reviewed literature as much as they were through my own experiences. What follows is therefore a selective account of the influences on my praxis, and this is purposefully done so as to prevent this chapter from becoming a full-blown autoethnography. My aim is to restrict my discussion to those experiences that have had the most significant influence on my praxis as a musician–educator–researcher since undertaking doctoral study, in order to illustrate the intra-active nature of theory and practice.

Socially engaged student performances at Sage Gateshead

In this section, I discuss a number of practical examples of 'socially engaged' (Helguera 2011) performance projects by third-year students on the UK's first BA (Hons) Community Music programme, situated within the artistic programme of Sage Gateshead between 2012 and 2018, where I was a Senior Lecturer. The choice to share this particular experience is because the range of student performances in response to this module's primary assignment – a socially engaged musical performance – was significant in helping to refine the music in three dimensions model discussed in Chapter 4 and which was the focus of my doctoral studies. The diversity of responses to a socially engaged assignment brief also raised many questions about how to assess the relative quality of very different kinds of musical performances, and which in turn led to me summarizing my reflections in a journal article which problematized the notion of 'quality' in musical performance (Camlin 2015b). I elaborate on the insights developed in that article in what follows.

Rather than a more traditional demonstration of their individual musical talent, the third-year 40-credit Performance Project module required students to engage with specific social, philosophical or ethical considerations in devising and curating a musical performance, resulting in a wide range of performance events with different kinds of social engagement. The resulting performance events illustrate the wide range of positions it is possible to take up along a continuum between the aesthetic and participatory dimensions of musical traditions outlined in Chapter 4. While some of these student events were more recognizable as 'presentational' performances, others were more clearly from participatory traditions, including performances in schools with and for children with special educational needs and disabilities; a one-day community folk festival; an installation celebrating the musical faith traditions of the diaspora of Ap Chau island; collaborative performances with service users of mental health organizations; a Blue Light Choir to support the well-being of emergency services personnel.

Being expected to explore the creative tensions between 'presentational' and 'participatory' dimensions of performance meant that few students choose to curate events that were either wholly 'presentational' – a recital, for example – or a wholly 'participatory' musicing situation where there are 'no artist-audience distinctions, only participants and potential participants' (Turino 2008: 28). In the former, demonstrating social, philosophical or ethical considerations became more challenging, although not impossible. In the latter, it became harder for students to present a performance event that could be distinguished from a participatory workshop. However, in the dialogic space between these two dimensions, there was much opportunity for a rich exploration of some of the tensions and inconsistencies which constitute more socially engaged performance, and which I hope these brief examples illustrate.

Example 1: We are who we can be

In Emily's performance event, she fronted a large house band as part of an uplifting funk/soul revue, supported by an amateur adult choir. She worked with a local mental health recovery group to collect the stories of individuals recovering from their mental health, and with their informed consent used the resulting narratives as song lyrics for new compositions which formed the bulk of the house band's repertoire. The adult choir, too, included some patients from the mental health recovery group, so there were several ways for participants to engage with the performance event. Some participants made narrative contributions that were realized as song lyrics, where hearing their words sung back to them in performance was very validating of their experience. They might also have been involved in the performance of those lyrics through membership in the choir, taking their involvement to a deeper level. Audience members could participate simply as listeners, enjoying the uplifting groove-based music, or their experience of the event might be heightened through their personal connection to some of the performers, finding a deeper meaning in their friends'/relatives' public appearance as a performance of their recovery.

In Chapter 4, I discussed this kind of musical performance as 'performance-as-participation'. While ostensibly a very presentational performance – a high-quality funk/soul review with a tight house band and choir performing to a capacity crowd in the prestigious environment of Sage Gateshead's Hall 2 – the level of social engagement beneath the surface underlined a potent sense of transformation for many of the individuals involved. For Emily, finding a way to combine participatory elements into her band's performance also helped her to find a stronger performing identity:

> The performance has altered my thinking around my identity as a musician. Now I feel that I could build a career completely out of music, which includes performance. It has enabled me to celebrate my identity as a musician and music leader. My 'cartoon' version of myself has been developed, and I hope to expand this even more at future events. I feel very proud of the participants, especially my choir who have worked really hard throughout the year.
>
> (Emily 2015: n.pag.)

Example 2: Big about Corby

Starting much more from the participatory end of the spectrum, Callum worked with a number of schools in Corby, Lincolnshire to curate a showcase event featuring performers from all of the schools involved. A sell-out audience for a large local venue ensured a great atmosphere and community spirit on the night, with opportunities for everyone present to be involved as co-performers during the final songs of the evening. There was much evidence of civic pride throughout the evening, involving large numbers of performers who got to 'appear' in public in front of a large cross-section of their community. Callum joined in with some of the groups on his trumpet, but the focus of the evening was always on the 'appearance' in public of the less-experienced performers, marking this event out as a kind of 'participation-as-performance', as discussed in Chapter 4.

> I would best describe this whole process as an inspirational learning journey that has taught me so much about myself, and my practice. This whole project has identified and supported local talent, and encouraged people to develop their interests and expertise in music at whatever level it may be. My main aim was to encourage participation; not to pressurise individuals to be the world's best singers, but to nurture the creativity of the children, empowering them to believe in themselves and their artistic abilities, as when they start to do this, they become more involved.
> (Callum 2017: n.pag.)

Other students' performance events blurred the boundaries of aesthetic and participatory dimensions of musicing still further. Resisting attempts to categorize them as either 'presentational' or 'participatory' performances, they integrated aspects of both dimensions to powerful effect.

Example 3: Fram fest

Ellie curated a one-day folk festival in the Northumbrian village of Longframlington, involving local heritage community musical groups alongside international performers like fiddler Stuart Hardie as well as her own student ensemble. The day started with singing workshops and a maypole dance, featuring showcase performances throughout the day including the premiere of her arrangement of a neglected local folk song, Longframlington Fair, and culminated with a community ceilidh. Genuinely community-focused, but with a strong emphasis on musical quality, attendees spent the day seamlessly moving between the contrasting roles of listening audience and co-participant.

For Ellie too, casting herself in the multiple roles of performer–producer–facilitator helped her to achieve a stronger professional identity:

> I have become more confident as a person, as a musician and a facilitator, having experienced this process. The whole journey was a learning curve, as I have never

> attempted a project like this before. When I performed with my band in the evening, I was more relaxed into the performance because of everything else that I had achieved that day. I like to think I have come out the other side with better organisational skills, and overall, more confidence in what I can achieve in life.
>
> (Ellie 2012: n.pag.)

Example 4: Disability dilemmas

Sarah also used the opportunity of her performance event to launch her career as a performing artist, enlisting fellow performers from her section of the Pandemonium Drummers from the 2012 Olympics opening ceremony, alongside a house percussion band, various collaborations with other musicians and a solo piano set. Turning her speech disability into a performing asset, she conceived a stand-up routine using pre-recorded sequences and live dialogue to invite the audience to join her in 'laughing about' disability. Her performance event provided her with a unique opportunity to control and re-invent her public musical identity, from that of a 'disabled musician' to that of a 'musician with a disability':

> I felt there was apprehension before my first event where people didn't know how I would combine music, disability and humour or compere the event. I felt people focused on my challenges more and not my ability, but people then saw me for my ability. This has led to me performing and presenting more about music, disability and humour at other events, including developing my own show again.
>
> (Sarah 2015: n.pag.)

Assessing quality

As many of these performance events drew on *both* aesthetic and participatory dimensions of musicing – the performance of 'works' *and* the 'performance' of relationships – to different degrees, it raised an interesting challenge of how to assess the quality of these contrasting events consistently and fairly, despite their obvious differences in character. What I hope is revealed through this brief discussion of students' contrasting responses to the same brief to curate a socially engaged performance event is that the sheer diversity of responses even in this small sample renders a more 'fixed' understanding of quality largely insufficient. Each of the performances was successful in its own right, even though they were all very different, highlighting the importance of a more nuanced understanding of musical quality.

Some of the students' comments reflecting back on the experience and its legacy for their artistic development further highlight the rich and transformative power of this approach to performance:

> I created this event as a way of pushing myself past what I thought I could be capable of. I had struggled with crippling self-doubt and confidence as a musician throughout my time at university. To put on this event, I would have to become a cartoon 'diva' version of myself and try to turn my nerves into excitement. The performance was a massive success. Everyone seemed to enjoy it, and I surprised myself by becoming this diva on the stage! The performance really showed me that I can do anything that I set my mind to. Now, if I'm ever faced with a situation where I start to doubt my abilities, I remember my performance and realise that it's only the self-doubt that is stopping me. The performance has also shown me a way to help the participants of my choir when we perform. A lot of the participants get terrible stage fright, and so now I encourage them to adopt the idea of turning the nerves into excitement.
>
> (Emily 2015: n.pag.)

> It was an extremely important event that encouraged community cohesion through the love of music. It provided children with a fantastic performance opportunity whilst also developing their musical skills/knowledge and networking with others who had similar interests. From a personal perspective, it highlighted the wealth of community spirit that my hometown holds and the songs that I decided to use emphasised to the children, their schools and their families that they are capable of anything if they put their minds to it – a view that I strongly believe and encourage.
>
> (Callum 2017: n.pag.)

> My 'FramFest' performance project will always mean an awful lot to me as it was ultimately put together in memory of my grandad who had died of cancer the year previously. It was also evidence that a grand idea can be seen all the way through to fruition if you want to achieve something enough. I still talk about it in job interviews today as one of my proudest achievements – I literally learned how to be organised through completing this project. I have used the skills I learnt through organising this event in all my jobs since graduating, but even more so with my current job because I am in the process of curating small local events for community-based art projects with the aim of raising money for charity. Although FramFest was possibly one of the most stressful 'jobs' I've (naively) taken on, I learned so much through doing it and always look back on it with the fondest of memories.
>
> (Ellie 2012: n.pag.)

> Doing [my performance event] allowed me to share my experience of living with my disabilities and break down the barriers around disability being a taboo subject, proving that you can laugh *about* it and disability isn't a bad thing. As well as being able to show my full musical ability, which is the most important part for me.
>
> (Sarah 2015: n.pag.)

What all of the students' reflections highlight is a sense of the 'social/ethical responsibility [that] lies at the heart of responsible artistic practice' (Elliott et al. 2016: 3), and the opportunity to locate themselves authentically within such a responsibility. In each case, curating a socially engaged performance event provided them with the opportunity to develop and realize an authentic artistic identity which was as unique and distinctive as themselves as individuals – in the particular sociocultural situations they found themselves in. Freed from the narrow constraints of a more 'rational' understanding of quality, the students were able to create instances of musical performance which were powerful and transformative for all involved, not least themselves.

Working with these students – and many others during my time at Sage Gateshead – taught me that a more authentic understanding of musical quality is therefore contingent on its context, on the specific ways in which practices are materialized in relation to aesthetic, participatory and paramusical dimensions which co-constitute musical practice. It is also perhaps to be found in how well an individual musician develops a critical understanding of their capabilities in relation to the particular circumstances of the different and complementary musical dimensions and traditions they find themselves operating within. Furthermore, the quality of a musical experience is only partially revealed in the realization of a musical event itself; a fuller understanding of quality only really emerges in the subsequent reflections on the experience, and the evolution of a musician's 'praxis' in relation to those experiences. In turn, this has significant implications when it comes to making assessments of such quality, as I discuss in Chapter 8; any basis for assessment needs to be flexible and account for the complex creative tensions and intra-actions between aesthetic, participatory and paramusical dimensions of musicing.

Student encounters with participatory music at the Royal College of Music

In 2014, I was appointed as Lecturer in Music Education at Trinity-Laban Conservatoire in London as a part of the team delivering the institution's new Master's programme, The Teaching Musician. In 2018, I also took up a lecturing role within the Music Education team at the Royal College of Music (RCM) in London and began teaching on the institution's new Master in Music Education (MEd) as well as the established undergraduate programme. The students in both Master's programmes come from a wide range of international backgrounds in music education, from 1:1 instrumental tutors and classroom-based teachers and community musicians working across a diverse range of settings. The diversity of their experiences constantly affirms the notion that music education is a deeply situated practice, and I have learned a great deal about the very different ways that music education is approached in different contexts around the world. Many of the ideas in this book have been refined through the many dialogues and provocations to my thinking which have resulted from working closely with these inspirational musicians over the last decade or so, and for which I am extremely grateful.

One of the modules I lead with the undergraduate music students at RCM serves as an introduction to what may be an unfamiliar world for them of participatory music. As a prestigious international conservatoire, the students are steeped in aesthetic traditions – they have to be if they are to succeed in (i) securing a place at the college in the first instance and (ii) fulfilling their primary ambition of developing and sustaining a career as a professional musician in the highly competitive field of classical music. Developing the skills, values, attitudes and social networks to inhabit an authentic position within this 'rational community' is the main focus of their study so that when they graduate, they are able to integrate themselves within that community as smoothly as possible. Entry into such a competitive professional environment represents a considerable achievement, and students require talent, determination and focus to emerge successfully from their studies into that professional world.

Of course, most of the undergraduates also go on to develop professional capabilities as teachers and educators – and perhaps even community musicians – and the development of music education within the core curriculum is a direct means of preparing them for this reality. Encountering participatory music in a professional context can be an unfamiliar experience for these students, and it has been both fascinating and rewarding to be able to witness them making sense of such encounters. I conducted a short piece of research with a focus group of students and community musicians to explore some of the issues that arise for musicians from these kinds of backgrounds in their encounters with participatory music (Camlin 2022). The findings were very illuminating, and I discuss them in more detail in Chapter 8.

For my own praxis, it confirmed many of the things that I suspected about the particular challenges facing any musician who has developed their musical knowledge and skills primarily within any one of music's dimensions to the relative neglect of the others. My own musical background – as someone who learned to be musical through more informal and participatory traditions – has meant that I have had to work hard to understand the musical world of the conservatoire and the centrality of notation to its practices. For the conservatoire students, the opposite was generally true. Encountering music as a 'performance' of relationships represents quite a radical shift – from the 'rational community' of the conservatoire and its perfectionist ethic where individuals can feel alienated and ultimately replaceable, to a more relational ethic where everyone's contribution is taken at face value. Such a shift is not just an attitudinal one, but an epistemological 'break' as well, requiring a willingness to consider musical quality in more holistic terms than the orthodox discourse of the conservatoire.

Students described the excitement of having to respond to musical situations that were not just different to their usual experiences of music but also *uniquely* different in their specifically situated configurations of people, places and practices, and it was heartening to hear students talking about re-connecting with their sense of 'fun' in music through these encounters. What was perhaps more surprising was how they also recognized that such encounters helped them to develop their own expressive musical capabilities; performing music with and for individuals that they were able to form bonds of attachment which enabled them to find more emotional engagement in their own musical expression.

In all of these higher educational settings, it is the experiences such as the ones described above that have most shaped my own ideas about music. Having to think about the complexities of how musicians from different backgrounds and traditions make sense of musical experiences which are different to their own biographical histories in music – without losing sight of the fact that *all* of these experiences are equally valid in a holistic understanding of music – is what has driven much of my research and my teaching. What language can help us to articulate the complexity of our diverse and dissensual truths about music? What ideas can help us to recognize the humanity in one another through the unique expressions of our musical selves? It is through the asking of such questions that the full potential of music – as a uniquely human resource for developing kinship relations – can begin to be revealed.

Participatory projects

I conclude this chapter with a brief discussion of some of the more recent practical projects I have also been involved in as a music practitioner–researcher while the ideas for this book were evolving. Again, the purpose of such a discussion is to highlight the ways in which these ideas have taken shape through their intra-action with musical practices. This is not to make any general claim about their value – either of practices or ideas – but rather to highlight their co-constitutive nature, 'as practices that systematically form the objects of which they speak' (Foucault 2002: 50).

A particularly potent connection made through my time at Sage Gateshead was with the other three singers in Mouthful, a vocal quartet who I've now sung with for over twenty years. Developing my close harmony skills also led to me developing skills and experience in vocal leadership, and my practice as a community musician has therefore increasingly focused on group singing. The questions which arise when one is immersed in that practice centre around trying to understand why it has the effect that it has on those who participate in it. Over time as a leader of group singing, the stories of participants who experience therapeutic benefits from the activity becomes impossible to ignore – such stories become part of the material fabric of the group. Hence a lot of my praxis – practice and research – has centred on building up a better understanding of what is going on during the activity which means that its participants can often have profound and sometimes spiritual responses to the experience.

Over that same period of two decades, a formidable body of research knowledge has been developed around the phenomenon of group singing, and which is perhaps best summarized in a systematic review of mental health and well-being outcomes of group singing for adults with a mental health condition (Williams et al. 2018) and the development of an agenda for best practice in group singing research (Dingle et al. 2019). Much of the research is able to demonstrate *what* group singing is good for, but the question of *why* it is good has remained more elusive. The research by Fancourt et al. 2021, referred to in Chapter 3, highlights the complex network of possible mechanisms which may be implicated in such an understanding. As I also discuss in Chapter 3, the experience of 'magic moments' (Gabrielsson 2011: 746; Pavlicevic 2013a: 197) seems to be as close as research can get to describing these kinds of musical experiences which represent the complex intra-action of multiple complementary mechanisms; they tend to defy linguistic articulation, in that they render participants literally speechless.

My best guess – and it just a hunch, a hypothesis because I suspect it is immeasurable – expressed in this book and elsewhere (Camlin et al. 2020; Camlin 2021c) is that group singing – like all musicing – involves participants in the experience of an entangled state; an intra-action between musical entrainment, individual biology and interpersonal neurobiology, as well as other cultural, social and psychological mechanisms. When people experience these transcendental 'magic moments' of 'communitas', what is invoked is a profound sense of building kinship relationships which capitalizes on the uniquely human capacity for communicative musicality, which is in turn evocative of our experiences of deep human connection and love.

As a practicing community musician and also a researcher, I've therefore become increasingly interested in understanding how the knowledge of what is going on for singers during these 'magic moments' can be expressed. What is their experience of such moments of transcendence, and why does it feel so significant for many of them? Moreover, from a practitioner's point-of-view, I'm interested to explore what I can do to curate the conditions which support such experiences. As this book has evolved, I have also become interested in the question of what can be *done* with such experiences? How might they be put to service in addressing some of the challenging questions that we currently face about human existence on an increasingly fragile planet?

A series of encounters with other researchers have been significant in leading to a reconfiguration of my practice. In my capacity as Head of Higher Education and Research at Sage Gateshead, I was fortunate enough to work in partnership with Dr Petia Sice and her team at the Department of Computer and Information Science at Northumbria University on a number of projects around 2013–15 which introduced me to complexity theory, interpersonal neurobiology and SenseMaker®, the software app which is now central to my own research. Through her, I had the opportunity to discuss ideas about interpersonal neurobiology and music with Dr Dan Siegel, a key thinker in the field of interpersonal neurobiology. She also introduced me to Dave Snowden and his team at the Cynefin Company who developed the Sensemaker® research method. Engaging with these discourses about complexity was instrumental in helping me to recognize music as a complex adaptive system, and the role of interpersonal neurobiology as part of the underpinning architecture of music's potential for well-being.

Another such catalyst to my praxis was a chance encounter with Dr Helena Daffern at a conference in York in 2016 where she was presenting some of her recent research on singing in virtual reality (VR), including Vocal Interaction in an Immersive Virtual Acoustic (VIIVA) – the virtual immersive singing environment that she and some of her colleagues at the University of York's Electronic Engineering department had created. This was my first experience of singing in VR – as the fourth member in a pre-recorded vocal quartet in the richly reverberant virtual recreation of the concert hall in the York Early Music centre, singing an improvisation of Amazing Grace. It was quite a remarkable experience – the immersive detail of the ambisonic environment alongside the 360-degree visual field of vision was initially disorienting in its realism, but settled into an enjoyable and exciting experience of virtual group singing. Because the activity involved singing with a pre-recording, it quickly became apparent that the virtual experience was not the same as a 'live' one because nothing I did with my voice was responded to by the other three singers. That aside, it was still a remarkable achievement of technology. After the virtual experience, we had a long discussion about the research and its direction and intentions and found sufficient common interest to consider possible collaboration.

As a result, Dr Daffern very generously involved me in the SINGSVR project with her colleagues at University of York, where we conducted experiments to explore the potential of group singing in VR using the VIIVA system (Daffern et al. 2018). Focusing on VR experiences in relation to group singing was an important avenue to explore, as clearly if the experience of group singing whilst physically isolated from the other singers was as potent as the in-person experience, it would cast doubt on the hypothesis that at least some of the well-being effect arises from interpersonal neurobiological attunement. The results were not so clear-cut. Singers in the VIIVA environment clearly had a positive experience, even though the methods of understanding their experiences suggested that they 'responded quite differently in the two conditions' (13). It was not the case that the virtual group singing experience was 'worse' than the real thing, simply a different experience. This distinction would prove invaluable when thinking about the complexity of replicating group singing in online/virtual environments, and ultimately lead to the realization that the specific configuration of 'apparatus' (in the broadest sense) for a musical experience is constitutive of that experience. As discussed in Chapter 3, the material disruption to the regular weekly singing experience of participants in the project was too much for a number of the singers involved; not only was the virtual experience very different to the 'real thing', but attempting to capture the 'real thing' to present it virtually disrupted the 'real' experience so significantly that the singers no longer recognized it as valid. At this point, as a practitioner I was sensing the limits of the virtual experience by the negative comments that my singers were sharing.

This place

However, the collaboration with Dr Daffern extended to a further project where the potential of group singing and VR was at least partially recovered. The Fellowship of Hill and Wind and Sunshine was a 2018 project delivered in partnership with the UK's National Trust (National Trust), involving taking 'scratch' choirs of singers onto Lake District mountain summits to perform a song cycle commemorating the 'great gift' of those summits to the nation. Following the Great War 1914–18, a group of Cumbrian mountaineers from the Fell and Rock-Climbing Club (FRCC) raised sufficient funds to buy 12 mountain summits in memory of their climbing comrades who had died in the war. Their story is a powerful testament in itself, evoking a spirit of remembrance and celebrating the sense of freedom that immersion in nature brings. The project brought all of us who participated in it in quite a profound way to the ideals of a previous generation who – scarred by war – sought to imagine a more hopeful and peaceful future. The opportunity to create a song cycle for the project – especially using the words of dedication given by poet-mountaineer Geoffrey Winthrop-Young at the unveiling of the commemorative plaque on the summit of Great Gable in 1924 – felt like a precious gift, and a responsibility. In many ways, this project has been instrumental in shaping the direction of my praxis since, as it brought together a number of connected threads, not the least of which is the centrality of place-based musicing within my artistic practice.

The Lake District fells have been the backdrop to most of my life – I was born here, and generations of my ancestors farmed and laboured here, so the Cumbrian landscape is where I feel most connected to my own history and my heritage. For all of us who call this remote part of the UK home – and the millions of tourists who are drawn to visit each year – the Lake District has a timeless quality where the wildness of nature is only ever just below the surface, a vivid reminder of its endurance, and of our own temporality. The story of the FRCC's 'great gift' highlights the powerful ways in which our lives find meaning through the connections we make with each other in our collective inhabitation of the natural world. As one of the participating singers said at the time, 'somehow it was the mountains that were reverberating with us, if you see what I mean, rather than an audience' (Camlin et al. 2020: 10).

The use of VR to make these kinds of experiences accessible to those unable to physically participate was also significant. Rather than VR as a disruptive interruption to regular weekly singing, it was used as a way of capturing the mountain-top choral performances, which were then installed as a VR experience in the local museum in Keswick so that people who had been unable to climb the mountains – for reasons of mobility or other health reasons – could still participate in the project. In this instance, the results were much more positive. Even though the experience of singing in VR was not the same as singing 'for real' on actual mountain-tops, because it was not set up as a comparative experience, participants were able to enjoy the virtual experience on its own terms, i.e. a remarkable opportunity to be transported to an amazing mountain landscape that one wouldn't otherwise be able to access, in a very immersive way, and to sing (albeit virtually) with familiar singing friends from one's choir. This was an important qualification about how to consider the VR experience – rather than asking the question 'is it as good as the real thing?' asking the question 'who is it good for, and under what circumstances?' revealed a very different discourse, where a more nuanced understanding of its value could be explored.

These people

The Fellowship project also gave me my first opportunity to fully implement an innovative research method that I had been developing with the Cynefin Company.

Sensemaker® is described as a 'distributed ethnography' (Snowden 2016) which collects people's narrative accounts of their experiences through an app, and then involves them in making sense of the narrative they shared through a series of interpretative software tools (Cynefin Company n.d.: n.pag.). The design of the Sensemaker® framework is done with the specific intention of collecting people's experiences of phenomena in their own terms – either as text, image, audio, video or in combination. However, rather than in more traditional ethnography where a researcher might immerse themselves in a community over an extended period in order to develop insights into people's experiences, Sensemaker® 'distributes' the researcher role across the research population such that every participant is actively involved in the research – both in sharing their story, and subsequently in interpreting it.

The findings from this research study have been reported elsewhere and are in the public domain (Camlin et al. 2020) so I won't elaborate extensively on them here. However, a salient point to this discussion of the intra-active nature of theory and practice concerns the rich accounts of the transformative experience that people underwent through participation in the project, and which were captured in vivid detail through the Sensemaker® process, which enabled me to distance myself somewhat from contaminating their reflections with my own preconceptions. In particular, the discussion in a research focus group with participants to draw out the themes emerging from their collective narratives explored the many accounts of 'transcendence' and the challenges of articulating it (10), highlighting many of the themes which I explore in this book, and especially in Chapter 3. The geometric patterns which arose from the Sensemaker® 'self-signification' process indicated a number of important findings. First, that the paramusical outcomes of musicing (discussed in Chapter 4) are significant in people's experience, and that these outcomes appear to be supported the best when both aesthetic and participatory dimensions are activated – in other words, when musical activities are fun and inclusive, and when they also focus on achieving a cohesive collective sound. Second, that the sense of connection people feel to one another during musicing tends to be uppermost in people's minds when they reflect on the experience.

Beyond the realization of the project's aims and the publication of its research findings, what the project also did was strengthen existing social bonds across those who participated in it, many of which have endured. Of course, some participants in the project only connected to this particular community through that one project, so it is only possible to speculate on any long-term impact for them, but for those who have remained within this singing community, the 'fellowship' has become an invisible bond between us (I include myself in the community) and part of our collective biography – sharing a profound experience which resists linguistic articulation means that it is only ever 'known' as a shared memory – you had to be there.

Of course, the extended singing community I find myself in is not restricted to those who participated in the Fellowship project; it includes several hundred singers who sing regularly in groups and workshops – primarily across the North of England – led by myself or one of the other musicians in Mouthful. Many of the members of the Mouthful community have been singing together for many years in their various local groups, and all of the projects and experiences they have shared over that time have added to the sense of collective identity. At a local level – the choir/singing group which sustains over time – the community is characterized by the unique contributions of the individuals involved – the quality and timbre of their particular voices, their characters, predilections and quirks. When key members of the community are absent for a protracted period of time – as happened during the pandemic – their absence is felt keenly by those who are accustomed to entraining to their presence. As new members 'appear' within the community, they in turn shape the group's collective identity as it evolves, in keeping with the principles of a 'community of practice' (Lave and Wenger 1991; Wenger 1999).

When I compose, arrange or lead music for/with these groups, it is very much with the voices and personalities of individuals within the group in mind. *These people* and their individual and collective capabilities, aspirations, sense of humour and sense of unity are fundamental to the materiality of my practice as a musician – they are the ground in which my practice is rooted. I assume that this is not an uncommon experience for many similar communities bonded through music in the long term. This ethic of mutuality towards the people one is involved with musically is a foundation of sustainable musical practice – whatever the circumstances of such practice – and is therefore something to be fostered in the education of musicians, which I elaborate on in Chapter 8.

Inspired by the Fellowship project and its impact on the singers who participated, in 2019 the focus of my praxis began to shift more explicitly towards themes of sustainability, peace and the 'wild' places which supported and amplified the moments of transcendence experienced by the Fellowship singers. I live very close to the Ennerdale valley – a stunningly peaceful location replete with childhood memories because of its central place in my maternal ancestors' origins.[2] In recent years, the valley has become an important site for re-wilding, with the emergence of the Wild Ennerdale project as 'one of the UK's largest wildland partnerships' (Wild Ennerdale). With the support of Arts Council England and the National Trust, we developed a project entitled Creative Ennerdale which enabled us to engage more closely with the valley's unique remote location. One of the events we organized was an artistic residential we called The Universe Next Door, conceived as an opportunity for participants to engage in creative ways with the wildness of the location. Over a weekend, working with a team of artists including Mouthful, percussionist Brendan Murphy, Dirk Proost and Sarah Verhulst from Belgium and UK willow artist Phil Bradley, we holed up in a remote field centre a few miles up the valley without mobile phone reception, and created a range of musical and other works.

One of these was the Girt Dog, a willow sculpture facilitated by Phil over the weekend as a representation of the legendary thylacine (now-extinct Tasmanian Tiger) which is believed to have escaped to the valley from a travelling circus in 1810 and which terrorized local sheep populations until it was hunted and killed. This symbolic reanimation in willow of an extinct species, in the place where one of its kind had miraculously found itself over 200 years ago, bestowed upon us a function similar to Donna Haraway's 'Speaker for the Dead', whose task is to 'bring the dead into the present, so as to make more response-able living and dying possible in times yet to come' (Haraway 2016: 69). 'Gertie' as she became affectionately known, was ritually welcomed back into the valley with a dance and a symbolic sacrifice: I fell into the river off the bridge where I was filming Arwen, the dancer. Being dragged under the bridge fully clothed with the river in full spate was an alarming experience – perhaps more so for the onlookers than myself, for whom time slowed down considerably over the six seconds I was underwater.

Since her reanimation, Gertie has taken up permanent residence as a guard dog in The Gather – the local community centre in Ennerdale Bridge where the Creative Ennerdale project also helped us to revive an old Cumbrian community tradition. Merry Neets were once a regular feature of Cumbrian social life, an opportunity for the local community to gather and share songs, stories, jokes and generally make merry. Perhaps the best account of one is in the Cumberland Bard Robert Anderson's (1770–1833) song 'The Bleckell Murry Neet' where 'the soun' o' the fiddle yet rings in mey ear' (Gregson 1980: 10) as he describes the various characters engaged in clogging, singing, drinking and smoking the night away. As a child, I remember listening to my Granda's accounts of Shepherd's Meets in local pubs which had a similar flavour. We revived the Merry Neet tradition by establishing our own series of events where people share songs, stories, poems and other creative offerings with a supportive and appreciative audience. The Creative Ennerdale project concluded with a community play, worked up over a number of weeks, presenting a fictionalized account in story and song of a final Merry Neet in the lakeside Anglers Hotel before it was demolished in 1968.

In bringing the past to life through these kinds of creative activities, we are not just remembering and celebrating past events, but using them as opportunities to scan the history of our collective imaginations for ways of being in the world which speak to our present circumstances, and our possible futures. As Haraway suggests, 'the Speakers for the Dead are also tasked with bringing into mind and heart the new things of earth, the emerging kinds of beings and ways of life of an always evolving home world' (Haraway 2016: 168). The Merry Neets have sustained since then, and have become a regular feature of this community's cultural life, providing a regular outlet for the collective expression of creativity. People bring songs, stories, jokes, dance, mini-lectures to share on a different theme at each event, and these modest gatherings affirm the strong social bonds which have been nurtured over time.

The greatest threat to this community spirit came in 2020, when the global COVID pandemic shut down all UK social life (except for a privileged elite in government) in one fell swoop. Faced with the stark choice of moving my choirs and musical activity entirely online, or stopping them altogether, I reluctantly invested in the necessary technology to convene online 'live'(-ish) group singing, facing all of the various challenges which are becoming well documented in research literature (Camlin and Lisboa 2021; Daffern et al. 2021), including the technological barriers to participation, the disruptions to normal social interactions and the ensuing compromises to musical quality. If we accept that music entangles us with one another through patterns of diffraction which are both musical *and* interpersonally neurobiological, then some obstacles are harder to overcome than others. We can compensate to some extent in the online environment for compromises in musical quality, and as technology progress, this will become easier. However, we cannot compensate for the removal of the body from musicing. We experience it as a loss of dynamism, and a loss of 'presence' (Daugvilaite 2021). Above all, this loss of the 'presence' of the other singers – which we might take here to include all of the complex ways in which 'diffraction' is experienced, as discussed in Chapter 3 – is insurmountable in an online musicing situation.

However, this absence is balanced against the over-riding need for 'choir continuity': 'a strong sense of willingness to put up with these difficulties and inconveniences by placing the virtual choir in the context of "doing something," no matter how difficult or unsatisfactory, [rather] than "doing nothing"' (Daffern et al. 2021: 7). The online experience literally polarized the community: some felt that the price of experiencing each other in a state of partial absence was too great to countenance – a painful reminder of what had been lost – and stayed away. Others found comfort and stability in the continuation of the community, however disrupted. Like singers' experiences of the SINGSVR project, what was highlighted was that group singing and *online* group singing are *materially* different activities, albeit with many resemblances which help to mediate their differences. Attempting to compare online and face-to-face musicing is often to miss the complexity of how they materialize in different ways: the 'agential cut' that is made by replacing analogue diffraction with its digital counterpart means that they are essentially different phenomena, with different 'apparatus' which intra-act to produce different particular effects.

Literally, the materials involved are different – in the instance of group singing, the materials are embodied human agents in complex diffractive, intra-active and interpersonal relationships with one another in real time and space. In *online* group singing, a simulacrum of group singing is materialized, with an attendant emphasis on maintaining social connections with one's community and finding individual pleasure in entraining to musical sounds together. Not the same thing as singing together in person, but nonetheless significant in terms of maintaining well-being and social connection.

In response, we explored a whole manner of different activities as ways of bridging some of the perceived experiential gaps. We established labour-intensive 'virtual choir' projects where group members submitted home-made recordings of themselves to be incorporated into video and audio 'performances' shared on Youtube. We also used the audio recordings in weekly singing rehearsals to provide a more immersive sense of singing within a choir – re-creating the full group sound across a stereo image for people to locate themselves within, able to recognize the voices of their fellow singers around them as they sang. We built a prototype 'car choir' technical setup using wireless microphones transmitting FM frequencies into people's cars in real time. We continued the Merry Neets on the Zoom teleconferencing platform, increasing audience numbers considerably beyond the capacity of The Gather's intimate space, and welcoming people from across the United Kingdom and the world into our little hub of community creativity.

Our most ambitious projects sought to work within the limitations of the online medium to achieve something resembling 'live' performance. In Hearth Songs (Mouthful 2020), Bex Mather and myself worked with singers from across the Mouthful community and story-teller Malcolm Green to bring a Northumbrian folk tale to life, using pre-recorded 'virtual choir' recordings, video clips and the Zoom choir performing a dramatic interpretation of the songs with various props, backgrounds and costumes. In Trip to the Lakes (Mouthful 2021), during a period when limited social mixing was permitted, we created a blended performance in a local Arts Centre using a wide range of materials to create a unique performance: previously unseen video recordings (including spectacular drone footage) from the Fellowship project used as a basis for a 'virtual choir' recording which was then mixed in with the original recording; a small acoustic ensemble performing 'live' in the venue alongside a small socially distanced choir; a Zoom choir performing online, and projected in a live mix with the video footage onto the venue's projection screen; the entire performance – 'live' and pre-recorded performances alongside the video projections – broadcast on Facebook and Youtube as a live stream.

While these experiments came as close as it was possible for us to get to a sense of 'live' performance with online elements, they also highlighted a more poetic truth that was at least partially grasped beforehand, that 'a world of made is not a world of born' (Cummings 1944). Online and virtual singing experiences can clearly be beneficial for some (*these* people in *this* situation) but do not *compare* favourably with the analogue experiences they are meant to emulate. They fare much better as experiences when they are taken on their own terms rather than in comparison, highlighting the fact that these practices are *materially* different, whilst maintaining considerable resemblance.

This point was further emphasized in a piece of research I undertook during the lockdown as part of an international study. The Ethno project brings groups of young people together at a series of annual international summer music camps, providing 'a unique opportunity for young people from across the globe to come together and engage through music in a manner that is characterised by respect, generosity and openness' (JM International). During lockdown, all of this activity moved online by necessity, and in investigating this move, Gibson (2021) had already identified similar conclusions to the ones drawn here, that the 'turn' towards online musical experiences highlighted 'what was possible to achieve from one's home' whilst recognizing that 'it cannot replace the offline experience' (Gibson 2021: 151). In our research using Sensemaker® to explore the experiences of organizers of Ethno events reflecting on their histories of working on different Ethno events over time, the same themes of 'communitas' identified in previous research (Camlin et al. 2020: 10) came to the fore – the sense that when people make music together, they connect with one another in profoundly intra-active ways (Camlin and Reis 2022). Moreover, this research highlighted the sense that when people engage in musicing in these transnational contexts, they forge new biographical identities together which transcend national ones and that it is in the act of musicing itself where such transcendences occur (31). What is palpable in Gibson's account is the same sense of loss pervading the online musicing experience when compared with the 'real thing' that Daffern et al. (2021) discuss.

The ongoing resonances of the Fellowship project, felt through the Trip to the Lakes performance in lockdown, led to a reimagining of one of my choirs as Wild Chorus, with an express commitment around 'connecting with each other; with our collective creativity; with audiences; with, in and through nature in the promotion of living more sustainably – freeing our voices to sing together in wild places!' (Mouthful n.d.). The particular dialects of civic imagination at work here are to do with community solidarity in addressing complex social problems – in this instance environmental degradation which has a particular resonance for a community living next to a remote UNESCO World Heritage Site, and with a long tradition of coal and iron ore mining. More specifically, what the lockdown experience threw into sharp relief was the powerful nature of *in-person* group singing, and also its fragility in the face of pandemic social restrictions.

Emerging from the second wave of the pandemic in the summer of 2021, the Communitas project addressed this issue directly, curating a series of 'pop-up' outdoor performances in wild places across the north of England, from the Holy Island of Lindisfarne and the Northumberlandia monument near Newcastle, along Hadrian's Wall and through caves, rivers and fells of the Lake District National Park in Cumbria down to deserted beaches and Roman forts in the wilder and more remote parts of the county, less frequented by tourists. At each location, groups of singers gathered to renew old acquaintances, establish new friendships, and above all connect with one another again through the diffractive intra-action of our collective voices surrounded by the majesty of the natural world.

In the autumn of 2021, we gradually returned to regular weekly indoor singing and lent our voices to global music initiatives surrounding Cop26. There have been more outdoor singing in the last twelve months than I can remember, and the joy of this new-found means of connecting music and people and place is still reverberating with freshness and promise. At the time of writing, I have started leading an additional 'Recovery Choir' with the local Recovery College, aimed at supporting those in the recovery of their mental health as we emerge, blinking and a bit bewildered, into our 'new normal'. Earthsong, our summer singing project for 2022 had a renewed focus on how singing might help us connect with what Haraway (2016) terms our 'companion species', especially those under threat of extinction, and captured so beautifully in The Lost Words (Macfarlane and Morris 2017), with performance events in wildflower meadows and public gardens, by rivers and firesides, at scarecrow and music festivals, in libraries and museums, and of course at Merry Neets.

In this chapter, I have outlined a selection of practical experiences which have most influenced the development of ideas presented in Part 2 of this book. I reiterate the point that this is no way to suggest that the practices themselves are in any way more special than those of any other musician. The general tenor of this book is that all musical practice is uniquely situated, and therefore highlighting the different elements which configure my own practice is not to make any special claims about it, but merely to illustrate the point about the particularly situated ways in which musical practice is configured. While elements of particular musical traditions will no doubt be evident within my account, I hope that the detail of that account is sufficient to convince you of the particular nature of its configuration, which is dependent on being *this* musician, making music in *this* situation with *these* people and *these* materials, within *these* cultures and traditions. In the following chapter, I consider some of the implications of this way of thinking, as it might apply to the education of musicians in general, and specifically with regard to those intending to pursue music as a career.

NOTES

1. A wonderful musician called Joe Wilson, remembered fondly by all who knew him.
2. For a historical flavour of life in the Ennerdale valley, my late Great Aunt Janie had many stories to tell (Pearson 2004).

8

Musician Education

FIGURE 8.1: Earthsong Loweswater 2022. Photographer: Dave Camlin.

In this final chapter, I discuss some of the implications of the contents of the rest of the book for the education of musicians. To return to my original definition, what I mean by the term 'musician' is anyone who is actively engaged in music making, whether they do so professionally or as recreation, for their physical and/or mental health, with family/friends or as part of a community-based activity. In this chapter, my primary focus is on the education of musicians who aspire to a professional career in music, where such a career might also involve them in an educative role themselves, as teachers or community/health musicians. I start with a question, what are we educating musicians for?, which is another way of asking, what do we imagine musicians are going to *do* with the education they receive? After consideration of the increasing need for professional musicians to develop educational capabilities alongside their musicianship skills as part of what is referred to as a 'portfolio' career covering multiple kinds of creativity, I then consider what skills, attributes and values musicians may need to mobilize in order to develop such a career. I conclude the chapter with some implications for pedagogy in general, not just in how music education might be approached in formal settings like schools and universities, but how a more 'diffractive' and situational approach to pedagogy might be of relevance to all instances of musicing, from the classroom and concert hall through to community, healthcare, leisure and other settings.

Debates in education often return to the inherent tensions contained in the word itself, which is believed to have two Latin derivations which are not only complementary but also contradictory: *educare* to 'train or to mold', and *educere* to 'lead out' (Craft 2017; Bowman 2018: 172; Elliott and Silverman 2015: 115–16). While *educare* might be to do with 'the preservation and passing down of knowledge and the shaping of youths in the image of their parents' (Bass and Good 2004: 162), *educere* is more about 'preparing a new generation for the changes that are to come – readying them to create solutions to problems yet unknown' (162): 'Educare sees learners as consumers of knowledge, while educere sees them as creators of new knowledge. Educere nurtures independence of mind, the courage to swim upstream against prevailing currents – and the ability to discern when that is necessary' (Bowman 2018: 172).

These two traditions within education tend to exist in a creative tension with one another, providing a sense of balance between them, although this balance can of course be more or less stable under different ideological conditions. Administrations which champion *educare* are often interested in the education system producing effective and efficient trained workers, while those which champion *educere* may be more interested in the education system resulting in the emergence of unique individuals with a capacity for critical thinking. The classical German framing of education – as outlined by Gert Biesta (Biesta 2006, 2014, 2017, 2021) – presents these inherent tensions within education in a slightly different way, as three complementary domains:

> There are (at least) three domains in which education can function and thus three domains in which educational purposes can be articulated. One is the domain of qualification (ausbildung), which has to do with the acquisition of knowledge, skills, values, and dispositions. The second is the domain of socialisation (bildung), which has to do with the ways in which, through education, we become part of existing traditions and ways of doing and being. The third is the domain of subjectification (erziehung), which has to do with the interest of education in the subjectivity or 'subject-ness' of those we educate. It has to do with emancipation and freedom and with the responsibility that comes with such freedom.
>
> (Biesta 2014: 4)

The domains of qualification and – perhaps to a lesser extent – socialization are perhaps more implicitly understood as being central to education. However, the domain of subjectification – like the ethical principles implied by *educere* – is perhaps more overlooked in the ideological context of 'increasing neglect or sidelining (other than in rhetoric) of the social purposes of education' (Ball 2008: 8).

What are we educating musicians for?

Therefore, if education in the fullest sense means accounting for all its complementary domains, and its capacity to 'lead out', then before we can fully address the issues surrounding the education of musicians, we first need to consider the more philosophical question of what are we educating musicians *for*? Where are we *leading them out to?* Is it to train them to be able to take up roles within established 'rational communities' (Lingis 1994) of music? Or is it to prepare them to be able to apply their acquired musical capabilities in diverse sociocultural situations outside of those communities? Is it to help them demonstrate that those same capabilities have satisfied the expectations of a particular standard which 'qualifies' them to assert a particular identity? Or is it to help them integrate themselves into complex communities of musical practice? Is it to support their actualization as unique and singular human beings?

Naturally, 'when faced with a choice, do both' (Eno and Schmidt 1979) and the answer to all of the above questions might indeed be 'yes'. However, there are good reasons for emphasizing some of these aspects of musician education more than others, because of the way that they may be more neglected. Because all musicians are likely to have developed their musical capabilities within a particular set of practices and traditions, if they are to work in music education in its broadest sense, they need leading out of those traditions – whatever they may be – into a more holistic understanding of music, as outlined in Part 2 of this book, and implied by the above rhetorical questions.

This tension between pedagogical traditions – of musician *training* on the one hand, and musician *education* in its fullest sense on the other – has a long history, and continues to permeate contemporary discourse in music education, where 'the problem of musical instruction's sociopolitical insularity remains a significant problem' (Bowman and Frega 2012: 28), because of the 'unexamined assumption [...] that *educating in* music is the fundamental point of musical instruction, and that *educating through* music is largely non-musical' (28, original emphasis). Such an inherent inconsistency within music education has a destructive impact on the discipline's potential social and cultural value to broader society:

> Infatuated with efficiency and technical rationality, music educators have gravitated toward training rather than education, toward definitive answers rather than better questions. Our understandings of music, of education, and of music education are in urgent need of repair. A crucial part of that project is recovery of their nature as ethical and ethically-guided practices as rich resources for exploring crucial questions about what kind of people music making and musical education should enable us to become.
>
> (Bowman 2018: 167)

Thinking about music as a complex adaptive system which invokes entangled states and is experienced as a vitality; considering the aesthetic, participatory and paramusical dimensions of music and how they intra-act; recognizing music's role in political life and how 'vigilance' is necessary to prevent it becoming a part of the problem of structural inequalities; understanding the potential of musicing as a resource for civic imagination, through the performance of humanist values of love, reciprocity and justice: all of these considerations about music's value to people and society deserve a place in a broad education of musicians. As Mellizo highlights, the most emancipatory forms of music education are about fostering global citizenship as much as individual musicianship:

> If today's students develop strong in-group affiliations at every level of community they will need to navigate through in the future, they can become the types of citizens who will work together to solve problems that extend beyond geographical borders, and collectively transform our world into a more just and humane place.
>
> (Mellizo 2019: 8)

If musicians are to be part of a more general 'leading out' of the existential challenges we currently face as a species, their role as educators needs to be critically informed so as not to simply re-create or reinforce existing structures which might mitigate against sustainable development and social/environmental justice. As part of that process of 'leading out' or 'going visiting' (Arendt 1989: 43), one can also expect musicians to develop not just greater awareness of other musical traditions and contexts but also greater self-awareness of their own:

> In venturing forth and 'living in' the inherent and delineated meanings of an unfamiliar musical context, all students gain what only such 'moving out' can provide: insight into one's 'self' (musical and otherwise) and the relationship of one's self to one's own and other music cultures.
>
> (Elliott 1990: 160)

I hope it is not unfair to say that many – if not most – musicians in formal music education are being *trained*, so to speak, rather than *educated*, by which I mean that they are being socialized to fulfil particular roles within particular performing musical traditions, developing the capacity to communicate authentically within the 'rational community' of such traditions. From quite an early age, many aspiring musicians are encouraged – or perhaps drawn – to the music examination system, which provides a valuable assessment of their developing capability to integrate themselves within a rational community of musical practice in due course. The qualifications they obtain as a result of their studies represent the necessary cultural capital to assert access to the next level of that community; enrolment on the next grade examination; securing a place at a music college or conservatoire. As a result, there may be a corresponding de-emphasis within such an educational journey on the capabilities surrounding participatory music and of music's paramusical benefits. Paradoxically, asserting membership of any rational community is also to accept that membership is contingent on 'speaking' with the 'interchangeable voice' (Biesta 2006: 64) of that community, which ultimately renders its members replaceable. Hence, great emphasis is placed on maintaining membership by continuing to demonstrate the capacity to 'speak' as a representative of the community – perfecting and maintaining precise means of performing the canonized repertoire of the musical works of that community, for example.

What is music for?

This capacity to 'speak' as a member of a rational community – socialization or *bildung* – is clearly an important function of education, as the system of examination and resulting qualifications clearly demonstrates, but education in the fullest sense is about more than that. As Bowman (2009b) says, 'music education is not just about music, it is about students, and it is about teachers, and it is about the kind of societies we hope to build together' (75). For this reason, musicians may also need leading out into a broader understanding of education itself. To address the question of what we are educating musicians for is therefore also to ask the broader question of what is *music education* for, which is in turn bound up itself in a still broader question of what is *music* for? What I hope is clear from this book is that music has many purposes, many of which overlap, intersect and intra-act. Therefore, music education (in its broadest sense) is about preparing musicians (also in the broadest sense) to potentially take up active musical roles in a very broad plurality of practices, which are uniquely situated.

The 'subjectification' work of music education – how music becomes integral to our sense of ourselves as unique and singular individuals in a complex and changing world – is therefore essential to an understanding of what someone will *do* with the knowledge and skills they acquire through their education or participation. At both Sage Gateshead and Royal College of Music, I have witnessed first-hand the confusion and uncertainty that many emerging musicians have over how to engage with Community Music (CM) and participatory traditions. Many of them struggle to see how to fit their own musical identity into what they perceived as an existing 'community of practice' (Lave and Wenger 1991; Wenger 1999) with apparently normative behaviours and approaches. The undergraduate students at Sage Gateshead saw other musicians enacting their diverse practices in many different situations, and often judged themselves – quite harshly at times – against their own perceptions of what was lacking in their own capabilities, rather than celebrating the things that made them unique as musicians. Whatever it was they happened to be less confident about doing – whether that be composition/songwriting, sight reading, improvisation, singing, notating and arranging, group leading, or a host of other musical practices – often appeared to them to be the thing that excluded them from becoming part of the perceived community they aspired to graduate into.

We learned to reassure these students that CM starts with *you*, *your* practice as a musician, and the people *you* work with – *this* musician, in *this* place, with *these* people and so on. It is a fundamentally humanistic and dialogic approach to educating musicians, as it emphasizes the relational nature of music and the pluralistic ways in which musicing occurs in different situations with different groups of people worldwide. Becoming the subject in your own narrative about what music is to you, and moreover what it *does* for you, is what lies at the heart of a progressive music education, and it applies to all musicians, whether or not they are seeking to develop a career in music, or simply wanting to enjoy being musical as part of their everyday life.

As I hope I have implied in the rest of this book, it is to this question that the education of musicians really needs to turn. Chris Philpott asserts that,

> Music should be considered as a [communication] system that is vital to the ways in which we construct meaning, culture and ideology[...] music educators at all levels need to engage with a critical pedagogy which aims to facilitate pupils, students and teachers to engage with the complex webs of meaning which arise as part of making music.
>
> (Philpott 2012: 27)

At this point in our history, developing ways of engaging with these 'complex webs of meaning' which constitute our lives and our futures is of critical importance, if we are to navigate a course through the uncertainty of the next decades.

Music has an important potential in that regard, which means that the education of musicians needs to widen its focus from training to education in the broadest sense. In our journey to Terrapolis, *every* community needs a musician. If living more sustainably means travelling less and organizing more locally, *every* community needs ways of building and sustaining more local biographical identities in a globally connected world, which musicing is well placed to deliver. It is therefore imperative, as Mellizo (2019) suggests, 'for practitioners and scholars to consider the ways in which learning experiences in the music classroom can cultivate higher levels of global competency without diminishing musical learning' (Mellizo 2019: 1).

Although the 'community' aspects of professional musicianship may have taken a back seat during music's ascendancy as a source of economic capital, now that its symbolic value is recovering some relative status once again, there are lessons from our not-so-distant history which can help us re-imagine the role of the musician in society. Even for musicians steeped in the aesthetic traditions of the classical world, the musician in the community has a long and honourable history. Although it may not be even on the radar of young people embarking on a career in music, developing a modest musical practice which is woven into the heart of a community's social life can be a deeply rewarding profession. Consider the town band leader, or the village organist:

> By tradition the organist was the general practitioner of the musical world and, whether based at the diocesan cathedral or a large town parish church, [s]he was likely to find – or make – [them]self the focal point of much local music-making, directing the local choral society or orchestra, and often being the principal grammar school music teacher.
>
> (Wright 2013: 13)

Portfolio careers in music

Establishing what is referred to as a 'portfolio' career 'characterized by multiple concurrent roles' (Bennett and Burnard 2016: 123) is essential for most musicians who manage to sustain a career in the current economic climate (Bennett 2012: 15; Hallam and Gaunt 2012: 14). Although 'it is not uncommon for students to feel 'second-rate' if they redefine their career aims to include activities beyond performance' (Perkins 2012: 27), being able to say 'yes' to new opportunities and adapt one's practice accordingly, becomes not only a pragmatic approach to professional security but can also lead to careers which are deeply fulfilling in their creative diversity. Such an approach to professional life requires 'the sophisticated application of a wide range of musical and generic/transferable skills, and more entrepreneurial attitudes towards work' (Hallam and Gaunt 2012: 14). These attitudes of entrepreneurship which lie at the heart of a 'protean' career are characterized as 'career creativities' which Bennett and Burnard (2016) summarize as:

- Community-building creativity represents professional networks and communities of practice.
- Inspiration-forming creativity includes role models, inspirational figures and supporters.
- Career-positioning creativity represents the creation of capacity through interest, recognition, new markets (including market 'engagement') and professional learning.
- Bestowed gift-giving creativity refers to capital that is 'given away' in forms such as mentorship and pro-bono work (126).

In research undertaken with students at Sage Gateshead where they interviewed respected musicians within their own community of practice (Camlin 2021a), we found that teaching and music education more generally had become a key part of professional musicians' portfolios, providing some financial security against the vicissitudes of a career in music: on average, music education took up about 30 per cent of their time but accounted for nearly 50 per cent of their income (80–81). Perhaps more significant is that this dimension of their portfolio also provided clear opportunities to feel like they were doing something useful with their musical skills, e.g. 'supporting others to get more joy from music' (82).

Traditionally, models of formal music education set up the professional identity of a music educator as the *negation* of a professional identity as a performing musician, and this can be a significant barrier to musicians identifying with such a role (Freer and Bennett 2012). Many of us have probably heard – or even given – the advice to aspiring musicians that you can *train* as a musician, and if that doesn't work out, you can always become a music teacher, thereby suggesting that music educators are in some sense 'failed' or non-musicians. This negative perception of music educator as a professional identity mitigates against musicians being able to develop the necessary skills and knowledge within their own education to function successfully *as* music educators. However, because of the way the music industry has changed into a very different landscape to that known by previous generations (Anderson 2009), most musicians will need to be adept at teaching music as well as performing it, if they are to sustain a career in music in the long term.

Hence, an important corollary of the approach of providing students with authentic 'real-world' experiences across the continuum of presentational and participatory musical practices – as described in Chapter 7 – is that it provides them with a better understanding of what a professional life in music might actually be like once they graduate. Musicians need more than just the traditional skills of musicianship if they are to form and sustain long-term careers in music. Rather than the outdated perception of becoming a music educator as the *negation* of a professional identity in music, approaching a professional career in music with a more holistic understanding of music's complexity sees musicians as more versatile agents, with the knowledge and skills to be able to operate competently and effectively across all of music's different dimensions.

Embracing a more holistic understanding of music does require some conceptual shifts and changes in the understanding of what it means to be a musician. For the conservatoire students I referred to in the previous chapter, their 'encounters' with participatory music prompted some of them to reconsider their own relationship to music. While this process wasn't necessarily an entirely comfortable one it ultimately led them to a deeper awareness of their own motivations and capabilities as musicians (Camlin 2022). Recognizing the 'fun' in music – rather than feeling alienated and restricted by a more competitive striving for perfection in their musical performances – led them to develop a more relaxed approach to their musicing, which they could 'channel' even in more presentational situations, thus (ironically) enhancing their expressive potential, and mediating their experiences of musical performance anxiety. Similarly, explicitly focusing on music as the 'performance' of relationships gave them a different frame through which to view their own chamber music practices, becoming more sensitized to the intra-action of individual personalities, collective capabilities and expressive characteristics, and how these factors are negotiated within a group dynamic. Above all, answering the call to respond musically to situations outside of their familiar experiences required them to increase their situated awareness and develop insights – both into the complexity of these unfamiliar situations and also into themselves as musicians. They described these epistemological shifts as changes in 'mindset', being willing to consider a more nuanced notion of what constitutes 'quality' in a musical situation, and recognizing the many different factors which could co-constitute such quality, in a similar fashion to their counterparts studying CM at Sage Gateshead.

Praxis

An important factor in this epistemological shift is through the way that practice and theory are called into a closer relationship, the foundations of a musical 'praxis'. Being able to justify any practical approach to a musical situation – in relation to any of music's complementary dimensions – on the basis of relevant theoretical understanding and research findings is important for contemporary musicians as it fosters a sense of rigour in practice, and is an important means of underpinning quality. It supports musicians to inhabit the role of 'artistic citizen' more fully by supporting them to create artistic work as necessary and/or relevant responses to the situations, communities and localities where they find themselves, and calls on them to be 'critically reflective, person-centered, creative, and ethically guided' (Elliott and Silverman 2019: 73). In supporting them to engage with research and be pro-active about responding to findings, it also helps musicians to be, 'critical consumers of the new research findings that will come out during the many decades of their career' as well as helping them to 'generate new research questions' (Goldacre 2013: 214–15) themselves, seeking out their own understanding of the complexities, tensions and discontinuities of practice through their creative work. This sense of praxis as 'theory imbricated within practice' (Nelson 2013: 33) is important not just for the emergence of effective approaches to complex 'real-world' musical situations, but also for the way that theories of such situations can evolve too. Rather than allowing a separation between theory and practice to emerge – with the resulting risk that theories of music are developed by researchers from outside those practices – praxis calls on practitioners to find ways of articulating the truth of their own experiences in ever more critical terms.

Skills, attributes and values

Hence, rather than a prescriptive 'toolkit' of pedagogical devices to be deployed in music education situations, an approach to musician's education which recognizes the uniquely situated nature of musical practice across its multiple dimensions requires more of a focus on the epistemological manoeuvres which musicians will need to undertake to engage authentically in a plurality of situations which may vary in terms of their familiarity. Many toolkits of repertoire and approaches already exist, which can be useful in shaping ideas, but here the emphasis is rather on responding to the uniqueness of situations appropriately, as an essential part of the development of a musician's praxis.

In a previous publication focused on the education of community musicians, Katherine Zeserson and I suggested that 'despite the situatedly diverse nature of CM practice, we believe that there is a sufficient alignment of practice amongst CM's "many ways" to be able to infer a number of generalizable characteristics of CM practitioners' (Camlin and Zeserson 2018: 713). We summarized these as a set of skills and attributes which are situated, musical, pedagogical, ethical and praxial, and that the inculcation of these skills and attributes is done with broadly humanistic intentions – to foster human flourishing – and are therefore representative of humanistic values. Rather than repeat these previous insights, in the following section I refine them a little to suggest that these skills and attributes are largely applicable to all musicians who think of themselves also as educators, not just those who call themselves 'community' musicians. I also expand on this previous discussion to suggest that the quality of one's practice as a music educator is also dependent on the extent to which such practice is authentically held and ethically enacted, by which I mean how one's self-awareness as a musician can function as a mediator of one's agency.

Above all, the education of musicians is about preparing them for plurality and difference. Even if we are more formally 'training' them to take up positions within established communities of practice, acknowledging that such 'rational' communities are themselves 'situated' in particular sociocultural circumstances is an important intellectual reminder to be 'vigilant' to the many other ways that people may have of being musical, and to respond accordingly. As each situation of musicing is different – because the people are different, if not in name, then at least in the fluid and unpredictable way that people's personalities can vary and intra-act with others over time – then each such situation is effectively 're-made' each time it is materialized. Such 're-makings' of practical experience might happen over years, months, weeks, days or moment-by-moment, and the role of the musician is to respond to those changes as they occur, in whatever capacity – performer, educator, composer and producer – they find themselves. Having a wealth of experiences to draw on in different situations – not just of practical things that have worked previously but also a more processual understanding of reflexivity and one's feelings and responses to disruptions to practice and how they have been overcome previously – equips the musician with the practical and cognitive means of adaptation to the unfamiliar.

Although it may really go without saying, a musician 'must be a practitioner *of* something musical to be authentic' (Camlin and Zeserson 2018: 714) as an educator. Even in educational settings where one's own musicianship may not be called into play – e.g. some contexts of rock/pop musicing where the role of the facilitating musician is not to become 'part of the band' but rather to let the band get on with it without undue interference – being *able* to respond musically to a particular situation is what establishes a musician's authority to teach. Thus, any kind of musician education has to have at its heart the development of musical skills, otherwise it is not really *music* education. In a similar vein, if musicians are also expected to be educators, there needs to be a corresponding emphasis on their pedagogical capability – their ability to respond to music education/musicing situations with appropriate pedagogical sensitivity and skill. The complexity of these pedagogical approaches is explored in the final part of this chapter, on diffractive pedagogy.

Beyond these practical – musical and pedagogical – capabilities, we might also recognize an underpinning ethic of care for the other people involved in our musicing, which extends to an empathic awareness of how they might be feeling, and what kinds of musical and/or pedagogical actions and behaviours will support their engagement and development, rather than impede it. For example, bringing an awareness of the similar neurobiological underpinnings of musicing and love (outlined in Chapter 3) has direct implications for the facilitation of musicing, recognizing the ethical importance of well-boundaried supportive relationships which facilitate students'/participants' 'ontological and historical vocation to be more fully human' (Freire 1970: 37). If we facilitate musicing with the awareness that as well as any musical outcomes we may be working towards, we are also facilitating a basic human need for attachment and growth, our work will be all the stronger for it. As the story in Chapter 3 about the student's question 'do you love us?' highlights, this principle is only congruent if it applies equally to students of music education as much as it does to musicing participants. If any musician is to facilitate a 'loving' space for participants, they will do so more congruently if they have direct first-hand experience of being held in 'unconditional positive regard' (Rogers 1961) by their own educators – in other words, if music education is undertaken with an ethic of love (Silverman 2012; Bartleet 2016).

Authenticity

However, within this broad set of musical and pedagogical skills/attributes and humanistic values, no two musicians' praxis is the same. I am always *this* (unique) musician, making music in *this* (unique) situation with *these* (unique) people and *these* materials, within *these* cultures and traditions. To inhabit my praxis *authentically* is to be aware of its constitution, and the possibilities for it to be otherwise; to accept that the work I do – here and now – calls on me alone to do it, and that no one else can do it for me.

Authenticity is an elusive quality. Our self-system – 'made up of a number of self-images including those relating to self-esteem, self-efficacy, ideal selves, and possible selves' (Hallam 2017: 475) – is about how we think of ourselves. From a perspective of 'authentic' leadership, we might say that our artistic and leadership practices are strengthened by heightened meta-cognition of our self-system, referred to as 'self-awareness' (Chan et al. 2005: 5). As authenticity is 'a self-referential state of being [which] has to do primarily with *being* one's true self' (6, original emphasis), when we develop self-awareness, what we do – our agency – becomes more authentic. Authentic artists – of any discipline – are therefore authentic *because* what they do expresses something true about themselves; without authenticity, any artistic practice is more craft than art.

In other words, in order to express oneself authentically, one has to know oneself. With self-awareness comes confidence, and in particular the confidence to actualize one's highest personal ideals, to *be* authentic. Of course, a potential paradox surrounding authenticity is that claims to actualize individual authenticity are mitigated somewhat by the social nature of our existence:

> Being human always points, and is directed, to something, or someone, other than oneself – be it a meaning to fulfil or another human being to encounter. The more one forgets oneself – by giving oneself to a cause to serve or another person to love – the more human one is and the more one actualises oneself. What is called self-actualisation is not an attainable aim at all, for the simple reason that the more one would strive for it, the more one would miss it. In other words, self-actualisation is possible only as a side effect of self-transcendence.
>
> (Frankl 1946: 2)

We therefore only really come to know ourselves through our relationships with others, through the ways in which our authentic selves are seen and felt by others, what I referred to in Chapter 4 as the Arendtian power of 'appearance' (Arendt 1958: 50; Camlin et al. 2020: 10). Because musicing fosters kinship and the conditions for 'feeling felt' – for revealing and recognizing one another's 'true selves' in the musical moment – it provides a valuable opportunity to experience relationship, not just in general terms, but with *these* people in *this* situation. In so doing, it provides all involved with the opportunity to *be* authentic, and it is therefore imperative that musicians inhabit the role of music educator authentically, being their true self in the musicing so that others can similarly engage. By definition, this means that no two *authentic* musicians' musicing practices will ever look or feel the same.

Diffractive pedagogy

Pedagogically, this raises a number of issues, some of which I've already touched on. Rather than a 'toolkit' approach to music education, musicians require both reflexive and reflective capabilities – being able to choose to do something different at the moment, in response *to* the moment (reflection-in-action, or reflexivity) and being able to learn from experience (reflection-on-action) – in order for their authentic musical selves to respond to a musical situation. In the following section, I outline what I refer to as a 'diffractive' approach to pedagogy, by which I mean one which accounts for the entangled ways in which diverse material 'apparatus' – including people, instruments, sounds, repertoires, contexts, cultures and traditions – are differently configured through complex intra-actions to co-constitute unique musical situations over time. This conception of pedagogy borrows heavily from Barad's (performative) new materialist perspective, where 'diffraction does not concern homologies but attends to specific material entanglements' (Barad 2007: 88) and represents a different methodological approach to pedagogy:

> A diffractive methodology is a critical practice for making a difference in the world. It is a commitment to understanding which differences matter, how they matter, and for whom. It is a critical practice of engagement, not a distance-learning practice of reflecting from afar.
>
> (Barad 2007: 105)

This approach emphasizes the diffractive nature of musical experience, both metaphorically and literally, recognizing that the diffraction/interference of audio (and other) waveforms during musicing lies at the heart of such experience. Music education is preparing its subjects to be able to participate in real-world musicing situations, where groups of humans organize sound through the manipulation of their bodies and instruments to produce patterns of diffraction/interference which communicate emotions, intentions and vitality. Pedagogy is also diffractive in the sense of a practice that is configured and reconfigured over time, in response to situational variations, where 'teachers, students, objects and spaces are equally material phenomena and similarly entwined with one another' (Hickey-Moody et al. 2016: 220), and where – as part of the pedagogical 'apparatus' – they 'must be tuned to the particularities of the entanglements at hand' (Barad 2007: 87). These variables might include but are not limited to: participant (and educator) previous experience and skill level; situational purpose; performative factors; changes in collective – or individual – group identity and aspiration; negotiations around leadership and followership; instrumental arrangements; musical genre.

Organizational dynamics

A diffractive pedagogy also accounts for the ways in which groups themselves change over time, and how fluctuations in group membership, commitment and purpose have a material impact on practice, as represented in 'classic' models including Bruce Tuckman's characterization of group process as a series of recursive 'stages' (forming – storming – norming – performing – mourning) (Tuckman 1965; Tuckman and Jensen 1977). While the model implies a linear progression through these stages, it is rarely ever so – groups emerge and develop, split, re-form, hit their stride, lose it again, change key personnel, re-group and so on in endless cycles. Effective pedagogy is about accounting for all of these diffractive and disruptive influences on a group's ongoing evolution.

Eric Berne's conception of organizational dynamics highlights the importance of the 'imago' in shaping group experience, where the 'imago' is simply 'any mental picture, conscious, preconscious or unconscious, of what a group is or should be like' (Berne 1973: 244), and how that imago evolves collectively over time (Camlin 2021b: 29–30). At the outset, the imago is 'provisional', an expectation of how the group will be, but becomes an 'adapted' imago in response to the reality which is actually encountered – in particular the actual characteristics of the group leader and other members, but by extension the practices, repertoires, settings and other material circumstances which co-constitute the group's existence. It becomes an 'operative' imago once an individual has found their place within the group, and finally, an 'adjusted' imago when the individual 'relinquishes some of their own proclivities in favor of the group cohesion' (Berne 1973: 244). Of course, the process of development of a group imago is highly dynamic, as individuals will move back and forth through the different stages of imago formation at their own pace, and changes in group membership will disrupt and re-set the collective imago for all involved, including the leader.

Hence, in a musicing situation, different pedagogical approaches are required at different stages in the process towards a more 'performative' imago. At the outset, there is much emphasis within CM traditions of the 'welcome' (Higgins 2009) and the establishment of 'a safe and creative atmosphere where everyone feels accepted as they are' (Huhtinen-Hildén and Pitt 2018: 90). Psychological safety is a necessary part of risk-taking, especially where it involves 'revealing' something hidden about yourself – which is an implicit part of the process of interpersonal attunement and entrainment in musicing. Hence, how the conditions of 'safe danger' (Camlin et al. 2020: 11) are established as the group adapts to the material circumstances of its existence becomes an important part of a group dynamic, as it will determine the extent to which authentic exchanges of vitality can occur within a group's musical activities.

These conditions of shared vitality, mutuality and trust take time and patience to establish, and 'grow stronger as the leader and the group members get to know each other' (Huhtinen-Hildén and Pitt 2018: 52), but are not susceptible to measurement as such, despite everyone being aware of them. Reaching an 'adjusted' imago with a musical group – where all of the individuals involved are able to actualize their own musical potential and put it to the service of the group – is an elusive and often temporary state of affairs which takes considerable pedagogical skill to maintain, ensuring that there is a sufficient level of challenge for everyone without leaving others behind. Above all, for it be done well, this kind of collaborative maintenance of an 'adjusted' imago is a process of dialogue and negotiation which 'takes into account all members of the group, respecting their different views and personalities' (Huhtinen-Hildén and Pitt 2018: 53).

Central to all of these considerations is that in thinking of pedagogy as diffractive is also to recognize that as educators, we are never *outside of* the educational situations where we wish to apply our musical and pedagogical knowledge; rather we are inescapably a fundamental part of such situations. We can never be a neutral carrier or transmitter of musical knowledge; rather, we are entangled within it, an intrinsic part of its materialization in the world. Diffractive pedagogy therefore builds on notions of 'pedagogical sensitivity' (van Manen 2008) which Huhtinen-Hildén and Pitt describe as 'the professional knowing that allows us to feel, to analyse in action and to combine this with the knowledge that we have, merging them all in our pedagogical actions to support learning in the specific moment and context' (Huhtinen-Hildén and Pitt 2018: 26). Pedagogical sensitivity implies a more nuanced kind of responsive attention to situations where people are developing their musical capabilities than 'reflection-in-action' and/or reflexivity, which can suggest more internalized responses to situations and deciding to do something different in the moment. Being pedagogically sensitive implies 'tuning in' to more covert individual group processes like vitality dynamics, micro-expressions and barely perceptible gestures and shifts in the energetic and diffractive qualities of a musical situation.

Diffractive pedagogy is also not meant to be a substitute for curriculum. Especially when it comes to training musicians to be able to take up positions within established traditions or 'rational communities' of musicing (especially aesthetic traditions), there is a fulsome discourse on how to do so across many musical disciplines and genres, and many schools of praxis which have evolved over time to provide reliable and effective means of such integration. However, the principle of diffraction implies that all music education situations are materially different, in that the people involved are different in their uniqueness even if the subject content is the same. Hence, a diffractive pedagogy accounts for such individual and situated differences and is willing to explore ways of reconfiguring the educational apparatus (including the pedagogical strategy) to refine the efficacy of any approach.

A further implication of a diffractive pedagogy is that it implies no separation between educator and students, between subject and object. All of those present are part of the same apparatus, and all have the potential to influence the process of musicing and its outcomes. The responsibility of leadership, therefore, carries with it the need to be sensitive to the capabilities of all present (including themselves) in order to facilitate a positive 'process in which all grow' (Freire 1970: 61).

Outside of more established musical traditions, where the emphasis of musicing might be more on the 'performance' of relationships or the realization of paramusical outcomes, a diffractive approach to pedagogy can be even more present as a praxis, 'tuning in' to sociocultural contexts, individual personalities and (medical) conditions, group dynamics and vitality dynamics, individual and collective musical aspirations, place-based considerations and other material circumstances, to develop a way of working which best addresses the intra-action of those complex variables. As above, experimenting with different ways of configuring and reconfiguring the educational apparatus – making different choices about where to apply or foster different kinds of agency or influence – becomes an iterative process which is constantly evolving, entangled within the practices themselves.

Situational music education pedagogy

Despite the obvious conclusion that – if the material circumstances of all musicing are uniquely situated – it is less possible to devise fixed curricula which do not change over time, it is nevertheless possible to identify some general pedagogical principles which can help an aspiring music educator to know in which direction to look for promising approaches to support the development of their students'/participants' musical capabilities. At Sage Gateshead, my colleague Bex Mather and I drew on a business leadership model of Situational Leadership developed by Ken Hersey (1997) to support CM students to reflect on potential pedagogical approaches to the great diversity of CM practices (Mather and Camlin 2016). In the following section, I outline some of these ideas, which have relevance beyond CM practice in terms of a more diffractive approach to pedagogy.

As the field of music education is so diverse, and the nature of such practice subject to much change, it requires a flexible, responsive and adaptable approach to conceiving of pedagogy: one size does not fit all. The idea of situational pedagogy was therefore developed with the intention of supporting music educators 'consciously to adopt a range of pedagogies, adapting them to their students and institutional requirements' (Cain 2013: 89, 90), specifically, to:

- emphasize the needs, capabilities and aspirations of participants when designing and planning musical activities,
- resist the common trap of teaching the way they themselves were taught (Regelski 2009: 3; Zeserson 2014: 23) and
- appreciate and adopt a wider range of teaching styles and approaches.

Pedagogical approaches used by music educators vary according to the situation, not just because the situation demands it (Harrison and Mullen 2013) but also because within these different situations, the context may shift as a project develops. Groups of participants might expect to be led from initial engagement with simple musical forms, to more complex musical forms as part of their natural evolution as a musical group. Pedagogy therefore needs to be able to adapt and respond not just to these basic changes in an evolving musical context, but also to subtle differences in group makeup, individual preferences, pre-existing and emerging capabilities and a host of other factors which are particular to each situation.

Music education naturally occurs across a number of inter-related continuums of practice, including formal–informal (Department for Education 2004; Green 2008), pedagogic–heutagogic (Price 2013) and technical–ethical (Bowman 2005) and with groups of individuals of all ages and abilities. While some music educators may work more exclusively in one fixed setting, many more operate *across* all of these kinds of contexts and therefore need to navigate shifts in pedagogical approaches which are responsive to those differences. An 'average' day for a music educator – if such a thing existed – may include giving private music instruction in the morning, leading group music making in the afternoon, and facilitating a more informal drop-in session for local bands in the evening, all in the same day. Practitioners naturally adapt their pedagogy to suit the situation.

Rather than viewing leadership as a fixed quality of the leader (Lewin 1944), the reality of effective leadership in the context of difference is that it is contingent and situational; it depends on the circumstances of its existence for meaning. Moreover, it is fluid – in the sense of being subject to change – and responsive to the needs of its 'followers'. In that sense, it emerges from educational situations in response to them. Music educators need to be able to move between the more 'instructional learning' of formal 'pedagogy', the 'self-directed learning' of andragogy' and the 'self-determined learning' of heutagogy (Price 2013: 212) as the situation requires. In a similar vein, while 'we may engage in musicing and teaching either technically or ethically' (Bowman 2009a: 117), the reality is that we are often called on to do both. We are concerned with our participants' development as musicians, and we are also concerned with their development as people. Mullen advocates that the CM practitioner, 'moves through a range of roles' as part of what he terms the 'facilitraining rainbow' (Mullen 2008), and Higgins echoes this, suggesting that, 'facilitators are never static in one approach or another but move in and out of roles as the group dictates' (Higgins 2012: 148).

Situational leadership

As a way of navigating such pedagogical complexity, Bex Mather and I found ourselves referring to a model of leadership which had largely fallen out of use – and print – but which we thought nevertheless had some value. Situational leadership

(Hersey 1997) was developed as a management leadership framework by Dr Paul Hersey in the 1990s. The model recognizes the complex inter-relationship between what Hersey terms 'leaders' and 'followers', emphasizing the 'importance of a leader's diagnostic ability' (57), i.e. their ability to understand the 'readiness' of 'followers'. At its simplest, the model emphasizes a dynamic interplay between:

1. the amount of task behaviour a leader provides,
2. the amount of relationship behaviour a leader provides,
3. the readiness level that followers demonstrate in performing a specific task or activity. (Hersey 1997: 57–58)

In this context, 'readiness' consists of ability and willingness, where ability is, 'the knowledge, experience and skill that an individual or group brings to a particular task or activity' and willingness, 'has to do with confidence, commitment, and motivation to accomplish a specific task or activity' (46). 'Followers' may be more or less able, and more or less willing to participate in an activity. Tuning into these levels of 'readiness' then guides the deployment of a corresponding pedagogical approach, particularly in terms of the relative emphasis on 'task' and 'relational' behaviour. The model developed by Hersey has become a global leadership brand, used by businesses in leadership development programmes worldwide (Situational Leadership n.d.).

The full model is perhaps too corporate and too 'fixed' to be of practical service in musicing situations, as it may encourage a view of groups as homogenous entities, suggesting that specific group 'followership' behaviours are met with a particular leadership style. As discussed above, the reality is considerably more complex. However, the general principles of Hersey's model have some value in suggesting that one size does not fit all, and implying the need to adjust pedagogical approaches in response to different groups of people and situations. Reminding the 'leader' to attend to the capabilities of their 'followers' is an important pedagogical attitude, which encourages the movement away from set curricula. The distinction between 'task' and 'relational' behaviour is also valuable. If someone needs to learn how to perform a particular technique on their voice or instrument, some clear instructions (directing) may help them to understand the most efficient ways of doing so, whereas a more 'relational' approach may be more effective in encouraging or supporting students/participants to build engagement, motivation and resilience.

In a musical context, follower 'ability' might relate to a number of things, including the current levels of general musicianship skills of individuals or the group, e.g. ability to work with 'pulse', hold their part against contrasting parts; their technical skills – ability to produce good 'tone' on their instrument/voice; their practical knowledge of musical concepts. Follower 'willingness' might be to do with their engagement – as individuals or collectively – in the group musical process, and their general confidence in any/all of the above. Assessing where students/participants are located in terms of their willingness, skill and confidence is not an easy task, especially in a group setting with high levels of individual difference, and also as none of those things can be easily measured with much objectivity. Willingness might well be a function of someone's confidence, learned behaviour and/or expectations of the environment, culture or situation, while skills are often situation-dependent – for example, some very skilled musicians used to working exclusively from notated scores can quickly experience a dip in their competence and confidence when called upon to improvise, making them much less willing to do so, and vice versa. The model invites critical reflection, by bringing the needs of students/participants, their existing capabilities and their aspirations to the fore.

The range of possible leadership responses to the many variables of 'followership' then becomes a complex and sensitive pedagogical process. In terms of 'task' behaviour, individuals may need additional support to acquire the particular musical skills which will facilitate their participation. Or the whole group may need to work on aspects of collaboration to strengthen their collective musical expression. In terms of 'relational' aspects, there may be social aspects of group process and collective working which need addressing. Ways of differentiating roles and responsibilities, and structuring activities so that everyone is able to contribute to the best of their ability whilst being sufficiently challenged requires negotiation and experimentation:

> Structures and scaffolds provide space for creativity, improvisation and skills development. On the other hand, an inflexible structure, or following the leader´s instructions alone, will not lead to creative freedom or flow. The delicate balance between freedom and structure is hard to describe yet important to aim for.
>
> (Huhtinen-Hildén and Pitt 2018: 75)

How leadership is distributed in more 'dialogic' situations becomes an important aspect of the group's – and individual – development, similar to the kind of 'self-determined learning' (Price 2013: 212) of more heutagogic situations exemplified by ensembles like the Orpheus Ensemble where musical leadership is distributed across the musicians themselves (Hackman et al. 2001).

More experienced music educators might take all of this as a 'given' – as we acquire pedagogical capabilities, we have to think about them less and can perform them more automatically, as the expression of more tacit ways of knowing. However, the acquisition of situational pedagogical skills – matching an appropriate pedagogical approach to the students/participants within a group – is something that requires time and practice. At the outset of a developing practice in music education, musicians may be thinking less about the students/participants, and more about a host of other concerns, including the musical content they want to cover; remembering the different parts they have to teach; their own insecurities or anxieties about their leadership; communicating their musical ideas clearly; enacting responsibility for the overall group sound through conduction and gestures to manage dynamics. Using the situational pedagogy model as a reflective tool supports emerging music educators to place their awareness in the complex materialization of their practice amidst the other people involved, rather than more exclusively on their own performance.

Therefore, the skill of musical leadership is in being able to adopt a range of pedagogical approaches to suit the particular teaching–learning situation, but always in response to the dialogical shifts within that situation: 'Because teaching occurs not in isolation but in relation to students, a teacher's knowledge-in-action is what gives meaning to the teaching-learning situation' (Elliott 1995: 251). While more experienced practitioners might do this automatically, drawing on their tacit knowledge of such teaching–learning situations, the situational pedagogy model provides a helpful framework for less-experienced practitioners to reflect on the situation and the developing needs of the students/participants within it – literally, to de-construct the teaching–learning dialogue – and deploy an appropriate pedagogical response which will maintain students'/participants' engagement and support the development of their musical capabilities. The emphasis on relational approaches also opens up the possibilities of a more dialogic pedagogy, i.e. 'where dialogue and collaborative inquiry allow possibilities for working together [and] directs the focus to group dynamics, removing the emphasis on managing behaviour, searching for a 'right solution' or applying ready-made strategies to solve problems' (Huhtinen-Hildén and Pitt 2018: 49).

Limitations

There are, of course, some obvious limitations to working with Hersey's situational leadership as a pedagogical framework. The risk of any kind of categorization of students/participants is in many ways to go against the fluid and emergent nature of a diffractive pedagogy; the reality of situations where people are developing their musical capabilities is more complex than this simple model allows. Moreover, the model seems to place the development of the group squarely as the responsibility of the leader, rather than in a 'dialogic' process with the group. Who decides when a 'follower' is 'ready', and for what? How the model might be applied in practice reveals further inconsistencies. For example, a more directive 'telling' approach with disengaged young people who might be sceptical about their own ability as well as education and music in general might be a sure-fire way of ensuring their ongoing disengagement, whereas learning about their own motivations and interests through a more relational approach might be a more effective starting place for a dialogue about what might be achieved together. Furthermore, people may be competent in one context, but not another, e.g., working with score/improvisation, respectively. Therefore, the model does not replace *common sense* as a key informant for how to work with people.

However, the strength of the model is in inviting music 'leaders' to consider the 'followers' in a given situation – and their capabilities and interests – as a priority in any consideration of how to proceed pedagogically. Effective leadership in music education consists in reading the subtle changes in levels of students'/participants' competence and confidence in different situations, and tailoring an appropriate pedagogical response in each case, rather than assuming a more 'fixed' style of leadership with a group or an individual. A shift in focus from the pedagogical skills of the music 'leader' to the musical capabilities and aspirations of the 'followers' – and the material circumstances which mediate their engagement – brings with it a compelling need for educators to broaden their own pedagogical capabilities to be more responsive to the particular circumstances of music education settings.

To summarize, a diffractive approach to pedagogy is a means of attending to some of the more subtle influences on group musicing and bringing them to the fore, such as the issues of entrainment and attunement discussed in Chapter 3, the creative tensions between aesthetic, participatory and paramusical traditions discussed in Chapter 4, the political dimensions of music and social/biographical identities discussed in Chapter 5 and music's potential as a resource for civic imagination, as discussed in Chapter 6. Rather than a prescriptive and pre-determined set of teaching and learning activities designed to underpin the development of particular musical skills, a diffractive pedagogy is a reminder that the purposes of music education are only partially fulfilled unless and until we have an idea of what students/participants are going to *do* with the knowledge/skills they acquire. It is also a call to music educators to take a step back from their own experience of developing musical capabilities, and recognize the fundamentally situated nature of such development – however, we have learned to be musical is just *one* way of doing so, and does not therefore necessarily apply to all people in all situations. Taking such a step back reveals a more holistic understanding of how human beings come to be musical, and moreover, what being musical *means* to them. Additionally, it calls musicians into a pedagogical and ethical responsibility to attend to the differences between individual experiences, as it is into such differences that civic imagination is born.

Music education is such an important part of how musicing might be realized as a resource for civic imagination, that I have chosen to give it the final word in this book. To borrow from John Fox and Sue Gill, what I hope may be accomplished through a diffractive approach to music education pedagogy is the realization of an opportunity to re-position musicians as 'engineers of the [civic] imagination' (Coult and Kershaw 1983) where together, in the musical moment, in the blending of our voices, instruments and hearts, in the resonances that linger in the air when the music ceases, we can not only imagine the kinds of worlds and futures we actually want to live in but begin to inhabit them.

Conclusions

> When I close my eyes and envision the crossroads that our elders foresaw, it runs like a movie in my head. The fork in the road stands atop a hill.
>
> To the left the path is soft and green and spangled with dew. You want to go barefoot.
>
> The path to the right is ordinary pavement, deceptively smooth at first, but then it drops out of sight into the hazy distance. Just over the horizon, it is buckled with heat, broken to jagged shards.
>
> (Robin Wall Kimmerer 2020: 368)

In this short vignette from indigenous prophecy, Kimmerer epitomizes the current human condition neatly. At this point in human history, we are indeed approaching a crossroads, where continuing on the jagged path of exploitation of the earth's natural resources is almost inevitably leading us to environmental catastrophe. Finding alternative ways of being in the world as the dominant species on an increasingly fragile planet means equipping ourselves with the resources that will help us to live on the earth differently from the way we have become accustomed, during the period of industrialization and attendant human population explosion which has characterized the last few hundred years. In this book, I have suggested that musicing – as a uniquely human activity which has persisted throughout our long evolutionary history – might be one such resource. Not a solution in itself to the climate emergency, but one of the tools we can carry with us in our metaphorical rucksacks as we set out on a journey to an uncertain future as Terrapolitans. Music has been a feature of all known human communities and has been instrumental in the development of our current highest levels of political and biographical affiliation, citizens of a network of nation-states that now cover the earth. The developmental task facing us is to collectively imagine ourselves as citizens of the planet, rather than any of the more partisan identities which put us in direct competition for limited resources – not just with our fellow humans, but with all other species and indeed the natural world herself.

Musicing – when undertaken with ethical intent – represents 'a value-imbued practice that mediates our social relations' (Väkevä 2012: 87), and as such can be viewed as a valuable means of orienting ourselves ethically to our responsibilities – to each other as fellow humans and – by extension – to all other life on the planet. In this book, I have attempted to trace how such an ethical responsibility might be mobilized. In recognizing music as a complex adaptive system where multiple mechanisms intra-act in highly situated and ever-changing ways, I have highlighted music's polyvalent significance, or how it comes to 'mean' so many things in so many different ways to so many different people. A fundamentally human activity, the effects of musicing are experienced in vital ways which illuminate the unique character of our humanity.

From a holistic perspective, musicing is about the 'performance' of relationships as much as it is the performance of 'works', and these complementary traditions are united when considered alongside the 'paramusical' benefits that musicing affords. While this complex web of musical meaning has a dishonourable as well as an honourable tradition, when undertaken with ethical intent 'to achieve the kinds of lives we want in relation to our ideals' (Elliott and Silverman 2015: 20), it carries the potential to transform our experience of existence in profound ways. While the origins of musicing lie in the way that all humans communicate with their infants to facilitate social bonding, this feature of musicing has been used over many thousands of years to forge attitudes of kinship with other humans we will never know socially. Because of music's 'floating intentionality' (Cross 1999: 22), the same 'trick of the imagination' that we use music for when we sing national anthems to reinforce a national identity could be put to service in the fostering of attitudes of global solidarity (terrapolitanism) in the face of existential threats to life as we know it.

Re-imagining music as a resource for civic imagination in the service of a global world order is not something likely to be achieved overnight. Over the next 30 years, we are likely to face increasingly disruptive challenges to our existence from a wide range of environmental, economic and political crises. As these complex disruptions play out, we need simple resources we can keep a tight hold of to help us orient ourselves in unfamiliar situations, and which will help to remind us of the qualities and characteristics that bind us to the other members of our species, rather than those which divide us. As a ubiquitous and accessible resource with the capacity for establishing and strengthening bonds of kinship across divisions, musicing is a potent way in which we can face an uncertain future together, infused with moments of collective joy, and in solidarity with the earth.

References

Abrahams, F. (2013), 'Critical pedagogy for music education', http://www.frankabrahams.com/index.html. Accessed 11 April 2013.

Adams, P., McQueen, H. and Hallam, S. (2010), 'Contextualising music education in the UK', in S. Hallam and A. Creech (eds), *Music Education in the 21st Century in the UK*, London: Institute of Education, pp. 18–33.

Adorno, T. W. (1973), *Negative Dialectics*, Rpt ed., New York: Continuum.

Aiello, L. and Dunbar, R. (1993), 'Neocortex size, group size, and the evolution of language', *Current Anthropology*, 34:2, pp. 184–93, https://doi.org/10.1086/204160.

Ainsworth, M. (1963), 'The development of infant–mother interaction among the Ganda', in B. M. Foss (ed.), *Determinants of Infant Behaviour II*, London: Methuen, pp. 67–112.

All-Party Parliamentary Group on Arts, Health and Wellbeing (2017), *Creative Health*, London: All-Party Parliamentary Group on Arts, Health and Wellbeing, https://www.culturehealthandwellbeing.org.uk/appg-inquiry/. Accessed 25 October 2017.

Anderson, C. (2009), *The Longer Long Tail: How Endless Choice Is Creating Unlimited Demand*, New York: Random House Business.

Angelou, M. (1995), 'On the Pulse of Morning', *The Complete Collected Poems of Maya Angelou*, London: Virago, pp. 267–73.

Anthropocene Working Group (2019), *Subcommission on Quaternary Stratigraphy*, May, *What Is the Anthropocene? – Current Definition and Status*, http://quaternary.stratigraphy.org/working-groups/anthropocene/. Accessed 8 December 2021.

Appiah, K. A. (2007), *Cosmopolitanism: Ethics in a World of Strangers*, London: Penguin.

Appiah, K. A. (2016), 'Mistaken identities: Colour', *BBC News*, Reith Lecture Series, 5 November, Accra, http://www.bbc.co.uk/programmes/b080t63w. Accessed 5 November 2016.

Arendt, H. (1958), *The Human Condition*, Chicago: University of Chicago Press.

Arendt, H. (1989), *Lectures on Kant's Political Philosophy*, Rpt ed. (ed. R. Beiner), Chicago: University of Chicago Press.

Arts & Humanities Research Council (2014), *Cultural Value Project, Cultural Value Mid-Term Report*, May 2014, http://www.ahrc.ac.uk/Funded-Research/Funded-themes-and-programmes/Cultural-Value-Project/Pages/Mid-Term-Report.aspx. Accessed 19 December 2014.

Arts Council England (n.d.), *Strategy 2020–2030, Arts Council England*, https://www.artscouncil.org.uk/lets-create/strategy-2020-2030. Accessed 28 October 2021.

Baiocchi, G., Bennett, E., Cordner, A., Klein, P. and Savell, S. (2015), *Civic Imagination: Making a Difference in American Political Life*, 1st ed., London: Routledge.

Bakhtin, M. M. (1981), *The Dialogic Imagination: Four Essays* (eds M. Holquist and V. Liapunov), Austin: University of Texas Press.

Bakhtin, M. M. (1984), *Problems of Dostoevsky's Poetics* (ed. C. Emerson), Minneapolis: University of Minnesota Press.

Ball, S. J. (2008), *The Education Debate: Policy and Politics in the Twenty-First Century,* Birstol: Policy Press.

Barad, K. (2007), *Meeting the Universe Halfway: Quantum Physics and the Entanglement of Matter and Meaning*, Illustrated ed., Durham: Duke University Press.

Barenboim, D. (2009), *Everything Is Connected: The Power of Music*, London: Phoenix.

Barrett, M. (2017), 'Laying the foundations for narrative identities in and through music', in R. MacDonald, D. J. Hargreaves and D. Miell (eds), *Handbook of Musical Identities*, 1st ed., Oxford: OUP Oxford, pp. 101–22.

Bartleet, B.-L. (2016), 'The role of love in intercultural arts theory and practice', in *The Routledge International Handbook of Intercultural Arts Practice*, New York: Routledge, pp. 91–101.

Bartleet, B.-L. and Higgins, L. (2018), 'An overview of community music in the twenty-first century', in *Oxford Handbook of Community Music*, New York: Oxford University Press. pp. 1–20.

Bartleet, B.-L. and Higgins, L. (eds) (2018), *Oxford Handbook of Community Music*, New York: OUP USA.

Bass, R. and Good, J. W. (2004), 'Educare and educere – Is a balance possible in the educational system?', *The Educational Forum*, 68:2, pp. 161–68.

Bauer, A. M., Edgeworth, M., Edwards, L. E., Ellis, E. C., Gibbard, P. and Merritts, D. J. (2021), 'Anthropocene: Event or epoch?', *Nature*, 597:7876, p. 332, https://doi.org/10.1038/d41586-021-02448-z.

BBC News (2021), 'Greta Thunberg mocks world leaders in "blah, blah, blah" speech – BBC News', YouTube, https://www.youtube.com/watch?v=ZwD1kG4PI0w. Accessed 30 November 2021.

BBC News (2019), 'Singing Hong Kong's new protest anthem', *BBC China News*, 14 September, https://www.bbc.co.uk/news/av/world-asia-china-49688548. Accessed 30 November 2021.

Begum, T. (2021), 'What is mass extinction and are we facing a sixth one?', *Anthropocene*, 19 May, https://www.nhm.ac.uk/discover/what-is-mass-extinction-and-are-we-facing-a-sixth-one.html. Accessed 8 December 2021.

Belfiore, E. and Bennett, O. (2008), *The Social Impact of the Arts: An Intellectual History*, London: Palgrave Macmillan.

Bennett, D. (2012), *Life in the Real World: How to Make Music Graduates Employable*, Champaign: Common Ground Publishing.

Bennett, D. and Burnard, P. (2016), 'Human capital career creativities for creative industries work: Lessons underpinned by Bourdieu's tools for thinking', in *Higher Education and the Creative Economy: Beyond the Campus, Regions and Cities*, Abingdon: Routledge, pp. 123–42.

Berne, E. (1973), *The Structure and Dynamics of Organizations and Groups*, New York: Ballantine Books.

Biesta, G. (2006), *Beyond Learning: Democratic Education for a Human Future*, 1st ed., Boulder: Paradigm Publishers.

Biesta, G. (2014), *Beautiful Risk of Education*, 1st ed., Boulder: Routledge.

Biesta, G. (2017), *The Rediscovery of Teaching*, 1st ed., New York: Routledge.

Biesta, G. (2021), *World-Centred Education: A View for the Present*, 1st ed., New York: Routledge.

Bishop, C. (ed.) (2006). *Participation*, London: Whitechapel Art Gallery.

Bishop, C. (2006), 'The social turn: Collaboration and its discontents', *Artforum*, February, pp. 179–85.

Blacking, J. (1974), *How Musical Is Man?* Rpt ed., Seattle, London: University of Washington Press.

Bookchin, M. (2005), *The Ecology of Freedom: The Emergence and Dissolution of Hierarchy*, Edinburgh: AK Press.

Bookchin, M. (2015), *The Next Revolution: Popular Assemblies and the Promise of Direct Democracy* (eds D. Bookchin-Taylor and M. Bookchin), London and New York: Verso Books.

Bourdieu, P. (1977), *Outline of a Theory of Practice* (ed. J. Goody), Cambridge, New York: Cambridge University Press.

Bourdieu, P. (1979), *Distinction*, 1st ed., London: Routledge.

Bourdieu, P., Chamboredon, J.-C. and Passeron, J.-C. (1991), *The Craft of Sociology: Epistemological Preliminaries*, Berlin, New York: de Gruyter.

Bourdieu, P. and Passeron, J. (1977), *Reproduction in Education, Society and Culture*, London, Newbury Park: Sage Publications, Inc.

Bourdieu, P. and Wacquant, L. (1992), *An Invitation to Reflexive Sociology*, Chicago: Polity Press.

Bourriaud, N. (1998), *Relational Aesthetics*, Dijon: Les Presse Du Reel.

Bowlby, E. J. M. (1969), *Attachment: Volume One of the Attachment and Loss Trilogy*, Rev. ed., New York: Vintage Digital.

Bowlby, J. (1988), *A Secure Base*, London and New York: Routledge.

Bowman, W. D. (2002), 'Why do humans value music?', *Philosophy of Music Education Review*, 10:1, pp. 55–63.

Bowman, W. D. (2005), 'The limits and grounds of musical praxialism', in D. Elliott (ed.), *Praxial Music Education: Reflections and Dialogues*, New York: Oxford University Press, pp. 52–78.

Bowman, W. D. (2009a), 'The community in music', *International Journal of Community Music*, 2:2&3, pp. 109–28, https://doi.org/10.1386/ijcm.2.2-3.109_1.

Bowman, W. D. (2009b), 'Why musical performance? Views praxial to performative', in *Praxial Music Education: Reflections and Dialogues*, New York and Oxford: OUP USA, pp. 142–63.

Bowman, W. D. (2016), 'Artistry, ethics, and citizenship', in D. Elliott, M. Silverman and W. D. Bowman (eds), *Artistic Citizenship: Artistry, Social Responsibility, and Ethical Praxis*, New York: Oxford University Press, pp. 59–80.

Bowman, W. D. (2018), 'The social and ethical significance of music and music education', *Revista da ABEM*, 26:40, pp. 167–75, https://doi.org/10.33054/ABEM2018a4010.

Bowman, W. D. and Frega, A. L. (2012), 'What should the music education profession expect of philosophy?', in W. D. Bowman and A. L. Frega (eds), *The Oxford Handbook of Philosophy in Music Education,* Rpt ed., Oxford: Oxford University Press, pp. 17–36.

Braidotti, R. (2013), *The Posthuman*, 1st ed., Cambridge, Malden: Polity Press.

Brannen, P. (2019), 'The anthropocene is a joke', *The Atlantic*, 13 August, https://www.theatlantic.com/science/archive/2019/08/arrogance-anthropocene/595795/. Accessed 8 December 2021.

Brown, T., Higham, B. and Rimmer, M. (2014), 'Whatever happened to community music?' *AHRC*, February, https://ueaeprints.uea.ac.uk/id/eprint/47880/1/Whatever_Happened_to_Community_Music_AHRC_CM_Research_Network_Report_final_.pdf. Accessed 2 June 2014.

Burnard, P. and Trulsson, Y. H. (2015), *Bourdieu and the Sociology of Music Education*, Rev. ed., Burlington, Farnham: Routledge.

Cain, T. (2013), 'Passing it on: Beyond formal or informal pedagogies', *Music Education Research*, 15:1, pp. 74–91.

Camlin, D. A. (2012), *ArtWorks NE Peer Artist Learning Project Report*, Gateshead: Sage Gateshead, https://doi.org/10.13140/RG.2.1.3601.9288.

Camlin, D. A. (2014), 'Whose quality is it anyway?', *Journal of Arts and Communities*, 6:2&3, pp. 99–118, https://doi.org/10.1386/jaac.6.2-3.99_1.

Camlin, D. A. (2015a), 'This is my truth, tell me yours: Emphasising dialogue within participatory music', *International Journal of Community Music*, 8:3, pp. 233–57, https://doi.org/10.1386/ijcm.8.3.233_1.

Camlin, D. A. (2015b), 'Whose quality is it anyway? Inhabiting the creative tension between presentational and participatory music', *Journal of Arts and Communities*, 6:2&3, pp. 99–118.

Camlin, D. A. (2016a), 'Music in three dimensions', Doctoral thesis, Sunderland: University of Sunderland.

Camlin, D. A. (2016b), 'Music in three dimensions', in D. Camlin (ed.), *International Society for Music Education Conference*, July. Glasgow: ISME.

Camlin, D. A. (2016c), 'Whatever you say I am, that's what I'm not', in D. Camlin (ed.), *Community Music Activity Commission*, July, Edinburgh: ISME, https://www.isme.org/other-publications/cma-proceedings-2016. Accessed 25 January 2023.

Camlin, D. A. (2017a), 'Beyond binaries', *Musoc*, September, https://learn.rcm.ac.uk/courses/1240/pages/dc-perspectives. Accessed 22 January 2019.

Camlin, D. A. (2017b), 'Singing the rights we do not possess', in *Community Music: beitrage zur theorie und praxis aus internationaler und Deutscher perspektive*, Munich: Waxmann, pp. 137–48.

Camlin, D. A. (2018a), 'Assessing quality in socially engaged musical performances', in H. Gaunt (ed.), *Reflective Conservatoire*, February, London: Barbican-Guildhall, pp. 1–12.

Camlin, D. A. (2018b), 'The word "Cope" and the word "Change"', *Musoc*, March, https://learn.rcm.ac.uk/courses/1240/pages/dave-camlin-perspectives-on-intervention. Accessed 22 January 2019.

Camlin, D. A. (2021a), 'Mind the gap!', in L. Willingham (ed.), *Community Music at the Boundaries*, Waterloo: Wilfrid Laurier University Press, pp. 72–95.

Camlin, D. A. (2021b), 'Organisational dynamics in community ensembles', in R. Timmers, F. Bailes and H. Daffern (eds), *Together in Music*, Sheffield: Oxford University Press, pp. 24–34.

Camlin, D. A. (2021c), 'Recovering our humanity – What's love (and music) got to do with it?', in J. Boyce-Tillman and K. Hendricks (eds), *Authentic Connection: Music, Spirituality, and Wellbeing, Music and Spirituality*, Oxford, New York: Peter Lang UK, pp. 293–312.

Camlin, D. A. (2022), 'Encounters with participatory music', in M. Dagantan-Dack (ed.), *The Chamber Musician in the 21st Century*, Oxford: OUP, Cambridge University, pp. 43–71.

Camlin, D. A., Daffern, H. and Zeserson, K. (2020), 'Group singing as a resource for the development of a healthy public: A study of adult group singing', *Humanities and Social Sciences Communications*, 7:1, pp. 1–15, https://doi.org/10.1057/s41599-020-00549-0.

Camlin, D. A. and Lisboa, T. (2021), 'The digital "turn" in music education (editorial)', in D. Camlin and T. Lisboa (eds), *Music Education Research*, London: Routledge, pp. 1–10, https://doi.org/10.1080/14613808.2021.1908792.

Camlin, D. A. and Reis, H. (2022), *Ethno Organizers Research Report*, York St John University: International Centre for Community Music, Ethno Research, https://www.ethnoresearch.org/publication/ethno-organizers/. Accessed 25 January 2023.

Camlin, D. A. and Zeserson, K. (2018), 'Becoming a community musician: A situated approach to curriculum, content, and assessment', in B. Bartlett and L. Higgins (eds), *Oxford Handbook of Community Music*, Oxford: OUP Oxford, pp. 711–33, https://www.oxfordhandbooks.com/view/10.1093/oxfordhb/9780190219505.001.0001/oxfordhb-9780190219505-e-7?rskey=4wPQqK&result=1. Accessed 25 January 2023.

Chaffin, R. and Lemieux, A. F. (2004), 'General perspectives on achieving musical excellence', in A. Williamon (ed.), *Musical Excellence: Strategies and Techniques to Enhance Performance*, Oxford: Oxford University Press, pp. 19–40.

Chan, A., Hannah, S. T. and Gardner, W. L. (2005), 'Veritable authentic leadership: Emergence, functioning and impacts', in W. L. Gardner, B. J. Volio and F. O. Walumbwa (eds), *Authentic Leadership Theory and Practice: Origins, Effects and Development*, Bingley: Emerald, pp. 3–42.

Chernoff, J. M. (1979), *African Rhythm and African Sensibility: Aesthetics and Social Action In African Musical Idioms*, Chicago: University of Chicago Press.

CHWA, *Culture Health and Wellbeing Alliance*, https://www.culturehealthandwellbeing.org.uk/. Accessed 24 March 2022.

Clarke, E., Dibben, N. and Pitts, S. (2010), 'Music in people's lives', in *Music and Mind in Everyday Life*, Oxford: OUP Oxford, pp. 1–14.

Clayton, M. (2012), 'What is entrainment? Definition and applications in musical research', *Empirical Musicology Review*, 7:1&2, pp. 49–56, https://doi.org/10.18061/1811/52979.

Clayton, M., Will, U. and Sager, R. (2004), 'In time with the music – The concept of entrainment and its significance for ethnomusicology', *ESEM CounterPoint*, 1, pp. 1–84.

Clift, S., Nicol, J., Raisbeck, M., Whitmore, C. and Morrison, I. (2010), *Group Singing, Wellbeing and Health*, Melbourne: UNESCO Observatory: University of Melbourne, pp. 1–24.

Comunian, R. and Gilmore, A. (eds) (2016), *Higher Education and the Creative Economy: Beyond the Campus*, Abingdon, Oxon, New York: Routledge.

Cooper, B. (2013), *Music Lab Evaluation Report*, Evaluation Report, Gateshead: Sage Gateshead, http://davecamlin.com/music-lab. Accessed 29 October 2013.

Coult, T. and Kershaw, B. (eds) (1983), *Engineers of the Imagination: Welfare State Handbook*, London: Methuen Drama.

Craft, M. (ed.) (2017), *Education and Cultural Pluralism*, 1st ed., London: Routledge.

Creech, A. (2014), *Active Ageing with Music: Supporting Wellbeing in the Third and Fourth Ages*, Dulles: Institute of Education Press.

Cross, I. (1999), 'Is music the most important thing we ever did? Music, development and evolution', in *Music, Mind and Science*, Seoul: Seoul National University Press, pp. 10–39.

Cross, I. and Morley, I. (2010), 'The evolution of music: Theories, definitions and the nature of the evidence', in *Communicative Musicality: Exploring the Basis of Human Companionship*, Oxford: Oxford University Press, pp. 61–81.

Cross, I. and Woodruff, G. E. (2009), 'Music as a communicative medium', in *The Prehistory of Language*, vol. 1, Oxford: Oxford University Press, pp. 113–44.

Crossick, G. and Kaszynska, P. (2016), *Understanding the Value of Arts and Culture: The AHRC Cultural Value Report*, Swindon: Arts & Humanities Research Council, http://www.ahrc.ac.uk/documents/publications/cultural-value-project-final-report/. Accessed 21 March 2016.

Crotty, M. J. (1998), *The Foundations of Social Research: Meaning and Perspective in the Research Process*, London: Sage Publications Ltd.

Cummings, E. E. (1944), *1x1. Early Rpt ed*, New York: Henry Holt.

Cynefin Company, *SenseMaker®*, https://cognitive-edge.com/sensemaker/. Accessed 8 November 2019.

Dabla-Norris, E., Kochhar, K., Suphaphiphat, N., Ricka, F, and Tsouta, E. (2015), *Causes and Consequences of Income Inequality: A Global Perspective*, Washington, DC: International Monetary Fund, https://www.imf.org/external/pubs/ft/sdn/2015/sdn1513.pdf. Accessed 12 December 2021.

Daffern, H., Camlin, D. A., Egermann, H., Gully, A. J., Kearney, G., Neale, C. and Rees-Jones, J. (2018), 'Exploring the potential of virtual reality technology to investigate the health and wellbeing benefits of group singing', *International Journal of Performance Arts and Digital Media*, 15:1, pp. 1–22, https://doi.org/10.1080/14794713.2018.1558807.

Daffern, H., Balmer, K. and Brereton, J. (2021), 'Singing together, yet apart: The experience of UK choir members and facilitators during the Covid-19 pandemic', *Frontiers in Psychology*, 12, p. 624474, https://doi.org/10.3389/fpsyg.2021.624474.

Daugvilaite, D. (2021), 'Exploring perceptions and experiences of students, parents and teachers on their online instrumental lessons', in *Music Education Research*, London: Routledge, pp. 1–15, https://doi.org/10.1080/14613808.2021.1898576.

Deane, K. and Mullen, P. (2013), 'Community music in the United Kingdom', in *Community Music Today*, Lanham: Rowman & Littlefield Education, pp. 25–40.

Deer, C. (2008), 'Doxa', in: *Pierre Bourdieu: Key Concepts*, 2nd ed., London, New York: Routledge, pp. 119–30.

DeNora, T. (2000), *Music in Everyday Life*, Cambridge: Cambridge University Press.

DeNora, T. (2013), *Music Asylums: Wellbeing through Music in Everyday Life*, Farnham: Ashgate.

Department for Education (2004), *The Music Manifesto*, London: Department for Education.

Diamond, J. (2013), *The World Until Yesterday: What Can We Learn from Traditional Societies?*, London: Allen Lane.

Dingle, G., Clift, S., Finn, S., Gilbert, R., Groarke, J. M., Irons, J. Y., Bartoli, A. J., Lamont, A., Launay, J., Martin, E. S., Moss, H., Sanfilippo, K. R., Shipton, M., Stewart, L., Talbot, S., Tarrant, M., Tip, L. and Williams, E. J. (2019), 'An agenda for best practice research on group singing, health, and well-being', *Music and Science*, 2, pp. 1–15, https://doi.org/10.1177/2059204319861719.

Dissanayake, E. (2010), 'Bodies swayed to music: The temporal arts as integral to ceremonial ritual', in *Communicative Musicality: Exploring the Basis of Human Companionship*, Oxford: Oxford University Press, pp. 533–44.

Dueck, B. (ed.) (2017), 'Imagining identifications: How musicians align their practices with publics', *Handbook of Musical Identities*, 1st ed., Oxford: OUP Oxford, pp. 383–402.

Dunbar, P. R. (2013), *The Science of Love and Betrayal*, London: Faber & Faber.

Dunbar, R. (2011), *How Many Friends Does One Person Need?: Dunbar's Number and Other Evolutionary Quirks*, Main ed., London: Faber & Faber.

Dunbar, R. (2012), 'On the evolutionary function of song and dance', in N. Bannon (ed.), *Music, Language and Human Evolution*, Oxford: OUP Oxford, pp. 201–14.

Dunbar, R. (2014), 'The origin of music', Triggers and Thresholds, 14 April, https://vimeo.com/90973920. Accessed 15 February 2015.

Eliot, T. S. (1942), *Four Quartets*, Main ed., London: Faber & Faber.

Elliott, D. J. (1990), 'Music as culture: Toward a multicultural concept of arts education', *Journal of Aesthetic Education*, 24:1, pp. 147–66, https://doi.org/10.2307/3332862.

Elliott, D. J. (1995), *Music Matters: A New Philosophy of Music Education*, New York, Oxford: OUP USA.

Elliott, D. J. (ed.) (2009), *Praxial Music Education: Reflections and Dialogues*, New York, Oxford: OUP USA.

Elliott, D. J. and Silverman, M. (2013), 'Why music matters: Philosophical and cultural foundations', in *Music, Health and Wellbeing*, Oxford: Oxford University Press, pp. 942–1447.

Elliott, D. J. and Silverman, M. (2015), *Music Matters: A Philosophy of Music Education*, New York: Oxford University Press.

Elliott, D. J. and Silverman, M. (2019), 'Change in music teacher education: A philosophical view', in *Oxford Handbook of Preservice Music Teacher Education in the United States*, Oxford: Oxford University Press, pp. 67–84, https://doi.org/10.1093/oxfordhb/9780190671402.013.13.

Elliott, D., Silverman, M. and Bowman, W. D. (2016), *Artistic Citizenship: Artistry, Social Responsibility, and Ethical Praxis*, New York: Oxford University Press.

Eno, B. and Schmidt, P. (1979), *Oblique Strategies: Over One Hundred Worthwhile Dilemmas*, London: Eno Publishing.

Erelli, M. (2006), *Passing Through*, Northampton: Signature Sounds.

Fancourt, D., Aughterson, H., Finn, S., Walker, E. and Steptoe, A. (2021), 'How leisure activities affect health: A narrative review and multi-level theoretical framework of mechanisms of action', *The Lancet*, 8:4, pp. 329–39, https://doi.org/10.1016/S2215-0366(20)30384-9.

Folkestad, G. (2002), 'National identity and music', in R. MacDonald, D. Hargreaves and M. Dorothy (eds), *Musical Identities*, New York: Oxford University Press, pp. 151–62.

Folkestad, G. (2017), 'Post-national identities in music', in R. MacDonald, D. J. Hargreaves and D. Miell (eds), *Handbook of Musical Identities*, 1st ed., Oxford: OUP Oxford, pp. 122–36.

Foot, M. (1974), *Aneurin Bevan: A Biography*, New York: Scribner.

Foucault, M. (1966), *The Order of Things*, London: Routledge.

Foucault, M. (2002), *Archaeology of Knowledge*, 2nd ed., London, New York: Routledge.

Fox, J. (2009), *New Ground, Lost Seeds*, Ulverston: Dead Good Guides, https://www.dead.goodguides.com/pages/handbooks.html. Accessed 14 June 2013.

Frankl, V. E. (1946), *Man's Search for Meaning: The Classic Tribute to Hope from the Holocaust*, New ed., Reading: Rider.

Freer, P. K. and Bennett, D. (2012), 'Developing musical and educational identities in university music students', *Music Education Research*, 14:3, pp. 265–84, https://doi.org/10.1080/14613808.2012.712507.

Freire, P. (1970), *Pedagogy of the Oppressed*, 2nd ed., London: Penguin.

Frith, S. (2007), *Taking Popular Music Seriously: Selected Essays*, 1st ed., Aldershot, Hampshire, Burlington: Routledge.

Gabrielsson, A. (2011), *Strong Experiences with Music: Music Is Much More than Just Music*, Oxford, New York: Oxford University Press.

Gamble, C. N., Hanan, J. S. and Nail, T. (2019), 'What is new materialism?', *Angelaki*, 24:6, pp. 111–34, https://doi.org/10.1080/0969725X.2019.1684704.

Gibson, S.-J. (2021), 'Shifting from offline to online collaborative music-making, teaching and learning: Perceptions of ethno artistic mentors', in *Music Education Research*, London: Routledge, pp. 1–16, https://doi.org/10.1080/14613808.2021.1904865.

Giroux, H. A. (2011), *On Critical Pedagogy*, New York: Continuum Publishing Corporation.

Godlovitch, S. (1998), *Musical Performance: A Philosophical Study*, 1st ed., Abingdon: Routledge.

Goldacre, B. (2013), *Building evidence into education, Department for Education*, March, https://assets.publishing.service.gov.uk/government/uploads/system/uploads/attachment_data/file/193913/Building_evidence_into_education.pdf. Accessed 25 March 2013.

Goldacre, B. (2014), *I Think You'll Find It's a Bit More Complicated Than That*, New York: Fourth Estate.

Goldberg-Vååg, R. (2018), 'Exploring critiques of cosmopolitanism', Bachelor thesis, Göteborg: Göteborgs Universitet, https://gupea.ub.gu.se/bitstream/2077/56719/1/gupea_2077_56719_1.pdf. Accessed 14 March 2021.

Government Office for Science (2013), *Foresight Future Identities: Final Project Report*, London: Government Office for Science, https://assets.publishing.service.gov.uk/government/uploads/system/uploads/attachment_data/file/273966/13-523-future-identities-changing-identities-report.pdf. Accessed 5 December 2021.

Graeber, D. and Wengrow, D. (2022), *The Dawn of Everything: A New History of Humanity*, 1st ed., London: Penguin.

Green, L. (2008), *Music, Informal Learning and the School: A New Classroom Pedagogy*, London: Ashgate.

Gregson, K. (ed.) (1980), *Cumbrian Songs and Ballads*, 1st ed., Clapham, North Yorkshire: Dalesman Publishing Co Ltd.

Gross, J., Wilson, N. and Bull, A. (2017), *Towards Cultural Democracy*, London: Kings College, https://www.kcl.ac.uk/cultural/resources/reports/towards-cultural-democracy-2017-kcl.pdf. Accessed 29 June 2017.

Hackman, J. R., Seifter, H. and Economy, P. (2001), *Leadership Ensemble: Lessons in Collaborative Management from the Worlds Only Conductorless Orchestra*, New York: Times Books.

Hallam, S. (2015), *The Power of Music*, London: Music Education Council, http://www.mec.org.uk/storage/power%20of%20music.pdf. Accessed 1 April 2015.

Hallam, S. (2017), 'Musical identity, learning and teaching', in R. MacDonald, D. J. Hargreaves and D. Miell (eds), *Handbook of Musical Identities*, 1st ed., Oxford: OUP Oxford, pp. 474–91.

Hallam, S., Creech, A. and McQueen, H. (2011), *Musical Futures: A Case Study Investigation*, London: Institute of Education.

Hallam, S. and Gaunt, H. (2012), *Preparing for Success: A Practical Guide for Young Musicians*, London: Institute of Education.

Hancock, M. (2018), 'The power of the arts and social activities to improve the nation's health', Department of Health and Social Care, 6 November, https://www.gov.uk/government/speeches/the-power-of-the-arts-and-social-activities-to-improve-the-nations-health. Accessed 8 November 2018.

Haraway, D. J. (2016), *Staying with the Trouble (Experimental Futures): Making Kin in the Chthulucene*, Illustrated ed., Durham: Duke University Press Books.

Haraway, D. J. and Goodeve, T. (2018), *Modest_Witness@Second_Millennium. FemaleMan_Meets_OncoMouse: Feminism and Technoscience*, 2nd ed., New York: Routledge.

Harrison, C. and Mullen, P. (2013), *Reaching Out: Music Education with Hard to Reach Children and Young People*, London: UK Association for Music Education – Music Mark.

Harvey, D. (2007), *A Brief History of Neoliberalism*, 1st ed., Oxford: Oxford University Press.

Hawking, S. (2016), 'This is the most dangerous time for our planet', *The Guardian*, 1 December, https://www.theguardian.com/commentisfree/2016/dec/01/stephen-hawking-dangerous-time-planet-inequality. Accessed 5 December 2016.

Hayles, K. (1999), *How We Became Posthuman*, Chicago, London: University of Chicago Press.

Helguera, P. (2011), *Education for Socially Engaged Art: A Materials and Techniques Handbook*, New York: Jorge Pinto Books.

Hersey, P. (1997), *The Situational Leader*, Escondido: Center for Leadership Studies.

Hesmondhalgh, D. (2013), *Why Music Matters*, Chichester, Malden: Wiley-Blackwell.

Hesser, B. and Bartleet, B.-L. (eds) (2020), *Music as a Global Resource: Solutions for Cultural, Social, Health, Educational, Environmental, and Economic Issues Compendium*, 5th ed., New York: Griffith University.

Hickey-Moody, A., Palmer, H. and Sayers, E. (2016), 'Diffractive pedagogies: Dancing across new materialist imaginaries', *Gender and Education*, 28:2, pp. 213–29, https://doi.org/10.1080/09540253.2016.1140723.

Higgins, L. (2007), 'Acts of hospitality: The community in Community Music', *Music Education Research*, 9:2, pp. 281–92, https://doi.org/10.1080/14613800701384441.

Higgins, L. (2009), 'Community music and the welcome', *International Journal of Community Music*, 1:3, pp. 391–400, https://doi.org/10.1386/ijcm.1.3.391/1.

Higgins, L. (2012), *Community Music: In Theory and In Practice*, New York: OUP USA.

Hinchliffe, S., Jackson, M., Wyatt, K., Barlow, A. and Barreto, M. (2018), 'Healthy publics: Enabling cultures and environments for health', *Palgrave Communications*, 4:1, p. 57, https://doi.org/10.1057/s41599-018-0113-9.

hooks, bell (2000), *All About Love*, 1st ed., New York: William Morrow.

Huhtinen-Hildén, L. and Pitt, J. (2018), *Taking a Learner-Centred Approach to Music Education: Pedagogical Pathways*, 1st ed., Abingdon, New York: Routledge.

Hunter, J., Micklem, D. and 64 Million Artists (2016), *Everyday Creativity*, London: 64 Million Artists, http://64millionartists.com/everyday-creativity-2/. Accessed 21 August 2016.

Husserl, E. (1931), *Ideas: General Introduction to Pure Phenomenology*, 1st ed., London and New York: Routledge.

Hyde, L. (2012), *The Gift: How the Creative Spirit Transforms the World*, Main-Canons Imprint Re-issue ed., Edinburgh: Canongate Canons.

Illari, P. M. and Williamson, J. (2012), 'What is a mechanism? Thinking about mechanisms across the sciences', *European Journal for Philosophy of Science*, 2:1, pp. 119–35, https://doi.org/10.1007/s13194-011-0038-2.

Jackson, S. (2011), *Social Works: Performing Art, Supporting Publics*, 1st ed., London: Routledge.

Jenkins, H., Shresthova, S. and Peters-Lazaro, G. (2020), *Popular Culture and the Civic Imagination: Case Studies of Creative Social Change*, New York: NYU Press.

JM International (n.d.), 'Ethno', JMI.net, https://jmi.net/programs/ethno. Accessed 22 August 2021.

Kaskla, E. (1992), 'Five nationalisms: Estonian nationalism in comparative perspective', *Journal of Baltic Studies*, 23:2, pp. 167–78.

KCLID (2021), *Reflections on the failures of COP26*, Forward Thinking Series, 16 December, https://www.kcl.ac.uk/reflections-on-the-failures-of-cop26. Accessed 24 March 2022.

Keil, C. (1987), 'Participatory discrepancies and the power of music', *Cultural Anthropology*, 2:3, pp. 275–83, https://doi.org/10.1525/can.1987.2.3.02a00010.

Kelly, K. (1997), 'New rules for the new economy', *Wired*, 1 September, https://www.wired.com/1997/09/newrules/. Accessed 17 October 2016.

Kelly, O. (1983), *Community, Art and the State: Storming the Citadels*, London and New York: Comedia.

Kertz-Welzel, A. (2016), 'Daring to question: A philosophical critique of community music', *Philosophy of Music Education Review*, 24:2, pp. 113–30.

Kimmerer, R. W. (2020), *Braiding Sweetgrass: Indigenous Wisdom, Scientific Knowledge and the Teachings of Plants*, 1st ed., London: Penguin.

Klickstein, G. (2009), *The Musician's Way: A Guide to Practice, Performance, and Wellness*, Oxford and New York: OUP USA.

Knudsen, J. S. (2011), 'Music of the multiethnic minority: A postnational perspective', *Music and Arts in Action*, 3:3, pp. 77–91.

Koch, R. (2020), 'In pursuit of a mastery of risk: Working with uncertainty, change, and surprise', in *Cynefin – Weaving Sense-Making into the Fabric of Our World*, Singapore: Cognitive Edge – The Cynefin Co, pp. 243–56.

Koelsch, S. (2013), 'From social contact to social cohesion – The 7 Cs', *Music and Medicine*, 5, pp. 204–09.

Lam, C. Y. (2022), 'A process of becoming', Doctoral thesis, London: Royal College of Music.

Latour, B. (2017), 'L'Europe est seule, mais seule l'Europe peut nous sauver', Tribune – Europe, 14 April, https://reporterre.net/L-Europe-est-seule-mais-seule-l-Europe-peut-nous-sauver. Accessed 23 January 2019.

Lave, J. and Wenger, E. (1991), *Situated Learning: Legitimate Peripheral Participation*, Cambridge: Cambridge University Press.

Law, N. and Fowler, E. (2021), *Freedom: How We Lose It and How We Fight Back*, London: Bantam Press.

Lee, D. (2015), 'Will a robot take your job?', *BBC News*, 11 September, http://www.bbc.co.uk/news/technology-34066941. Accessed 31 October 2016.

Levitin, D. J. (2008), *This Is Your Brain on Music: Understanding a Human Obsession*, New York: Atlantic Books.

Lewin, K. (1944), 'The dynamics of group action', *Educational Leadership*, 4, pp. 195–200.

Lewis, T., Amini, F. and Lannon, R. (2001), *A General Theory of Love*, Rpt ed., New York: Vintage Books.

Lingis, A. (1994), *The Community of Those Who Have Nothing in Common*, Bloomington: Indiana University Press.

MacDonald, R., Kreutz, G. and Mitchell, L. (eds) (2013a), *Music, Health, and Wellbeing*, 1st ed., Oxford: OUP Oxford.

MacDonald, R., Kreutz, G. and Mitchell, L. (2013b), 'What is music, health and wellbeing and why is it important?', in *Music, Health and Wellbeing*, Oxford: OUP Oxford, pp. 3–11.

Macfarlane, R. and Morris, J. (2017), *The Lost Words: Rediscover Our Natural World with this Spellbinding Book*, 1st ed., London: Hamish Hamilton.

MacIntyre, A. (1981), *After Virtue*, Rpt ed., London: Bloomsbury Academic.

MacLean, P. D. (1990), *The Triune Brain in Evolution: Role in Paleocerebral Functions*, New York: Springer.

Malloch, S. and Trevarthen, C. (2010), *Communicative Musicality: Exploring the Basis of Human Companionship*, Oxford: Oxford University Press.

van Manen, M. (2008), 'Pedagogical sensitivity and teachers practical knowing-in-action', *Peking University Education Review*, 1:1, pp. 1–23.

MARCH Network (n.d.), 'March legacy', https://www.marchlegacy.org/. Accessed 24 March 2022.

Mason, P. (2019), *Clear Bright Future: A Radical Defence of the Human Being*, London: Allen Lane.

Matarasso, F. (1997), *Use or Ornament? The Social Impact of Participation in the Arts*, Stroud: Comedia.

Matarasso, F. (2010), 'Rethinking cultural policy', in *Culture Watch Europe Conference 2010*, September, Brussels: Council of Europe, http://www.coe.int/t/dg4/cultureheritage/cwe/Rethink_EN.pdf. Accessed 29 November 2013.

Matarasso, F. (2013), 'Creative progression – Reflections on quality in participatory arts', *UNESCO Observatory Multi-Disciplinary Journal in the Arts*, 3:3, pp. 1–15.

Matarasso, F. (2014), *Music – What is it good for? Everyone Deserves Music*, Gateshead, 29 April, https://www.academia.edu/6912293/Music_-_What_is_it_good_for. Accessed 4 May 2014.

Mather, B. and Camlin, D. A. (2016), 'Situational pedagogy in Community Music', in *Community Music Activity Commission*, Edinburgh: ISME, https://www.isme.org/other-publications/cma-proceedings-2016. Accessed 22 January 2019.

McKay, G. and Higham, B. (2012), *Connected Communities – Community Music: History and Current Practice, Its Constructions of 'Community', Digital Turns and Future Soundings*, Salford: Arts & Humanities Research Council, http://www.ahrc.ac.uk/Funding-Opportunities/Research-funding/Connected-Communities/Scoping-studies-and-reviews/Documents/Community%20Music%20-%20History%20and%20Current%20Practice.pdf. Accessed 21 March 2013.

McLellan, R., Galton, M., Steward, S. and Page, C. (2012), *The Impact of Creative Partnerships on the Wellbeing of Children and Young People*, Cambridge: University of Cambridge.

McNiff, J. (2013), *Action Research: Principles and Practice*, 3rd ed., Milton Park, Abingdon, Oxon, New York: Routledge.

Mellizo, J. (2019), 'Music education as global education: A developmental approach', *Topics for Music Education Praxis*, 7 January, http://topics.maydaygroup.org/2019/01/. Accessed 3 February 2022.

Miller, M. L. and Ury, S. (2010), 'Cosmopolitanism: The end of Jewishness?' *European Review of History: Revue européenne d'histoire*, 17:3, pp. 337–59, https://doi.org/10.1080/13507486.2010.481923.

Mithen, S. (2007), *The Singing Neanderthals: The Origins of Music, Language, Mind, and Body*, Cambridge: Harvard University Press.

Mouthful (n.d.), 'Wild chorus', https://www.mouthfulway.co.uk/wild. Accessed 29 January 2022.

Mouthful (2020), 'Hearth songs', YouTube, https://www.youtube.com/watch?v=ga6qM8Yzrx4. Accessed 29 January 2022.

Mouthful (2021), 'Trip to the lakes', YouTube, https://www.youtube.com/watch?v=gCp1s0uV_HE. Accessed 29 January 2022.

Mullen, P. (2008), *Issues in Leadership for Community Music Workers. ISME Community Music Activity Commission*, Rome: ISME.

Mullen, P. (2015), 'What is "quality" in music work with children in challenging circumstances?', Youth Music Network, 11 January, http://network.youthmusic.org.uk/groups/musical-inclusion/discussions/what-%E2%80%98quality%E2%80%99-music-work-children-challenging-circumstances-in. Accessed 22 November 2015.

NAH, W. (2009), 'The community in music', *International Journal of Community Music*, 2:2&3, pp. 109–28.

National Trust (2018), 'Songs on the Summits 1918–2018', National Trust, 1 September, https://www.nationaltrust.org.uk/borrowdale-and-derwent-water/features/songs-on-the-summits-1918-2018. Accessed 14 March 2018.

Neelands, J., Belfiore, E., Firth, C., Hart, N. and Perrin, L. (2015), *Enriching Britain: Culture, Creativity and Growth*, Warwick: University of Warwick, https://warwick.ac.uk/research/warwickcommission/futureculture/finalreport/warwick_commission_report_2015.pdf. Accessed 24 May 2015.

Nelson, R. (2013), *Practice as Research in the Arts: Principles, Protocols, Pedagogies, Resistances*, New York: Palgrave Macmillan.

Norman-Haignere, S. V., Feather, J., Boebinger, D., Brunner, P., Ritaccio, A., McDermott, J. H., Schalk, G. and Kanwisher, N. (2022), 'A neural population selective for song in human auditory cortex', *Current Biology*, New York: Elsevier, https://doi.org/10.1016/j.cub.2022.01.069.

Nussbaum, M. C. (2007a), *Cultivating Humanity and World Citizenship*, Cambridge: Forum for the Future of Higher Education, pp. 37–40, http://forum.mit.edu/articles/cultivating-humanity-and-world-citizenship/. Accessed 23 March 2022.

Nussbaum, M. C. (2007b), *Frontiers of Justice Disability, Nationality, Species Membership*, New ed., Cambridge and London: Harvard University Press.

O'Dea, J. (2000), *Virtue or Virtuosity?: Explorations in the Ethics of Musical Performance*, Westport: Greenwood Press.

OECD (2014), *Policy Challenges for the Next 50 Years*, OECD Economic Policy Paper No. 9, July, https://www.oecd.org/economy/Policy-challenges-for-the-next-fifty-years.pdf. Accessed 17 October 2016.

OECD (2015), *In It Together: Why Less Inequality Benefits All*, Paris: OECD, http://www.keepeek.com/Digital-Asset-Management/oecd/employment/in-it-together-why-less-inequality-benefits-all_9789264235120-en#page1. Accessed 31 October 2016.

Office for Students (2021), *OfS Confirms Funding Reforms*, Bristol: Office for Students, https://www.officeforstudents.org.uk/news-blog-and-events/press-and-media/ofs-confirms-funding-reforms/. Accessed 6 February 2022.

Oxfam International (2020), *Time to Care*, Oxford: Oxfam International, https://www.oxfam.org/en/research/time-care. Accessed 5 February 2022.

Oxfam International (2022), *Inequality Kills*, Oxford: Oxfam International, https://webassets.oxfamamerica.org/media/documents/Inequality_Kills.pdf. Accessed 5 February 2022.

Pairon, L. and Sloboda, J. (n.d.), *Social Impact of Music Making*, http://www.simm-platform.eu/. Accessed 22 August 2021.

Pavlicevic, M. (2013a), 'Between beats: Group music therapy transforming people and places', in *Music Health and Wellbeing*, Oxford: Oxford University Press, pp. 196–212.

Pavlicevic, M. (2013b), 'Let the music work: Optimal moments of collaborative musicing', in *Where Music Helps*, Farnham: Ashgate, pp. 100–23.

Pavlicevic, M. and Ansdell, G. (2004), *Community Music Therapy*, London, Philadelphia: J. Kingsley Publishers.

Pearce, E., Launay, J. and Dunbar, R. (2015), 'The ice breaker effect. Singing mediates fast social bonding', *Royal Society Open Science*, 2:10, p. 150221, https://doi.org/10.1098/rsos.150221.

Pearson, J. (2004), 'Memories of an Ennerdale Lass', Dave Camlin, 28 January, http://www.davecamlin.com/ennerdale-lass. Accessed 28 January 2022.

Pentland, A. (2008), *Honest Signals: How They Shape Our World*, Cambridge: The MIT Press.

Perkins, R. (2012), 'Re-thinking "Career" for music students', in *Life in the Real World*, Champaign: Common Ground Publishing, pp. 11–26.

Perkins, R. and Williamon, A. (2014), 'Learning to make music in older adulthood: A mixed-methods exploration of impacts on wellbeing', *Psychol Music*, 42, pp. 550–67, https://doi.org/10.1177/0305735613483668.

Phelan, H. (2008), 'Practice, ritual and community music: Doing as identity', *International Journal of Community Music*, 1:2, pp. 143–58, https://doi.org/10.1386/ijcm.1.2.143_1.

Pierre, D. (2021), 'Hidden truths', *New Philosopher*, 34, pp. 41–43.

Pinker, S. (1995), *The Language Instinct: How the Mind Creates Language: The New Science of Language and Mind*, New ed., New York: Penguin.

Pinker, S. (2003), *How the Mind Works*, 1st ed., New York: W. W. Norton & Company.

Price, D. (2013), *Open: How We'll Work, Live and Learn in the Future*, England: Crux Publishing Ltd.

Price, D. (2014), 'Why pedagogy is no longer enough', *Engaged Learning*, April, http://engagedlearning.co.uk/?p=2212. Accessed 20 April 2014.

Public Health England, Daykin, N. and Joss, T. (2016), *Arts for Health and Wellbeing: An Evaluation Framework*, London: Public Health England, https://www.gov.uk/government/uploads/system/uploads/attachment_data/file/496230/PHE_Arts_and_Health_Evaluation_FINAL.pdf. Accessed 16 February 2016.

Putnam, R. (2001), *Bowling Alone: The Collapse and Revival of American Community*, New ed., New York: Simon & Schuster Ltd.

Ranciere, J. (2003), *Dissensus*, London and New York: Continuum.

Rawls, J. (1999), *A Theory of Justice*, Rev ed., Cambridge: Harvard University Press.

Reason, P. and Bradbury, H. (eds) (2013), *The SAGE Handbook of Action Research: Participative Inquiry and Practice*, 2nd ed., London: SAGE Publications Ltd.

Regelski, T. (2009), 'The ethics of music teaching as profession and praxis', *Visions of Research in Music Education*, 11:7, pp. 1–34.

Regelski, T. A. (2011), 'Praxialism and "Aesthetic This, Aesthetic That, and Aesthetic Whatever"', *Action, Criticism and Theory for Music Education*, 10:2, pp. 61–99.

Renshaw, P. (2008), *REFLECT Evaluation Report*, Gateshead: The Sage Gateshead.

Renshaw, P. (2010), *Engaged Passions: Searches for Quality in Community Contexts*, Delft: Eburon Academic Publishers.

Rifkin, J. (2015), *Zero Marginal Cost Society*, Rpt ed., New York: Griffin.

Rink, P. J. (2002), *Musical Performance: A Guide to Understanding*, Huntington: Cambridge University Press.

Robinson, K. (2010), 'Changing education paradigms', YouTube, 14 October, https://www.youtube.com/watch?v=zDZFcDGpL4U. Accessed 4 November 2014.

Roche, J. (2006), *Socially Engaged Art, Critics and Discontents: An Interview with Claire Bishop*, Saxapahaw: American Community Arts Network, https://contextualpractice.files.wordpress.com/2011/08/bishopinterview.pdf. Accessed 11 May 2014.

Roederer, J. G. (1984), 'The search for a survival value of music', *Music Perception: An Interdisciplinary Journal*, 1:3, pp. 350–56, https://doi.org/10.2307/40285265.

Rogers, C. (1961), *On Becoming a Person*, New ed., London: Constable.

Rusbridger, A. (2013), *Play It Again: An Amateur Against the Impossible*, London: Jonathan Cape.

Ruud, E. (2013), 'The new health musicians', in R. A. R. MacDonald, G. Kreutz and L. Mitchell (eds), *Music, Health and Wellbeing*, Oxford: OUP Oxford.

Sage Gateshead (2014), *Sage Gateshead Annual Review 2013–14*, Gateshead: Sage Gateshead, http://www.sagegateshead.com/about-us/annual-review/annual-review-13-14/. Accessed 5 February 2018.

Sage Gateshead (n.d.), Sage Gateshead, http://www.sagegateshead.com/. Accessed 19 June 2013.

Schön, D. A. (1984), *The Reflective Practitioner: How Professionals Think in Action*, New ed., London: Ashgate Publishing Limited.

Siegel, D. (2011), *Mindsight: Transform Your Brain with the New Science of Kindness*, Oxford: Oneworld Publications.

Siegel, D. (2015), informal interview with Dan Siegel (personal communication), 22 April.

Siegel, D. J. (2012), *Pocket Guide to Interpersonal Neurobiology: An Integrative Handbook of the Mind*, New York and London: W. W. Norton & Company.

Silverman, M. (2012), 'Community music and social justice: Reclaiming love', in *Oxford Handbook of Music Education*, vol. 2, Oxford: Oxford University Press, pp. 155–67.

Sing Up (n.d.), https://www.singup.org/. Accessed 1 October 2019.

Situational Leadership® (n.d.), https://situational.com/situational-leadership/. Accessed 4 October 2022.

Small, C. (1998), *Musicking: The Meanings of Performing and Listening*, Middletown: Wesleyan University Press.

Snowden, D. (2016), *Ethnography Part II*, Cognitive Edge, 10 February 2016, http://cognitive-edge.com/blog/ethnography-part-ii/. Accessed 1 March 2018.

Söderman, J., Burnard, P. and Hofvander-Trulsson, Y. (2015), 'Contextualising Bourdieu in the field of music and music education', in *Bourdieu and the Sociology of Music Education*, Burlington, Farnham: Routledge, pp. 1–12.

Stern, D. N. (2010), *Forms of Vitality: Exploring Dynamic Experience in Psychology, the Arts, Psychotherapy, and Development*, Illustrated ed., Oxford and New York: OUP Oxford.

Stern, M. J. and Seifert, S. C. (2009), *Civic Engagement and the Arts: Issues of Conceptualization and Measurement*, Philadelphia: University of Pennsylvania, http://animatingdemocracy.org/sites/default/files/CE_Arts_SternSeifert.pdf. Accessed 23 March 2022.

Stige, B. (ed.) (2002), *Culture-Centred Music Therapy*, Barcelona: Gilsum.

Stige, B. (2013), 'Health musicking: A perspective on music and health as action and performance', in *Music, Health and Wellbeing*, Oxford: OUP Oxford, pp. 183–95.

Stige, B., Ansdell, G., Elefant, C. and Pavlicevic, M. (2013), *Where Music Helps: Community Music Therapy in Action and Reflection*, Farnham, Burlington: Ashgate.

Symonds, J., Hargreaves, J. J. and Long, M. (2017), 'Music in IIN adolescence across school transition', in R. MacDonald, D. J. Hargreaves and D. Miell (eds), *Handbook of Musical Identities*, 1st ed., Oxford: OUP Oxford, pp. 510–26.

Tarr, B., Launay, J. and Dunbar, R. (2014), 'Music and social bonding: "Self-other" merging and neurohormonal mechanisms', *Frontiers in Psychology*, 5, Article 1096, https://doi.org/10.3389/fpsyg.2014.01096.

Tomasello, M. (2019), *Becoming Human: A Theory of Ontogeny*, Cambridge: Harvard University Press.

Tuckman, B. (1965), 'Developmental sequence in small groups', *Psychological Bulletin*, 63:6, pp. 384–99.

Tuckman, B. W. and Jensen, M. A. C. (1977), 'Stages of small-group development revisited', *Group & Organization Management*, 2:4, pp. 419–27, https://doi.org/10.1177/105960117700200404.

Turino, T. (2008), *Music as Social Life: The Politics of Participation*, Chicago: University of Chicago Press.

Turino, T. (2016), 'Music, social change, and alternative forms of citizenship', in *Artistic Citizenship*, New York: OUP USA.

Turner, E. (2012), *Communitas: The Anthropology of Collective Joy*, New York: Palgrave Macmillan.

Tusty, J. and Castle Tusty, M. (n.d.), The Singing Revolution, The Singing Revolution, https://singingrevolution.com/about/history/. Accessed 24 March 2021.

Twenge, J. (2017), *Igen: Why Today's Super-Connected Kids Are Growing Up Less Rebellious, More Tolerant, Less Happy – And Completely Unprepared for Adulthood – And What That Means for the Rest of Us*, New York: Atria Books.

UK Music (2021), This Is Music 2021, 19 October, https://www.ukmusic.org/news/uk-music-calls-for-government-action-to-boost-recovery-as-new-report-reveals-covid-wiped-out-one-in-three-music-jobs/. Accessed 6 February 2022.

United Nations Environment Programme and International Livestock Research Institute (2020), *Preventing the Next Pandemic: Zoonotic Diseases and How to Break the Chain of Transmission*, UNEP Frontiers, Nairobi, Kenya: UN Environment Programme, http://www.unenvironment.org/news-and-stories/statement/preventing-next-pandemic-zoonotic-diseases-and-how-break-chain. Accessed 29 July 2020.

Underhill, J. and ISM (2022), *Music: A Subject in Peril?*, London: Incorporated Society of Musicians, https://www.ism.org/music-in-peril?utm_medium=email&utm_campaign=Music%20a%20subject%20in%20peril%20-%20Non-corporate%20stakeholders&utm_content=Music%20a%20subject%20in%20peril%20-%20Non-corporate%20stakeholders+CID_8904e11a7942ae7b5ee1294f601f8e17&utm_source=&utm_term=Music%20A%20subject%20in%20peril. Accessed 24 March 2022.

United Nations (1948), 'Universal Declaration of Human Rights', http://www.un.org/en/universal-declaration-human-rights/. Accessed 20 April 2017.

United Nations (2015), *World Population Prospects*, New York: United Nations, https://esa.un.org/unpd/wpp/publications/files/key_findings_wpp_2015.pdf. Accessed 17 October 2016.

Väkevä, L. (2012), 'Philosophy of music education as art of life: A Deweyan view', in *Oxford Handbook of Philosophy in Music Education*, Oxford: Oxford University Press, pp. 86–110.

Varèse, E. and Wen-chung, C. (1966), 'The liberation of sound', *Perspectives of New Music*, 5:1, pp. 11–19, https://doi.org/10.2307/832385.

Vickhoff, B., Malmgren, H., Åström, R., Nyberg, G., Ekström, S., Engwall, M., Snygg, J., Nilsson, M. and Jörnsten, R. (2013), 'Music structure determines heart rate variability of singers', *Frontiers in Psychology*, 4, p. 334, http://journal.frontiersin.org/Journal/10.3389/fpsyg.2013.00334/full.

Vidal, C. M., Lane, C. S., Asrat, A., Barfod, D. N., Mark, D. F., Tomlinson, E. L., Tadesse, A. Z., Yirgu, G., Deino, A., Hutchison, W., Mounier, A. and Oppenheimer, C. (2022), 'Age of the oldest known Homo sapiens from eastern Africa', *Nature*, 601, pp. 579–83, https://doi.org/10.1038/s41586-021-04275-8.

Wegerif, R. (2012), *Dialogic: Education for the Internet Age*, Abingdon: Routledge.

Wenger, E. (1999), *Communities of Practice: Learning, Meaning, and Identity*, New ed., Cambridge: Cambridge University Press.

Whiten, A. (2007), 'The place of "deep social mind" in the evolution of human nature', in *What Makes Us Human?*, Oxford: Oneworld Publications, pp. 146–63.

Wild Ennerdale (n.d.), 'Wild Ennerdale – Shaping the landscape naturally', https://www.wildennerdale.co.uk/. Accessed 29 January 2022.

Wiles, D. (2016), 'Art and citizenship: The history of a divorce', in *Artistic Citizenship: Artistry, Social Responsibility, and Ethical Praxis*, New York: Oxford University Press, pp. 22–39.

Wilkinson, R. and Pickett, K. (2010), *The Spirit Level: Why Equality Is Better for Everyone*, London and New York: Penguin.

Williamon, A. (2004), *Musical Excellence: Strategies and Techniques to Enhance Performance*, Oxford: OUP Oxford.

Williams, E., Dingle, G. A. and Clift, S. (2018), 'A systematic review of mental health and well-being outcomes of group singing for adults with a mental health condition', *European Journal of Public Health*, 28:6, pp. 1035–42, https://doi.org/10.1093/eurpub/cky115.

Willingham, L. (2021), *Community Music at the Boundaries*, Waterloo: Wilfrid Laurier University Press.

Wright, D. C. H. (2013), *The Associated Board of the Royal Schools of Music: A Social and Cultural History*, Woodbridge, Cambridge: Boydell & Brewer, Cambridge Core, https://www.cambridge.org/core/books/associated-board-of-the-royal-schools-of-music/42EE7FE7A31FA69DB121EBC7B3EE7707. Accessed 25 January 2023.

Youth Music (2023), http://www.youthmusic.org.uk/. Accessed 1 September 2014.

Zeserson, K. (2014), *Inspiring Music for All*, London: Paul Hamlyn Foundation, http://www.phf.org.uk/news.asp?id=2232. Accessed 19 July 2014.

Zeserson, K. (2021), 'The magnificent territory: Pausing to reflect on a lifetime of working with people and music', *International Journal of Community Music*, 14:1, pp. 9–19, https://doi.org/10.1386/ijcm_00035_1.

Žižek, S. (2014), *Trouble in Paradise: From the End of History to the End of Capitalism*, London: Penguin.

Žižek, S. (2018), *Like a Thief in Broad Daylight: Power in the Era of Post-Humanity*, London: Allen Lane.

Index

www.ingramcontent.com/pod-product-compliance
Lightning Source LLC
LaVergne TN
LVHW081249151225
827617LV00002B/9